Parallelism in Production Systems

Anoop Gupta
Department of Computer Science
Carnegie-Mellon University

Parallelism in Production Systems

Pitman, London

Morgan Kaufmann Publishers, Inc., Los Altos, California

PITMAN PUBLISHING
128 Long Acre, London WC2E 9AN

First published 1987

Available in the Western Hemisphere from
MORGAN KAUFMANN PUBLISHERS, INC.,
95 First Street, Los Altos, California 94022

ISSN 0268-7526

British Library Cataloguing in Publication Data
Gupta, Anoop
　　Parallelism in production systems.—
　　(Research notes in artificial intelligence,
　　ISSN 0268-7526).
　　1. Artificial intelligence
　　I. Title　II. Series
　　006.3　　　　Q335

　　ISBN 0-273-08782-7

Library of Congress Cataloging in Publication Data
Gupta, Anoop.
　　Parallelism in production systems.

　　(Research notes in artificial intelligence;
ISSN 0268-7526)
　　Originally presented as the author's thesis
(doctoral-Carnegie-Mellon University, 1986)
　　Bibliography: p.
　　Includes index.
　　1. Parallel processing (Electronic computers)
2. Artificial intelligence.　3. Expert systems
(Computer science)　I. Title.　II. Series: Research
notes in artificial intelligence (London, England)
QA76.5.G857　1987　　　004'.35　　　87-20428
ISBN 0-934613-55-9 (U.S.)

Reproduced and printed by photolithography
in Great Britain by Biddles Ltd, Guildford

Contents

1 Introduction   **1**
  1.1 Preview of Results   3
  1.2 Organization of the Thesis   4

2 Background   **7**
  2.1 OPS5   7
    2.1.1 Working-Memory Elements   8
    2.1.2 The Left-Hand Side of a Production   8
    2.1.3 The Right-Hand Side of a Production   9
  2.2 Soar   10
  2.3 The Rete Match Algorithm   10
  2.4 Why Parallelize Rete?   15
    2.4.1 State-Saving vs. Non-State-Saving Match Algorithms   15
    2.4.2 Rete as a Specific Instance of State-Saving Algorithms   17
    2.4.3 Node Sharing in the Rete Algorithm   19
    2.4.4 Rete as a Parallel Algorithm   19

3 Measurements on Production Systems   **21**
  3.1 Production-System Programs Studied in the Thesis   21
  3.2 Surface Characteristics of Production Systems   22
    3.2.1 Condition Elements per Production   23
    3.2.2 Actions per Production   24
    3.2.3 Negative Condition Elements per Production   24
    3.2.4 Attributes per Condition Element   25
    3.2.5 Tests per Two-Input Node   25
    3.2.6 Variables Bound and Referenced   27
    3.2.7 Variables Bound but not Referenced   27
    3.2.8 Variable Occurrences in Left-Hand Side   28
    3.2.9 Variables per Condition Element   28
    3.2.10 Condition Element Classes   30
    3.2.11 Action Types   32
    3.2.12 Summary of Surface Measurements   32
  3.3 Measurements on the Rete Network   32
    3.3.1 Number of Nodes in the Rete Network   33
    3.3.2 Network Sharing   34
  3.4 Run-Time Characteristics of Production Systems   34
    3.4.1 Constant-Test Nodes   35
    3.4.2 Alpha-Memory Nodes   36

3.4.3 Beta-Memory Nodes   37
3.4.4 And Nodes   37
3.4.5 Not Nodes   39
3.4.6 Terminal Nodes   39
3.4.7 Summary of Run-Time Characteristics   39

4 Parallelism in Production Systems   **43**

4.1 The Structure of a Parallel Production-System Interpreter   43
4.2 Parallelism in Match   44
    4.2.1 Production Parallelism   45
    4.2.2 Node Parallelism   48
    4.2.3 Intra-Node Parallelism   50
    4.2.4 Action Parallelism   51
4.3 Parallelism in Conflict-Resolution   53
4.4 Parallelism in RHS Evaluation   53
4.5 Application Parallelism   54
4.6 Summary   54
4.7 Discussion   55

5 Parallel Implementation of Production Systems   **59**

5.1 Architecture of the Production-System Machine   59
5.2 The State-Update Phase Processing   62
    5.2.1 Hash-Table Based vs. List Based Memory Nodes 62
    5.2.2 Memory Nodes Need to be Lumped with Two-Input Nodes 64
    5.2.3 Problems with Processing Conjugate Pairs of Tokens 66
    5.2.4 Concurrently Processable Activations of Two-Input Nodes 67
    5.2.5 Locks for Memory Nodes   69
    5.2.6 Linear vs. Binary Rete Networks   69
5.3 The Selection Phase Processing   75
    5.3.1 Sharing of Constant-Test Nodes   75
    5.3.2 Constant-Test Node Successors   75
    5.3.3 Alpha-Memory Node Successors   77
    5.3.4 Processing Multiple Changes to Working Memory in Parallel 77
5.4 Summary   77

6 The Problem of Scheduling Node Activations   **81**

6.1 The Hardware Task Scheduler   82
    6.1.1 How Fast Need the Scheduler be?   82
    6.1.2 The Interface to the Hardware Task Scheduler 83
    6.1.3 Structure of the Hardware Task Scheduler   85
    6.1.4 Multiple Hardware Task Schedulers   86
6.2 Software Task Schedulers   88

7 The Simulator   **93**

7.1 Structure of the Simulator   94
    7.1.1 Inputs to the Simulator   94
        7.1.1.1 The Input Trace   94
        7.1.1.2 The Computational Model 94
        7.1.1.3 The Cost Model   95

	7.1.1.4 The Memory Contention Model	97
	7.1.2 Outputs of the Simulator	100
7.2	Limitations of the Simulation Model	101
7.3	Validity of the Simulator	102
8	**Simulation Results and Analysis**	**105**
8.1	Traces Used in the Simulations	105
8.2	Simulation Results for Uniprocessors	107
8.3	Production Parallelism	110
	8.3.1 Effects of Action Parallelism on Production Parallelism	115
8.4	Node Parallelism	117
	8.4.1 Effects of Action Parallelism on Node Parallelism	117
8.5	Intra-Node Parallelism	121
	8.5.1 Effects of Action Parallelism on Intra-Node Parallelism	121
8.6	Linear vs. Binary Rete Networks	126
	8.6.1 Uniprocessor Implementations with Binary Networks	126
	8.6.2 Results of Parallelism with Binary Networks	128
8.7	Hardware Task Scheduler vs. Software Task Queues	133
8.8	Effects of Memory Contention	140
8.9	Summary	145
9	**Related Work**	**147**
9.1	Implementing Production Systems on C.mmp	147
9.2	Implementing Production Systems on Illiac-IV	148
9.3	The DADO Machine and the TREAT Match Algorithm	148
9.4	The NON-VON Machine	152
9.5	Oflazer's Work on Partitioning and Parallel Processing of Production Systems	154
	9.5.1 The Partitioning Problem	154
	9.5.2 The Parallel Algorithm	155
	9.5.3 The Parallel Architecture	156
	9.5.4 Discussion	157
9.6	Honeywell's Data-Flow Model	159
9.7	Other Work on Speeding-up Production Systems	160
10	**Summary and Conclusions**	**161**
10.1	Primary Results of Thesis	161
	10.1.1 Suitability of the Rete-Class of Algorithms	161
	10.1.2 Parallelism in Production Systems	162
	10.1.3 Software Implementation Issues	165
	10.1.4 Hardware Architecture	165
10.2	Some General Conclusions	166
10.3	Directions for Future Research	167
References		**171**
Appendix A	**ISP of Processor Used in Parallel Implementation**	**179**
Appendix B	**Code and Data Structures for Parallel Implementation**	**185**
B.1	Code for Interpreter with Hardware Task Scheduler	185
B.2	Code for Interpreter Using Multiple Software Task Schedulers	204
Appendix C	**Derivation of Cost Models for the Simulator**	**211**
C.1	Cost Model for the Parallel Implementation Using HTS	211
C.2	Cost Model for the Parallel Implementation Using STQs	223

List of Figures

Figure 2-1: A sample production. 7
Figure 2-2: The Rete network. 12
Figure 3-1: Condition elements per production. 23
Figure 3-2: Actions per production. 24
Figure 3-3: Negative condition elements per production. 25
Figure 3-4: Attributes per condition element. 26
Figure 3-5: Tests per two-input node. 26
Figure 3-6: Variables bound and referenced. 27
Figure 3-7: Variables bound but not referenced. 28
Figure 3-8: Occurrences of each variable. 29
Figure 3-9: Variables per condition element. 29
Figure 4-1: OPS5 interpreter cycle. 43
Figure 4-2: Soar interpreter cycle. 44
Figure 4-3: Selection and state-update phases in match. 45
Figure 4-4: Production parallelism. 46
Figure 4-5: Node parallelism. 49
Figure 4-6: The cross-product effect. 51
Figure 5-1: Architecture of the production-system machine. 60
Figure 5-2: A production and the associated Rete network. 63
Figure 5-3: Problems with memory-node sharing. 65
Figure 5-4: Concurrent activations of two-input nodes. 67
Figure 5-5: The long-chain effect. 72
Figure 5-6: A binary Rete network. 73
Figure 5-7: Scheduling activations of constant-test nodes. 76
Figure 5-8: Possible solution when too many alpha-memory successors. 78
Figure 6-1: Problem of dynamically changing set of processable node activations. 82
Figure 6-2: Effect of scheduler performance on maximum speed-up. 83
Figure 6-3: Structure of the hardware task scheduler. 85
Figure 6-4: Effect of multiple schedulers on speed-up. 89
Figure 6-5: Multiple software task queues. 90
Figure 7-1: A sample trace fragment. 95
Figure 7-2: Static node information. 96
Figure 7-3: Code for left activation of an and-node. 97
Figure 7-4: Degradation in performance due to memory contention. 100
Figure 8-1: Production parallelism (nominal speed-up). 112
Figure 8-2: Production parallelism (true speed-up). 112
Figure 8-3: Production parallelism (execution speed). 112

Figure 8-4: Production and action parallelism (nominal speed-up).   116
Figure 8-5: Production and action parallelism (true speed-up).   116
Figure 8-6: Production and action parallelism (execution speed).   116
Figure 8-7: Node parallelism (nominal speed-up).   118
Figure 8-8: Node parallelism (true speed-up).   118
Figure 8-9: Node parallelism (execution speed).   118
Figure 8-10: Node and action parallelism (nominal speed-up).   120
Figure 8-11: Node and action parallelism (true speed-up).   120
Figure 8-12: Node and action parallelism (execution speed).   120
Figure 8-13: Intra-node parallelism (nominal speed-up).   122
Figure 8-14: Intra-node parallelism (true speed-up).   122
Figure 8-15: Intra-node parallelism (execution speed).   122
Figure 8-16: Intra-node and action parallelism (nominal speed-up).   124
Figure 8-17: Intra-node and action parallelism (true speed-up).   124
Figure 8-18: Intra-node and action parallelism (execution speed).   124
Figure 8-19: Average nominal speed-up.   125
Figure 8-20: Average true speed-up.   125
Figure 8-21: Average execution speed.   125
Figure 8-22: Production parallelism (nominal speed-up).   129
Figure 8-23: Production parallelism (execution speed).   129
Figure 8-24: Production and action parallelism (nominal speed-up).   129
Figure 8-25: Production and action parallelism (execution speed).   129
Figure 8-26: Node parallelism (nominal speed-up).   130
Figure 8-27: Node parallelism (execution speed).   130
Figure 8-28: Node and action parallelism (nominal speed-up).   130
Figure 8-29: Node and action parallelism (execution speed).   130
Figure 8-30: Intra-node parallelism (nominal speed-up).   131
Figure 8-31: Intra-node parallelism (execution speed).   131
Figure 8-32: Intra-node and action parallelism (nominal speed-up).   131
Figure 8-33: Intra-node and action parallelism (execution speed).   131
Figure 8-34: Average nominal speed-up.   132
Figure 8-35: Average execution speed.   132
Figure 8-36: Effect of number of software task queues.   135
Figure 8-37: Production parallelism (nominal speed-up).   136
Figure 8-38: Production parallelism (execution speed).   136
Figure 8-39: Production and action parallelism (nominal speed-up).   136
Figure 8-40: Production and action parallelism (execution speed).   136
Figure 8-41: Node parallelism (nominal speed-up).   137
Figure 8-42: Node parallelism (execution speed).   137
Figure 8-43: Node and action parallelism (nominal speed-up).   137
Figure 8-44: Node and action parallelism (execution speed).   137
Figure 8-45: Intra-node parallelism (nominal speed-up).   138
Figure 8-46: Intra-node parallelism (execution speed).   138
Figure 8-47: Intra-node and action parallelism (nominal speed-up).   138
Figure 8-48: Intra-node and action parallelism (execution speed).   138
Figure 8-49: Average nominal speed-up.   139

Figure 8-50: Average execution speed.   139
Figure 8-51: Processor efficiency as a function of number of active processors. 141
Figure 8-52: Intra-node and action parallelism (nominal speed-up).   143
Figure 8-53: Intra-node and action parallelism (execution speed).   144
Figure 9-1: The prototype DADO architecture.   149
Figure 9-2: The NON-VON architecture.   153
Figure 9-3: Structure of the parallel processing system.   157

List of Tables

Table 3-1:	VT: Condition Element Classes	30
Table 3-2:	ILOG: Condition Element Classes	30
Table 3-3:	MUD: Condition Element Classes	31
Table 3-4:	DAA: Condition Element Classes	31
Table 3-5:	R1-SOAR: Condition Element Classes	31
Table 3-6:	EP-SOAR: Condition Element Classes	31
Table 3-7:	Action Type Distribution	32
Table 3-8:	Summary of Surface Measurements	32
Table 3-9:	Number of Nodes	33
Table 3-10:	Nodes per Production	33
Table 3-11:	Nodes per Condition Element (with sharing)	33
Table 3-12:	Nodes per Condition Element (without sharing)	34
Table 3-13:	Network Sharing (Nodes without sharing/Nodes with sharing)	34
Table 3-14:	Constant-Test Nodes	35
Table 3-15:	Alpha-Memory Nodes	36
Table 3-16:	Beta-Memory Nodes	37
Table 3-17:	And Nodes	38
Table 3-18:	Not Nodes	39
Table 3-19:	Terminal Nodes	39
Table 3-20:	Summary of Node Activations per Change	40
Table 3-21:	Number of Affected Productions	40
Table 3-22:	General Run-Time Data	41
Table 7-1:	Relative Costs of Various Instruction Types	98
Table 8-1:	Uniprocessor Execution With No Overheads: Part-A	107
Table 8-2:	Uniprocessor Execution With No Overheads: Part-B	108
Table 8-3:	Uniprocessor Execution With Overheads: Part-A Node Parallelism and Intra-Node Parallelism	110
Table 8-4:	Uniprocessor Execution With Overheads: Part-B Node Parallelism and Intra-Node Parallelism	110
Table 8-5:	Uniprocessor Execution With Overheads: Part-A Production Parallelism	111
Table 8-6:	Uniprocessor Execution With Overheads: Part-B Production Parallelism	111
Table 8-7:	Uniprocessor Execution With No Overheads: Part-A	126
Table 8-8:	Uniprocessor Execution With No Overheads: Part-B	127
Table 8-9:	Uniprocessor Execution With Overheads: Part-A Node Parallelism and Intra-Node Parallelism	127
Table 8-10:	Uniprocessor Execution With Overheads: Part-B Node Parallelism and Intra-Node Parallelism	127

Table 8-11: Uniprocessor Execution With Overheads: Part-A Production Parallelism 127
Table 8-12: Uniprocessor Execution With Overheads: Part-B Production Parallelism 128
Table 8-13: Comparison of Linear and Binary Network Rete 128

Acknowledgements

I would like to thank my advisors Charles Forgy, Allen Newell, and HT Kung for their guidance, support, and encouragement. Charles Forgy helped with his deep understanding of production systems and their implementation. Many of the ideas presented in this thesis originated with him or have benefited from his comments. Allen Newell, in addition to being an invaluable source of ideas, has shown me what doing research is about, and through his own example, what it means to be a good researcher. He has been a constant source of inspiration and it has been a great pleasure to work with him. HT Kung has been an excellent sounding board for ideas. He greatly helped in keeping the thesis on solid ground by always questioning my assumptions. I would also like to thank Al Davis for serving on my thesis committee. The final quality of the thesis has benefited significantly from his comments.

The work reported in this thesis has been done as a part of the Production System Machine (PSM) project at Carnegie-Mellon University. I would like to thank its current and past members — Charles Forgy, Ken Hughes, Dirk Kalp, Ted Lehr, Allen Newell, Kemal Oflazer, Jim Quinlan, Milind Tambe, Leon Weaver, and Robert Wedig — for their contributions to the research. I would also like to thank Greg Hood, John Laird, Bob Sproull (my advisor for the first two years at CMU), and Hank Walker for many interesting discussions about my research.

I would like to thank all my friends in Pittsburgh who have made these past years so enjoyable. I would like to thank Greg Hood, Ravi Kannan, Gudrun and Georg Klinker, Roberto Minio, Bud Mishra, Pradeep Sindhu, Pedro Szekely, Hank Walker, Angelika Zobel, and especially Paola Giannini and Yumi Iwasaki for making life so much fun. Finally, I would like to thank my family, my parents and my two sisters, for their immeasurable love, encouragement, and support of my educational endeavors.

This research was sponsored by the Defense Advanced Research Projects Agency (DOD), ARPA Order No. 4864, monitored by the Space and Naval Warfare Systems Command under Contract N00039-85-0134. The views and conclusions contained in this document are those of the authors and should not be interpreted as representing the official policies, either expressed or implied, of the Defense Advanced Research Projects Agency or the US Government.

Abstract

Production systems (or rule-based systems) are widely used in Artificial Intelligence for modeling intelligent behavior and building expert systems. Most production system programs, however, are extremely computation intensive and run quite slowly. The slow speed of execution has prohibited the use of production systems in domains requiring high performance and real-time response. This thesis explores the role of parallelism in the high-speed execution of production systems.

On the surface, production system programs appear to be capable of using large amounts of parallelism — it is possible to perform match for each production in a program in parallel. The thesis shows that in practice, however, the speed-up obtainable from parallelism is quite limited, around 10-fold as compared to initial expectations of 100-fold to 1000-fold. The main reasons for the limited speed-up are: (1) there are only a small number of productions that are *affected* (require significant processing) per change to working memory; (2) there is a large variation in the processing requirement of these productions; and (3) the number of changes made to working memory per recognize-act cycle is very small. Since the number of productions affected and the number of working-memory changes per recognize-act cycle are not controlled by the implementor of the production system interpreter (they are governed mainly by the author of the program and the nature of the task), the solution to the problem of limited speed-up is to somehow decrease the variation in the processing cost of affected productions. The thesis proposes a parallel version of the Rete algorithm which exploits parallelism at a very fine grain to reduce the variation. It further suggests that to exploit the fine-grained parallelism, a shared-memory multiprocessor with 32-64 high performance processors is desirable. For scheduling the fine-grained tasks consisting of about 50-100 instructions, a hardware task scheduler is proposed.

The thesis presents simulation results for a large set of production systems exploiting different sources of parallelism. The thesis points out the features of existing programs that limit the speed-up obtainable from parallelism and suggests solutions for some of the bottlenecks. The simulation results show that using the suggested multiprocessor architecture (with individual processors performing at 2 MIPS), it is possible to obtain execution speeds of about 12000 working-memory element changes per second. This corresponds to a speed-up of 10-fold over the best known sequential implementation using a 2 MIPS processor. This performance is significantly higher than that obtained by other proposed parallel implementations of production systems.

To my parents

1 Introduction

Production systems (or rule-based systems) occupy a prominent position within the field of Artificial Intelligence. They have been used extensively to understand the nature of intelligence — in cognitive modeling, in the study of problem-solving systems, and in the study of learning systems [2, 45, 46, 65, 76, 77, 95]. They have also been used extensively to develop large expert systems spanning a variety of applications in areas including computer-aided design, medicine, configuration tasks, oil exploration [11, 14, 40, 42, 43, 56, 57, 84]. Production-system programs, however, are computation intensive and run quite slowly. For example, OPS5 [10, 19] production-system programs using the Lisp-based or the Bliss-based interpreter execute at a speed of only 8-40 working-memory element changes per second (wme-changes/sec) on a VAX-11/780.[1] Although sufficient for many interesting applications (as demonstrated by the current popularity of expert systems), the slow speed of execution precludes the use of production systems in many domains requiring high performance and real-time response. For example, one study that considered implementing the Harpy algorithm as a production system [66] for real-time speech recognition required that the program be able to execute at a rate of about 200,000 wme-changes/sec. The slow speed of execution of current systems also impacts the research that is done with them, since researchers often avoid programming styles and systems that run too slowly. This thesis examines the issue of significantly speeding up the execution of production systems (several orders of magnitude over the 8-40 wme-changes/sec). A significant increase in the execution speed of production systems is expected to open up new application areas for production systems, and to be valuable to both the practitioners and the researchers in Artificial Intelligence.

There also exist deeper reasons for wanting to speed up the execution of production systems. The cognitive activity of an intelligent agent involves two types of search: (1) *knowledge search*, that is, search by the agent of its knowledge base to find information that is relevant to solving a given problem; and (2) *problem-space search*, that is, search within the problem space [65] for a goal state. Problem-space search manifests itself as a combinatorial AND/OR search [68]. Since problem-space search when not pruned by knowledge is combinatorially explosive,

---

[1]This corresponds to an execution speed of 3-16 production firings per second. On average, 2.5 changes are made to the working memory per production firing.

1

a highly intelligent agent, regardless of what it is doing, must engage in a certain amount of knowledge search after each step that it takes. This results in knowledge search being a part of the *inner loop* of the computation performed by an intelligent agent. Furthermore, as the intelligence of the agent increases (the size of the knowledge base increases), the resources needed to perform knowledge search also increase, and it becomes important to speed up knowledge search as much as possible.

As an example, consider the problem of determining the next move to make in a game of chess. Problem-space search corresponds to the different moves that the player tries out before making the actual move. However, the fact that he tries out only a small fraction of all possible moves requires that he use problem and situation-specific knowledge to constrain the search. Knowledge search corresponds to the computation involved in identifying this problem and situation-specific knowledge from the rest of the knowledge that the player may have.

Knowledge search forms an essential component of the execution of production systems. Each execution cycle of a production system involves a knowledge-search step (the *match* phase), where the knowledge represented in rules is matched against the global data memory. Since the ability to do efficient knowledge search is fundamental to the construction of intelligent agents, it follows that the ability to execute production systems with large rule sets at high speeds will greatly help in constructing intelligent programs. In short, the match-phase computation (knowledge search) done in production systems is not something specific to production systems, but such computation has to be done, in one form or another, in any intelligent system. Thus, speeding up such computation is an essential part of the construction of highly intelligent systems. Furthermore, since production systems offer a highly transparent model of knowledge search, the results obtained about speed-up from parallelism for production systems will also have implications for other models of intelligent computation involving knowledge search.

There are several different methods for speeding up the execution of production systems: (1) the use of faster technology; (2) the use of better algorithms; (3) the use of better architectures; and (4) the use of parallelism. This thesis focuses on the use of parallelism. It identifies the various sources of parallelism in production systems and discusses the feasibility of exploiting them. Several implementation issues and some architectural considerations are also discussed. The main reasons for considering parallelism are: (1) Given any technology base, it is always possible to use multiple processors to achieve higher execution speeds. Stated another way, as technology advances, the new technology can also be used in the construction of multiple processor systems. Furthermore, as the rate of improvement in technology slows (as it must) parallelism becomes even more important. (2) Although significant improvements in speed have been obtained in the past through better compilation techniques and better algorithms [17, 20, 21, 22], we appear to be at a point where too much more cannot be expected. Furthermore, any improvements in compilation technology and algorithms will probably also carry over to the parallel implementations. (3) On the surface, production systems appear to be capable of using large amounts of parallelism — it is possible to perform the match for each production in parallel. This apparent mismatch between the inherently parallel production systems and the uniprocessor implementations, makes parallelism the obvious way to obtain significant speed up in the execution rates.

The thesis concentrates on the parallelism available in OPS5 [10] and Soar [47] production systems. OPS5 was chosen because it has become widely available and because several large, diverse, and real production-system programs have been written in it. These programs form an excellent base for measurements and analysis. Soar was chosen because it represents an interesting new approach in the use of production systems for problem solving and learning. Since only OPS5 and Soar programs are considered, the analysis of parallelism presented in this thesis is possibly biased by the characteristics of these languages. For this reason the results may not be safely generalized to production-system programs written in languages with substantially different characteristics, such as EMYCIN, EXPERT, and KAS [60, 96, 14].

Finally, the research reported in this thesis has been carried out in the context of the *Production System Machine* (PSM) project at Carnegie-Mellon University, which has been exploring all facets of the problem of improving the efficiency of production systems [22, 23, 30, 31, 32, 33]. This thesis extends, refines, and substantiates the preliminary work that appears in the earlier publications.

1.1. Preview of Results

The first thing that is observed on analyzing production systems is that the speed-up from parallelism is quite limited, about 10-fold as compared to initial expectations of 100-fold or 1000-fold. The main reasons for the limited parallelism are: (1) The number of productions that require significant processing (the number of *affected* productions) as a result of a change to working memory is quite small, less than 30. Thus, processing each of these productions in parallel cannot result in a speed-up of more than 30. (2) The variation in the processing requirements of the affected productions is large. This results in a situation where fewer and fewer processors are busy as the execution progresses, which reduces the average number of processors that are busy over the complete execution cycle. (3) The number of changes made to working memory per recognize-act cycle is very small (around 2-3 for most OPS5 systems). As a result, the speed-up obtained from processing multiple changes to working memory in parallel is quite small.

To obtain a large fraction of the limited speed-up that is available, the thesis proposes the exploitation of parallelism at a very fine grain. It also proposes that all working-memory changes made by a production firing be processed in parallel to increase the speed-up. The thesis argues that the Rete algorithm used for performing the match step in existing uniprocessor implementations is also suitable for parallel implementations. However, there are several changes that are necessary to the serial Rete algorithm to make it suitable for parallel implementation. The thesis discusses these changes and gives the reasons behind the design decisions.

The thesis argues that a highly suitable architecture to exploit the fine-grained parallelism in production systems is a shared-memory multiprocessor, with about 32-64 high performance processors. For scheduling the fine grained tasks (consisting of about 50-100 instructions), two solutions are proposed. The first solution consists of a hardware task scheduler. The hardware task scheduler is to be capable of scheduling a task in one bus cycle of the multiprocessor. The second solution consists of multiple software task queues. Preliminary simulation studies indicate that the hardware task scheduler is significantly superior to the software task queues.

The thesis presents a large set of simulation results for production systems exploiting different sources of parallelism. The thesis points out the features of existing programs that limit the speed-up obtainable from parallelism and suggests solutions for some of the bottlenecks. The simulation results show that using the suggested multiprocessor architecture (with individual processors performing at 2 MIPS), it is possible to obtain execution speeds of 5000-27000 wme-changes/sec. This corresponds to a speed-up of 4-fold to 23-fold over the best known sequential implementation using a 2 MIPS processor. This performance is significantly higher than that obtained by other proposed parallel implementations of production systems.

1.2. Organization of the Thesis

Chapter 2 contains the background information necessary for the thesis. Sections 2.1 and 2.2 introduce the OPS5 and Soar production-system formalisms and describe their computation cycles. Section 2.3 presents a detailed description of the Rete algorithm which is used to perform the match step for production systems. The Rete algorithm forms the starting point for much of the work described later in the thesis. Section 2.4 presents the reasons why it is interesting to parallelize the Rete algorithm.

Chapter 3 lists the set of production-system programs analyzed in this thesis and presents the results of static and run-time measurements made on these production-system programs. The static measurements include data on the surface characteristics of production systems (for example, the number of condition elements per production, the number of attribute-value pairs per condition element) and data on the structure of the Rete networks constructed for the programs. The run-time measurements include data on the number of node activations per change to working memory, the number of working-memory changes per production firing, etc. The run-time data can be used to get rough upper-bounds on the speed-up obtainable from parallelism.

Chapter 4 focuses on the sources of parallelism in production-system implementations. For each of the sources (production parallelism, node parallelism, intra-node parallelism, action parallelism, and application parallelism) it describes some of the implementation constraints, the amount of speed-up expected, and the overheads associated with exploiting that source. Most of the chapter is devoted to the parallelism in the match phase; the parallelism in the conflict-resolution phase and the rhs-evaluation phase is discussed only briefly.

4

Chapter 5 discusses the various hardware and software issues associated with the parallel implementation of production systems. It first describes a multiprocessor architecture that is suitable for the parallel implementation and provides justifications for the various decisions. Subsequently it describes the changes that need to be made to the serial Rete algorithm to make it suitable for parallel implementation. Various issues related to the choice of data structures are also discussed.

Chapter 6 discusses the problem of scheduling node activations in the multiprocessor implementation. It proposes two solutions: (1) the use of a hardware task scheduler, and (2) the use of multiple software task queues. These two solutions are detailed in Sections 6.1 and 6.2 respectively. The performance results corresponding to the two solutions, however, are not discussed until Section 8.7.

Chapter 7 presents details about the simulator used to study parallelism in production systems. It presents information about the input traces, the cost models, the computational model, the outputs, and the limitations of the simulator. More details about the derivation of the cost model are presented in Appendices A, B, and C.

Chapter 8 presents the results of the simulations. Section 8.1 lists the run-time traces used in the simulations. Section 8.2 discusses the overheads of a parallel implementation over an implementation done for a uniprocessor. Sections 8.3, 8.4, and 8.5 discuss the speed-up obtained using production parallelism, node parallelism, and intra-node parallelism respectively. Section 8.6 discusses the effect of constructing binary instead of linear Rete networks for productions. Section 8.7 presents results for the case when multiple software task queues are used instead of a hardware task scheduler. Section 8.8 presents results for the case when memory contention overheads are taken into account, and finally, Section 8.9 presents a summary of all results.

Chapter 9 presents related work done by other researchers. Work done on parallel implementation of production systems on C.mmp, Illiac-IV, DADO, NON-VON, Oflazer's production-system machine, and Honeywell's data-flow machine is presented.

Finally, Chapter 10 reviews the primary results of the thesis and presents directions for future research.

2 Background

The first two sections of this chapter describe the syntactic and semantic features of OPS5 and SOAR production-system languages — the two languages for which parallelism is explored in this thesis. The third section describes the *Rete* match algorithm. The Rete algorithm is used in existing uniprocessor implementations of OPS5 and SOAR, and also forms the basis for the parallel match algorithm proposed in the thesis. The last section describes the different classes of algorithms that may be used for match in production systems and gives reasons why the Rete algorithm is appropriate for parallel implementation of production systems.

2.1. OPS5

An OPS5 [10, 19] production system is composed of a set of *if-then* rules called *productions* that make up the *production memory*, and a database of assertions called the *working memory*. The assertions in the working memory are called *working-memory elements*. Each production consists of a conjunction of *condition elements* corresponding to the *if* part of the rule (also called the *left-hand side* of the production), and a set of *actions* corresponding to the *then* part of the rule (also called the *right-hand side* of the production). The actions associated with a production can add, remove or modify working-memory elements, or perform input-output. Figure 2-1 shows an OPS5 production named p1, which has three condition elements in its left-hand side, and one action in its right-hand side.

```
(p   p1   (C1   ^attr1 <x>      ^attr2 12)
          (C2   ^attr1 15       ^attr2 <x>)
     -    (C3   ^attr1 <x>)
     -->
          (remove 2))
```

Figure 2-1: A sample production.

The production-system *interpreter* is the underlying mechanism that determines the set of satisfied productions and controls the execution of the production-system program. The interpreter executes a production-system program by performing the following *recognize-act* cycle:

- **Match:** In this first phase, the left-hand sides of all productions are matched against the contents of working memory. As a result a *conflict set* is obtained, which consists of *instantiations* of all satisfied productions. An instantiation of a production is an ordered list of working memory elements that satisfies the left-hand side of the production. At any given time, the conflict set may contain zero, one, or more instantiations of a given production.

- **Conflict-Resolution**: In this second phase, one of the production instantiations in the conflict set is chosen for execution. If no productions are satisfied, the interpreter halts.

- **Act**: In this third phase, the actions of the production selected in the conflict-resolution phase are executed. These actions may change the contents of working memory. At the end of this phase, the first phase is executed again.

The recognize-act cycle forms the basic control structure in production system programs. During the match phase the knowledge of the program (represented by the production rules) is tested for relevance against the existing problem state (represented by the working memory). During the conflict-resolution phase the most relevant piece of knowledge is selected from all knowledge that is applicable (the conflict set) to the existing problem state. During the act phase, the relevant piece of knowledge is applied to the existing problem state, resulting in a new problem state.

2.1.1. Working-Memory Elements

A working-memory element is a parenthesized list consisting of a constant symbol called the *class* or *type* of the element and zero or more *attribute-value* pairs. The attributes are symbols that are preceded by the operator ^. The values are symbolic or numeric constants. For example, the following working-memory element has class **C1**, the value **12** for attribute **attr1** and the value **15** for attribute **attr2**.

```
(C1        ^attr1   12        ^attr2   15)
```

2.1.2. The Left-Hand Side of a Production

The condition elements in the left-hand side of a production are parenthesized lists similar to the working-memory elements. They may optionally be preceded by the symbol −. Such condition elements are called *negated* condition elements. For example, the production in Figure 2-1 contains three condition elements, with the third one being negated. Condition elements are interpreted as partial descriptions of working-memory elements. When a condition element describes a working-memory element, the working-memory element is said to *match* the condition element. A production is said to be *satisfied* when:

- For every non-negated condition element in the left-hand side of the production, there exists a working-memory element that matches it.

- For every negated condition element in the left-hand side of the production, there does not exist a working-memory element that matches it.

Like a working-memory element, a condition element contains a class name and a sequence of attribute-value pairs. However, the condition element is less restricted than the working-memory element; while the working-memory element can contain only constant symbols and numbers, the condition element can contain variables, predicate symbols, and a variety of other operators as well as constants. Only variables and predicates are described here, since they are sufficient for the purposes of this thesis. A variable is an identifier that begins with the character "<" and ends with ">" — for example, **<x>** and **<status>** are variables. The predicate symbols in OPS5 are:

```
<       =       >       <=      >=      <>      <=>
```

The predicates have their usual meanings for numerical and symbolic values. For example, the first predicate in the list, "<", denotes the *less-than* relationship, the second predicate, "=", denotes *equality*, and the last predicate, "<=>", denotes *of-the-same-type* relationship (a value in OPS5 is either of type *numeric* or *symbolic*). The following condition element contains one constant value (the value of **attr1**), one variable value (the value of **attr2**), and one constant value that is modified by the predicate symbol <> (the value of **attr3**).

```
(C1       ^attr1 nil       ^attr2 <x>       ^attr3 <> nil)
```

A working-memory element matches a condition element if the class-field of the two match and if the value of every attribute in the condition element matches the value of the corresponding attribute in the working-memory element. The rules for determining whether a working-memory element value matches a condition element value are:

- If the condition element value is a constant, it matches only an identical constant.

- If the condition element value is a variable, it will match any value. However, if a variable occurs more than once in a left-hand side, all occurrences of the variable must match identical values.

- If the condition element value is preceded by a predicate symbol, the working-memory element value must be related to the condition element value in the indicated way.

Thus the working-memory element

```
(C1       ^attr1   12       ^attr2   15)
```

will match the following two condition elements

```
(C1       ^attr1   12       ^attr2   <x>)
(C1       ^attr2 > 0)
```

but it will not match the condition element

```
(C1       ^attr1   <x>       ^attr2   <x>).
```

2.1.3. The Right-Hand Side of a Production

The right-hand side of a production consists of an unconditional sequence of actions which can cause input-output, and which are responsible for changes to the working memory. Three kinds of actions are provided to effect working memory changes. *Make* creates a new working-memory element and adds it to working memory. *Modify* changes one or more values of an existing working-memory element. *Remove* deletes an element from the working memory.

2.2. Soar

Soar [46, 48, 49, 77, 78] is a new production-system formalism developed at Carnegie-Mellon University to perform research in problem-solving, expert systems, and learning. It is an attempt to provide expert systems with general reasoning power and the ability to learn. In Soar, every task is formulated as heuristic search in a *problem space* to achieve a goal. The problem space [65] consists of a set of *states* and a set of *operators*. The operators are used to transform one problem state into another. Problem solving is the process of moving from some *initial state* through intermediate states (generated as a result of applying the operators) until a *goal state* is reached. Knowledge about the task domain is used to guide the search leading to the goal state.

Currently, Soar is built on top of OPS5 — the operators, the domain knowledge, the goal-state recognition mechanism, are all built as OPS5 productions. As a result most of the implementation issues, including the exploitation of parallelism, are similar in OPS5 and Soar. The main difference, however, is that Soar does not follow the match — conflict-resolution — act cycle of OPS5 exactly. The computation cycle in Soar is divided into two phases: a monotonic *elaboration phase* and a *decision phase*. During the elaboration phase, all directly available knowledge relevant to the current problem state is brought to bear. On each cycle of elaboration phase, all instantiations of satisfied productions fire concurrently. This phase goes on till quiescence, that is, till there are no more satisfied productions. During the decision phase a fixed procedure is run that translates the information obtained during the elaboration phase into a specific decision — for example, the operator to be applied next. With respect to parallelism, the relevant differences from OPS5 are: (1) there is no conflict-resolution phase; and (2) multiple productions can fire in parallel. The impact of these differences is explored later in the thesis.

Soar production-system programs differ from OPS5 programs in yet another way. Soar programs can improve their performance over time by adding new productions at run-time. An auxiliary process automatically creates new productions concurrently with the operation of the production system. The impact of this feature on parallelism is, however, not explored in this thesis.

2.3. The Rete Match Algorithm

The most time consuming step in the execution of production systems is the match step. To get a feeling for the complexity of match, consider a production system consisting of 1000 productions and 1000 working-memory elements, where each production has three condition elements. In a naive implementation each production will have to be matched against all tuples

of size three from the working memory, leading to over a trillion (1000×1000³) match operations for each execution cycle. Of course, more complex algorithms can achieve the above
computation using a much smaller number of operations, but even with specialized algorithms,
match constitutes around 90% of the interpretation time. The match algorithm used by
uniprocessor implementations of OPS5 and Soar is called Rete [20]. This section describes the
Rete algorithm in some detail as it forms the basis for much of the work described later in the
thesis.

The Rete algorithm exploits (1) the fact that only a small fraction of working memory changes
each cycle, by storing results of match from previous cycles and using them in subsequent
cycles; and (2) the similarity between condition elements of productions, by performing common tests only once. These two features combined together make Rete a very efficient algorithm for match.

The Rete algorithm uses a special kind of a data-flow network compiled from the left-hand
sides of productions to perform match. To generate the network for a production, it begins with
the individual condition elements in the left-hand side. For each condition element it chains
together test nodes that check:

- If the attributes in the condition element that have a constant as their value are
satisfied.

- If the attributes in the condition element that are related to a constant by a predicate
are satisfied.

- If two occurrences of the same variable within the condition element are consistently bound.

Each node in the chain performs one such test. (The three kinds of tests above are called
intra-condition tests, because they correspond to individual condition elements.) Once the algorithm has finished with the individual condition elements, it adds nodes that check for consistency of variable bindings across the multiple condition elements in the left-hand side. (These
tests are called *inter-condition* tests, because they refer to multiple condition elements.) Finally
the algorithm adds a special terminal node to represent the production corresponding to this part
of the network.

Figure 2-2 shows such a network for productions p1 and p2 which appear in the top part of the
figure. In this figure, lines have been drawn between nodes to indicate the paths along which
information flows. Information flows from the top-node down along these paths. The nodes
with a single predecessor (near the top of the figure) are the ones that are concerned with individual condition elements. The nodes with two predecessors are the ones that check for consistency of variable bindings between condition elements. The terminal nodes are at the bottom
of the figure. Note that when two left-hand sides require identical nodes, the algorithm shares
part of the network rather than building duplicate nodes.

To avoid performing the same tests repeatedly, the Rete algorithm stores the result of the

11

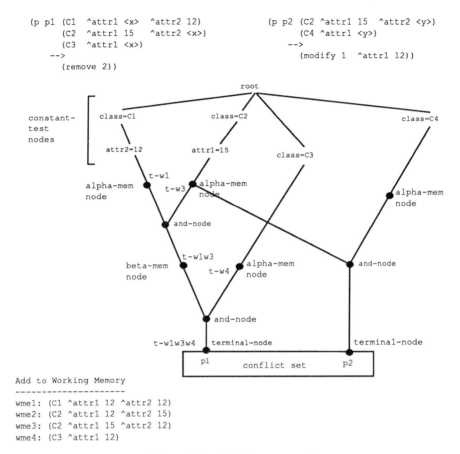

```
(p p1 (C1  ^attr1 <x>   ^attr2 12)          (p p2 (C2 ^attr1 15   ^attr2 <y>)
       (C2  ^attr1 15    ^attr2 <x>)                 (C4 ^attr1 <y>)
       (C3  ^attr1 <x>)                              -->
       -->                                           (modify 1   ^attr1 12))
       (remove 2))
```

```
Add to Working Memory
---------------------
wme1: (C1 ^attr1 12 ^attr2 12)
wme2: (C2 ^attr1 12 ^attr2 15)
wme3: (C2 ^attr1 15 ^attr2 12)
wme4: (C3 ^attr1 12)
```

Figure 2-2: The Rete network.

match with working memory as state within the nodes. This way, only changes made to the
working memory by the most recent production firing have to be processed every cycle. Thus,
the input to the Rete network consists of the changes to the working memory. These changes
filter through the network updating the state stored within the network. The output of the network consists of a specification of changes to the conflict set.

The objects that are passed between nodes are called *tokens*, which consist of a *tag* and an
ordered list of working-memory elements. The tag can be either a +, indicating that something
has been added to the working memory, or a −, indicating that something has been removed
from it. (No special tag for working-memory element modification is needed because a modify
is treated as a delete followed by an add.) The list of working-memory elements associated with
a token corresponds to a sequence of those elements that the system is trying to match or has
already matched against a subsequence of condition elements in the left-hand side.

12

The data-flow network produced by the Rete algorithm consists of four different types of nodes.[2] These are:

1. **Constant-test nodes:** These nodes are used to test if the attributes in the condition element which have a constant value are satisfied. These nodes always appear in the top part of the network. They have only one input, and as a result, they are sometimes called *one-input* nodes.

2. **Memory nodes:** These nodes store the results of the match phase from previous cycles as state within them. The state stored in a memory node consists of a list of the tokens that match a part of the left-hand side of the associated production. For example, the right-most memory node in Figure 2-2 stores all tokens matching the second condition-element of production p2.

   At a more detailed level, there are two types of memory nodes — the α-*mem* nodes and the β-*mem* nodes. The α-mem nodes store tokens that match individual condition elements. Thus all memory nodes immediately below constant-test nodes are α-mem nodes. The β-mem nodes store tokens that match a sequence of condition elements in the left-hand side of a production. Thus all memory nodes immediately below two-input nodes are β-mem nodes.

3. **Two-input nodes:** These nodes test for joint satisfaction of condition elements in the left-hand side of a production. Both inputs of a two-input node come from memory nodes. When a token arrives on the left input of a two-input node, it is compared to each token stored in the memory node connected to the right input. All token pairs that have consistent variable bindings are sent to the successors of the two-input node. Similar action is taken when a token arrives on the right input of a two-input node.

   There are also two types of two-input nodes — the *and-nodes* and the *not-nodes*. While the and-nodes are responsible for the positive condition elements and behave in the way described above, the not-nodes are responsible for the negated condition elements and behave in an opposite manner. The not-nodes generate a successor token only if there are no matching tokens in the memory node corresponding to the negated condition element.

4. **Terminal nodes:** There is one such node associated with each production in the program, as can be seen at bottom of Figure 2-2. Whenever a token flows into a terminal node, the corresponding production is either inserted into or deleted from the conflict set.

The following example provides a more detailed view of the processing that goes on inside the Rete network. The example corresponds to the two productions and the network given in Figure 2-2. It shows the match process as the four working-memory elements shown in the bottom-left corner of Figure 2-2 are sequentially added to the working memory.

---

[2]Current implementations of the Rete algorithm contain some other node types that are not mentioned here. Nodes of these types do not perform any of the conceptually necessary operations and are present primarily to simplify specific implementations. For this reason, they have been omitted from discussion in the thesis.

When the first working-memory element is added, token t-w1,

```
< + ,  (C1 ^attr1 12 ^attr2 12)  >
```

is constructed and sent to the root node. The root node broadcasts the token to all its successors. The associated tests fail at all successors except at one which is checking for "Class = C1". This constant-test node passes the token down to its single successor, another constant-test node, checking if "attr2 = 12". Since this is so, the token is passed on to the memory node, which stores the token and passes a copy of the token to the and-node below it. The and-node compares the incoming token on its left input to tokens in its right memory (which at this point is empty), but no pairs can be formed. At this point, the network has stabilized — in other words no further activity occurs, so we go on to the second working-memory element.

The token for the second working-memory element, t-w2,

```
< + ,  (C2 ^attr1 12 ^attr2 15)  >
```

is constructed and sent to the root node, which broadcasts the token to its successors. The token passes the "Class = C2" test but fails the "attr1 = 15" test, so no further processing takes place.

The token for the third working-memory element, t-w3,

```
< + ,  (C2 ^attr1 15 ^attr2 12)  >
```

passes through the tests "Class = C2" and "attr1 = 15", and is stored in the memory node below them. The memory node passes a copy of the token to the two successor and-nodes below it. The and-node on the right finds no tokens in its right memory, so no further processing is done there. The and-node on the left checks the token for consistency against token, t-w1, stored in its left memory. The consistency check is satisfied as the variable <x> is bound consistently. The and-node creates a new token, t-w1w3,

```
< + ,  ((C1 ^attr1 12 ^attr2 12), (C2 ^attr1 15 ^attr2 12))  >
```

and passes it down to the memory node below, which stores it. The memory node now passes a copy of the token to the and-node below it. The and-node finds that its right memory is empty, so no further processing takes place.

On addition of the fourth working-memory element, token t-w4,

```
< + ,  (C3 ^attr1 12)  >
```

is sent to the root node, which broadcasts it. The token passes the test "Class = C3" and passes on to the memory node below it. The memory node stores the token and passes a copy of the token to the and-node below it. The and-node checks for consistent bindings in the left memory and finds that the newly arrived token, t-w4, is consistent with token t-w1w3 stored in its left memory. The and-node then creates a new token, t-w1w3w4,

```
<+ ,  ((C1 ^attr1 12 ^attr2 12)
        (C2 ^attr1 15 ^attr2 12)
        (C3 ^attr1 12))>
```

and sends it to the terminal node corresponding to p1 below. The terminal node then inserts the instantiation of p1 corresponding to t-w1w3w4 into the conflict set.

The performance of Rete-based interpreters has steadily improved over the years. The most widely used Rete-based interpreter is the OPS5 interpreter. The Franz Lisp implementation of this interpreter runs at around 8 wme-changes/sec (about 3 rule firings per second) on a VAX-11/780, while a Bliss-based implementation runs at around 40 wme-changes/sec. In the above two interpreters a significant loss in the speed is due to the interpretation overhead of nodes. In OPS83 [21] this overhead has been eliminated by compiling the network directly into machine code. While it is possible to escape to the interpreter for complex operations during match or for setting up the initial conditions for the match, the majority of the match is done without an intervening interpretation level. This has led to a large speed-up and the OPS83 interpreter runs at around 200 wme-changes/sec on the VAX-11/780. Some further optimizations to the OPS83 have been designed which would permit it to run at around 400-800 wme-changes/sec. The aim of the parallel implementations is to take the performance still higher, in the range 2000-20000 wme-changes/sec. It is expected that this order of magnitude increase in speed over the best possible uniprocessor interpreters will open new application and research areas that could not be addressed before by production systems.

2.4. Why Parallelize Rete?

While being an extremely efficient algorithm for match on uniprocessors, Rete is also an effective algorithm for match on parallel processors. This section discusses some of the motivations for studying Rete and the reasons why Rete is appropriate for parallel implementations.

2.4.1. State-Saving vs. Non-State-Saving Match Algorithms

It is possible to divide the set of match algorithms for production system into two categories: (1) the *state-saving* algorithms and (2) the *non-state-saving* algorithms. The state-saving algorithms store the results of executing match from previous recognize-act cycles, so that only the changes made to the working memory by the most recent production firing need be processed every cycle. In contrast, the non-state-saving algorithms start from scratch every time, that is, they match the complete working memory against all the productions on each cycle.

In a state-saving algorithm the work done includes two steps: (1) computing the fresh state corresponding to the newly inserted working-memory elements and storing the fresh state in appropriate data structures; (2) identifying the state corresponding to the deleted working-memory elements and deleting this state from the data structures storing it. In a non-state-saving algorithm the work done includes only one step, that of computing the state for the match between the complete working memory and all the productions. (Note that this may involve temporarily storing some of the partial state that is generated.) In both state-saving and non-state-saving algorithms, state refers to the matches between condition elements and working-memory elements that are computed as an intermediate step in the process of computing the match between the complete left-hand sides of productions and the working-memory elements.

Whether it is advantageous to store state depends on (1) the fraction of working memory that changes on each cycle, and (2) the amount of state that is stored by the state-saving algorithm. To evaluate the advantages and disadvantages more concretely, consider the following simple model. Consider a production-system program for which the stable size of the working memory is s, the average number of inserts to working memory on each cycle is i, and the average number of deletes from working memory is d. Let the cost of step-1 (as described in the previous paragraph) for a single insert to working memory be c_1 and the cost for step-2 for a single delete from working memory be c_2. Further assume that the average cost of the temporary state computed and stored by the non-state saving algorithm is c_3 for each working-memory element. Then the average cost per execution cycle of the state-saving algorithm is $C_{state-sav}=i{\cdot}c_1+d{\cdot}c_2$. The average cost per execution cycle of the non-state-saving algorithm is $C_{non-state-sav}=s{\cdot}c_3$.

To evaluate the advantages of the state-saving algorithm, consider the inequality $C_{state-sav} < C_{non-state-sav}$. For the implementations being considered for the Rete algorithm, the cost of an insert to working memory is the same as the cost of a delete from the working memory. As a result, substituting $c_1=c_2$ in the inequality, we get $(i+d)/s < c_3/c_1$. Estimates based on simulations done for the Rete algorithm (see Chapter 8) indicate that c_1 is approximately equal to execution of 1800 machine-code instructions, and that c_3 is approximately equal to execution of 1100 machine-code instructions . Using these estimates we get the condition that state-saving algorithms are more efficient when $(i+d)/s < 0.61$, that is, state-saving algorithms are better if the number of insertions plus deletions per cycle is less than 61% of the stable size of the working memory. Measurements [30] on several OPS5 programs show that the number of inserts plus deletes per cycle constitutes less than 0.5% of the stable working memory size. Thus a non-state-saving algorithm will have to recover an inefficiency factor of 120 before it breaks even with a state-saving algorithm for OPS5-like production systems.[3]

The following example illustrates some of the points made in the previous paragraphs. Consider a production-system program whose stable working memory size is around 1000 elements and where each production firing makes 2-3 changes to the working memory. This is a common scenario for OPS5 programs. It is quite obvious in this case that since 99.8% of the working memory is unchanged, it is unwise to use a non-state-saving algorithm which performs match with this unchanged working memory all over again. Now consider a program whose stable working memory size is again 1000, but where each production firing changes 750 of these 1000 working-memory elements. In this case a state-saving algorithm will first have to identify

---

[3]In case the values of c_1, c_2, and c_3 are estimated from a different base algorithm, the above numbers will change somewhat.

and delete the state corresponding to the 750 deleted elements and then recompute and store state for the new 750 elements. The only saving corresponds to the unchanged 250 working-memory elements. The state-saving algorithm in this case no longer seems attractive.

The amount of state stored by a state-saving algorithm also influences the suitability of such an algorithm compared to a non-state-saving algorithm. The amount of state stored is important because it determines the amount of work needed to compute it when working-memory elements are inserted, and the amount of work needed to delete it when working-memory elements are deleted. In terms of the model described in the previous paragraphs, the amount of state that a state-saving algorithm stores affects the value of the constants c_1, c_2, and c_3, thus influencing the ratio $(i+d)/s$ when a non-state-saving algorithm becomes appropriate.

In summary, state-saving algorithms are appropriate when working memory changes slowly and when it costs more to recompute the state for the unchanged part of the working memory than to undo the state for the deleted working-memory elements. For OPS5 and Soar systems, the fraction of working memory that changes on every cycle is, in fact, very small. For this reason only state-saving algorithms are considered in the thesis.

2.4.2. Rete as a Specific Instance of State-Saving Algorithms

While it is generally accepted that state-saving algorithms are suitable for OPS5 and Soar production systems, there is no consensus about the amount of state that such algorithms should store. Of course, there are many possibilities. This section discusses some of the schemes that various research groups have explored, where the Rete algorithm fits amongst these schemes, and why Rete is interesting.

One possible scheme that a state-saving algorithm may use is to store information only about matches between individual condition elements and working memory elements. In the terminology of the Rete algorithm, this means that only the state associated with α-mem nodes is stored. For example, consider a production with three condition elements CE1, CE2, and CE3. Then the algorithm stores information about all working-memory elements that match CE1, all working-memory elements that match CE2, and all working-memory elements that match CE3. However, it does not store working-memory tuples that satisfy CE1 and CE2 together, or CE2 and CE3 together, and so on. This information is recomputed on each cycle. Such a scheme is used by the TREAT algorithm developed for the DADO machine at Columbia University [61]. This scheme stands at the low end of the spectrum of state-saving algorithms. A problem with this scheme is that much of the state has to be recomputed on each cycle, often with the effect of increasing the total time taken by the cycle.

A second possible scheme that a state-saving algorithm may use is to store information about matches between all possible combinations of condition elements that occur in the left-hand side of a production and the sequences of working-memory elements that satisfy them. For example, consider a production with three condition elements CE1, CE2, and CE3. Then, in this scheme, the algorithm stores information about all working memory elements that match CE1, CE2, and CE3 individually, about all working-memory element tuples that match CE1 and CE2 together, CE2 and CE3 together, CE1 and CE3 together, and so on. Kemal Oflazer, in his thesis [70], has proposed a variation of this scheme to implement a highly parallel algorithm for match. This scheme stands at the high end of the spectrum of state-saving algorithms, in that it stores almost all information known about the matches between the productions and the working memory. Two possible problems with such a scheme are: (1) the state may become very large; and (2) the algorithm may spend a lot of time computing and deleting state that never really gets used, that is, state that never results in a production entering or leaving the conflict set.

The amount of state computed by the Rete algorithm falls in between that computed by the previous two schemes. The Rete algorithm stores information about working-memory elements that match individual condition elements, as proposed in the first scheme. In addition, it also stores information about tuples of working-memory elements that match some *fixed* combinations of condition elements occurring in the left-hand side of a production. This is in contrast to the second scheme, where information is stored about tuples of working-memory elements that match *all* combinations of condition elements. The choice about the combinations of condition elements for which match information is stored is fixed at compile time.[4] For example, for a production with three condition elements CE1, CE2, and CE3, the standard Rete algorithm stores information about working-memory elements that match CE1, CE2, and CE3 individually. This information is stored in the α-mem nodes. In addition, it stores information about working-memory element tuples that match CE1 and CE2 together. This information is stored in a β-mem node, as can be seen in Figure 2-2. The Rete algorithm uses this information and combines it with the information about working-memory elements that match CE3 to generate tuples that match the complete left-hand side (CE1, CE2, and CE3 all together). The Rete algorithm does not store information about working memory tuples that match CE1 and CE3 together or those tuples that match CE2 and CE3 together, as is done by the algorithm in the second scheme.

The Rete algorithm has been successfully used in current uniprocessor implementations of OPS5 and Soar. It avoids some of the extra work done in the first scheme — work done in recomputing working-memory tuples that match combinations of condition elements. It is also less susceptible to the combinatorial explosion of state that is possible in the second scheme, because it can carefully select the combinations of condition elements for which state is stored. The combinations that are selected can significantly impact the efficiency of a parallel implementation of the algorithm. The thesis evaluates two of the many possible schemes for choosing these combinations, and discusses the factors influencing the choice in Section 5.2.6.

---

[4]Note that by varying the combinations of condition elements for which match information is stored, a large family of different Rete algorithms can be generated.

2.4.3. Node Sharing in the Rete Algorithm

As mentioned in Section 2.3, the Rete algorithm exploits the similarity between condition elements of productions by sharing constant-test nodes, memory nodes, and two-input nodes. For example, two constant-test nodes and an α-memory node are shared between productions *p1* and *p2* shown in Figure 2-2 (for some statistics on sharing of nodes in the Rete network, see Section 3.3.2). The sharing of nodes in the Rete network results in considerable savings in execution time, since the nodes have to be evaluated only once instead of multiple times. The sharing of nodes also results in savings in space. This is because sharing reduces the size of the Rete network and because sharing can collapse replicated tokens in multiple unshared memory-nodes into a single token in a shared memory-node. The main implication of the above discussion is that it is important for an efficient match algorithm to exploit the similarity in condition elements of productions to enhance its performance.

2.4.4. Rete as a Parallel Algorithm

The previous three subsections have discussed the general suitability of the Rete algorithm for match in OPS5 and Soar systems. They, however, do not discuss the suitability of Rete for parallel implementation. This subsection describes some features of Rete that make it attractive for parallel implementation.

The data-flow like organization of the Rete network is the key feature that permits exploitation of parallelism at a relatively fine grain. It is possible to evaluate the activations of different nodes in the Rete network in parallel. It is also possible to evaluate multiple activations of the same node in parallel and to process multiple changes to working memory in parallel. These sources of parallelism are discussed in detail in Chapter 4.

The parallel evaluation of node activations in the Rete network also corresponds to higher-level, more intuitive forms of parallelism in production systems. For example, evaluating different node activations in parallel corresponds to (1) performing match for different productions in parallel (also called *production-level* parallelism) and (2) performing match for different condition elements within the same production in parallel (also called *condition-level* parallelism) [22].

The state-saving model of Rete, where the state corresponding to only fixed combinations of condition elements in the left-hand side is stored, does impose some sequentiality on the evaluation of nodes, as compared to models where state corresponding to all possible combinations of condition elements is stored. It is, however, a plausible trade-off in order to avoid some of the problems associated with the other schemes, as discussed in the previous subsections.

Finally, although we have no way to prove that Rete is the most suitable algorithm for parallel implementation of production systems, for the reasons stated above, we are confident that it is a pretty good algorithm. Detailed simulation results for parallel implementations presented in

Chapter 8 of this thesis, and comparisons to the performance numbers obtained by other researchers (see Chapter 9) [31, 38, 61, 70], further confirm this view.

3 Measurements on Production Systems

Before proceeding on the design of a complex algorithm or architecture, it is necessary to identify the characteristics of the programs or applications for which the algorithm or the architecture are to be optimized. For example, computer architects refer to data about usage of instructions, depth of procedure call invocations, frequency of successful branch instructions, to optimize the design and implementation of new machine architectures [37, 71, 73]. Information about the target programs or applications serves two purposes: (1) it serves as an aid in the design process by identifying critical requirements; and (2) it serves as a means to evaluate the finished design.

This chapter describes the characteristics of six OPS5 and Soar production systems that have been used in the thesis for the design and evaluation of parallel implementations of production systems.[5] The data about the six production systems is divided into three parts. The first part consists of measurements on the textual structure of these production systems. The second part consists of information on the compiled form of the productions, and the third part consists of run-time measurements on the production-system programs.

3.1. Production-System Programs Studied in the Thesis

The six production-system programs that have been used to evaluate the algorithms and the architectures for the parallel implementation of production systems are given below. They are listed in order of decreasing number of productions, and this order is maintained in all the graphs shown later.[6]

1. VT [52] (Vertical Transport) is an expert system that selects components for a traction elevator system. It is written in OPS5 and consists of 1322 rules.

2. ILOG[7] [59] is an expert system that maintains inventories and production schedules for factories. It is written in OPS5 and consists of 1181 rules.

---

[5]The characteristics for another set of six production-system programs can be found in [30].

[6]Note: Many of the production-system programs listed below are still undergoing development. For this reason the data associated with the programs is liable to change. The number of rules listed with each of the programs below corresponds to the number of rules in the version on which data was taken.

[7]Referred to as PTRANS in the cited paper.

3. MUD [40] is an expert system that is used to analyze fluids used in oil drilling operations. It is written in OPS5 and consists of 872 rules.

4. DAA [43, 44] (Design Automation Assistant) is an expert system that designs computers from high-level specifications of the systems. It is written in OPS5 and consists of 445 rules.

5. R1-SOAR [77] is an expert system that configures the UNIBUS for Digital Equipment Corporation's VAX-11 computer systems. It is written in Soar and consists of 319 rules.

6. EP-SOAR [48] is an expert system that solves the Eight Puzzle. It is written in Soar and consists of 62 rules.

The above production-system programs represent a variety of applications and programming styles. For example, VT is a knowledge-intensive expert system which has been especially designed with knowledge acquisition in mind. It consists of only a small number of rule types and is significantly different from the earlier systems [56, 57] developed at Carnegie-Mellon University.[8] ILOG is a run-of-the-mill knowledge-intensive expert system. In contrast to the other five systems, the MUD system is a backward-chaining production system [4] and is primarily goal driven. The DAA program represents a computation-intensive task compared to the knowledge-intensive tasks performed by VT, ILOG, and MUD systems. Both R1-SOAR and EP-SOAR represent programming styles in Soar. R1-SOAR also represents an attempt at doing knowledge-intensive programming in a general weak-method problem-solving architecture. It can make use of the available knowledge to achieve high performance, but whenever knowledge is lacking, it has mechanisms so that the program can resort to more basic and knowledge-lean problem-solving methods.

3.2. Surface Characteristics of Production Systems

Surface measurements refer to the textual features of production-system programs. Examples of such features are — the number of condition elements in the left-hand sides of productions, the number of attributes per condition element, the number of variables per condition element. Such features are useful in that they give information about the code and static data structures that are generated for the programs, and they also help explain some aspects of the the run-time behavior of the programs.

The following subsections present the data for the measured features, including a brief description of how the measurements were made. Data about the same features of different production

---

[8]Personal communication from John McDermott.

systems are presented together, and have been normalized to permit comparison.[9] Along with each data graph the *average*, the *standard deviation*, and the *coefficient of variation*[10] for the data points are given.

3.2.1. Condition Elements per Production

Figure 3-1 shows the number of condition elements per production for the six production-system programs. The number of condition elements per production includes both positive elements and negative ones. The curves for the programs are normalized by plotting *percent* of productions, instead of *number* of productions, along the y-axis. The number of condition elements in a production reflects the specificity of the production, that is, the set of situations in which the production is applicable. The number of condition elements in a production also impacts the complexity of performing match for that production (see Section 5.2.6). Note that, on average, Soar productions have many more condition elements than OPS5 productions.

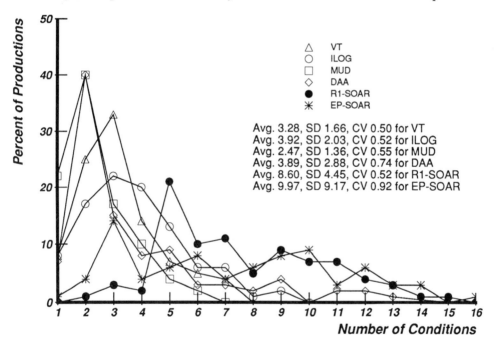

Figure 3-1:   Condition elements per production.

[9]The limits of the axes of the graphs have been adjusted to show the main portion of the graph clearly. In doing this, however, in some cases a few extreme points could not be put on the graph. For this reason, the reader should not draw conclusions about the maximum values of the parameters from the graph.

[10]Coefficient of Variation = Standard Deviation / Average.

3.2.2. Actions per Production

Figure 3-2 shows the number of actions per production. The number of actions reflects the processing required to execute the right-hand side of a production. A large number of actions per production also implies a greater potential for parallelism, because then a large number of changes to the working memory can be processed in parallel, before the next conflict-resolution phase is executed.

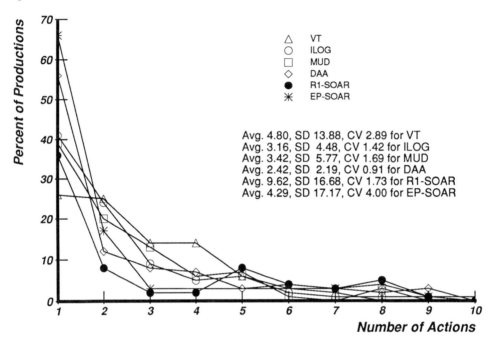

Figure 3-2: Actions per production.

3.2.3. Negative Condition Elements per Production

The graph in Figure 3-3 shows the number of negated condition elements in the left-hand side of a production versus the percent of productions having them. It shows that approximately 27% percent of productions have one or more negated condition elements. Since negated condition elements denote universal quantification over the working memory, the percentage of productions having them is an important characteristic of production-system programs. The measurements are also useful in calculating the number of not-nodes in the Rete network.

24

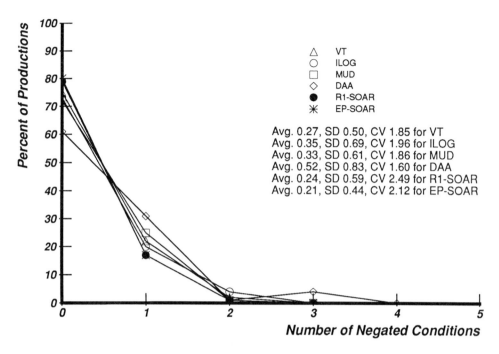

Figure 3-3: Negative condition elements per production.

3.2.4. Attributes per Condition Element

Figure 3-4 shows the distribution for the number of attributes per condition element. The *class* of a condition element, which is an implicit attribute, is counted explicitly in the measurements. The number of attributes in a condition element reflects the number of tests that are required to detect a matching working-memory element. The striking peak at three for R1-Soar and EP-Soar programs reflects the uniform encoding of data as triplets in Soar.

3.2.5. Tests per Two-Input Node

This feature is specific to the Rete match algorithm and refers to the number of variable bindings that are checked for consistency at each two-input node (and-node or not-node). A value of zero indicates that no variables are checked for consistent binding, while a large value indicates that a large number of variables are checked. For example, if the number of tests is zero, for every token that arrives at the input of an and-node, as many tokens as there are in the opposite memory are sent to its successors. This usually implies a large amount of work. Alternatively, if the number of tests is large, then the number of tokens sent to the successors is small, but doing the pairwise comparison for consistent binding now takes more time. The graph for the number of tests per two-input node is shown in Figure 3-5.

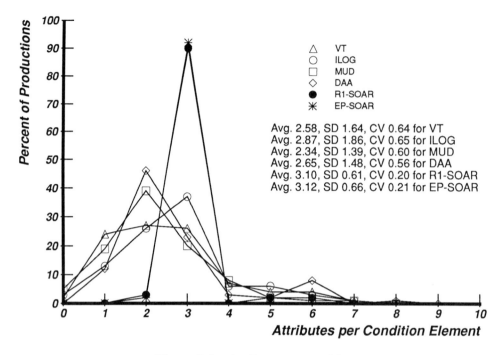

Figure 3-4: Attributes per condition element.

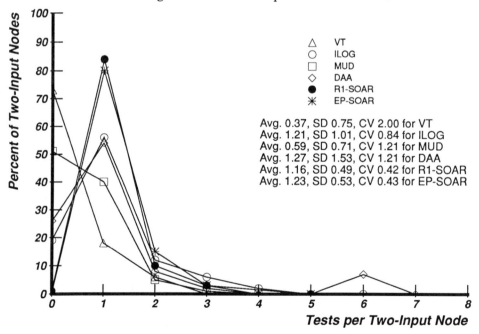

Figure 3-5: Tests per two-input node.

3.2.6. Variables Bound and Referenced

Figure 3-6 shows the number of distinct variables which are both bound and referenced in the left-hand side of a production. Consistency tests are necessary only for these variables. Beyond the α-mem nodes, all processing done by the two-input nodes requires access to the values of only these variables; values of other variables or attributes is not required. This implies that the tokens in the network may only store the values of these variables instead of storing complete copies of working-memory elements. For parallel architectures that do not have shared memory, this can lead to significant improvements in the storage requirements and in the communication costs associated with tokens.

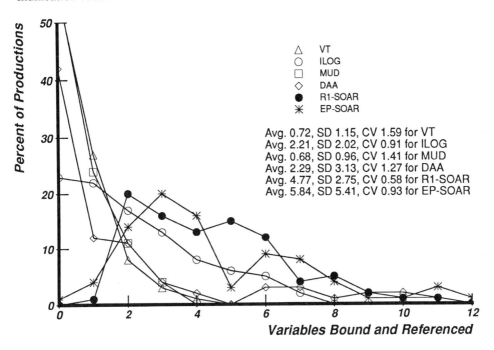

Figure 3-6: Variables bound and referenced.

3.2.7. Variables Bound but not Referenced

Figure 3-7 shows the number of distinct variables which are bound but not referenced in the left-hand side of a production. (These bindings are usually used in the right-hand side of the production.) This indicates the number of variables for which no consistency checks have to be performed.

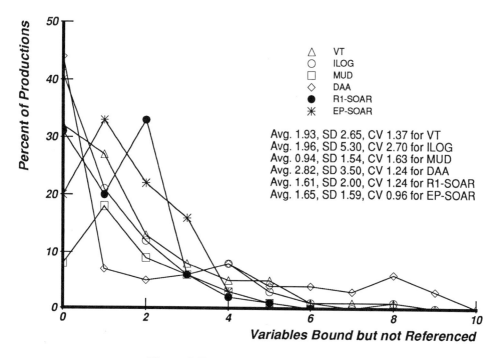

Figure 3-7: Variables bound but not referenced.

3.2.8. Variable Occurrences in Left-Hand Side

Figure 3-8 shows the number of times each variable occurs in the left-hand side of a production. Both positive and negative condition elements are considered in counting the variables. Our measurements also show that variables almost never occur multiple times within the same condition element (average of 1.5% over all systems). Under this assumption, the number of occurrences of a variable represents the number of condition elements within a production in which the variable occurs.

3.2.9. Variables per Condition Element

Figure 3-9 shows the number of variable occurrences within a condition element (not necessarily distinct, though as per Section 3.2.8 they mostly are). If this number is significant compared to the number of attributes for some class of condition elements, then it usually implies that the selectivity of those condition elements is small, or in other words, a large number of working-memory elements will match those condition elements.

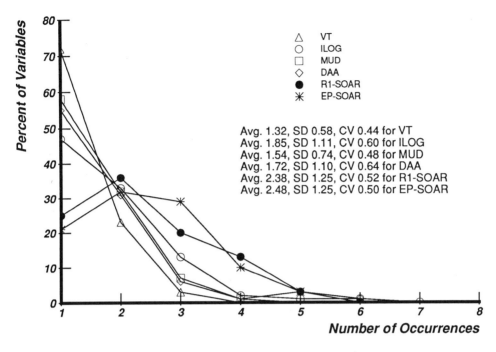

Figure 3-8: Occurrences of each variable.

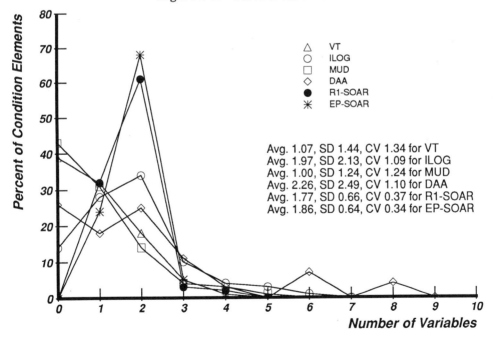

Figure 3-9: Variables per condition element.

3.2.10. Condition Element Classes

Tables 3-1, 3-2, 3-3, 3-4, 3-5, and 3-6 list the seven condition element classes occurring most frequently for the production-system programs. The tables also list the total number of attributes, the average number of attributes and its standard deviation, and the average number of variable occurrences in condition elements of each class. The total number of attributes for a condition element class gives an estimate of the size of the working-memory element. This information can be used to determine the communication overhead in transporting working-memory elements amongst multiple memories in a parallel architecture. It also has implications for space requirements for storing the working-memory elements. If we subtract the average number of variables from the average number of attributes for a condition element class, we obtain the average number of attributes which have a constant value for that class. This number in turn has implications for the selectivity of condition elements of that class.

Table 3-1: VT: Condition Element Classes

Class Name	# of CEs(%)	Tot-Attr	Avg-Attr	SD-Attr	Avg-Vars
1. context	1366 (31%)	4	1.59	0.75	0.22
2. item	756 (17%)	47	2.97	0.86	1.14
3. input	448 (10%)	19	3.06	1.24	1.56
4. needdata	239 (5%)	27	2.62	1.53	1.56
5. distance	228 (5%)	12	5.18	1.40	1.67
6. sys-measure	175 (4%)	11	4.87	1.47	1.71
7. io-stack	110 (2%)	4	1.05	0.35	1.02

Total number of condition element classes is 48

Table 3-2: ILOG: Condition Element Classes

Class Name	# of CEs(%)	Tot-Attr	Avg-Attr	SD-Attr	Avg-Vars
1. arg	1270 (27%)	4	2.99	0.14	1.91
2. task	1004 (21%)	2	1.76	0.44	0.77
3. datum	431 (9%)	58	4.16	2.15	2.89
4. period	143 (3%)	13	3.81	1.18	3.41
5. packed-with	106 (2%)	32	4.73	2.23	3.84
6. order	101 (2%)	37	3.16	2.29	3.08
7. capacity	91 (1%)	41	5.66	4.57	3.90

Total number of condition element classes is 86

Table 3-3: MUD: Condition Element Classes

Class Name	# of CEs(%)	Tot-Attr	Avg-Attr	SD-Attr	Avg-Vars
1. task	678 (31%)	4	2.35	0.85	0.58
2. data	547 (25%)	24	2.35	1.15	1.11
3. hyp	160 (7%)	9	1.99	0.72	0.60
4. datafor	111 (5%)	20	4.14	1.93	2.55
5. reason	74 (3%)	13	3.12	1.58	1.24
6. change	65 (3%)	6	1.40	0.87	0.88
7. do	65 (3%)	21	5.25	1.60	2.83

Total number of condition element classes is 38

Table 3-4: DAA: Condition Element Classes

Class Name	# of CEs(%)	Tot-Attr	Avg-Attr	SD-Attr	Avg-Vars
1. context	474 (24%)	3	2.40	0.52	2.05
2. port	241 (13%)	6	2.35	0.72	2.08
3. db-operator	197 (11%)	6	1.70	0.58	0.54
4. link	173 (9%)	6	5.28	1.53	5.55
5. module	170 (9%)	6	2.68	1.12	1.66
6. lists	134 (7%)	3	1.75	0.44	2.06
7. outnode	112 (6%)	11	2.37	0.87	2.14

Total number of condition element classes is 26

Table 3-5: R1-SOAR: Condition Element Classes

Class Name	# of CEs(%)	Tot-Attr	Avg-Attr	SD-Attr	Avg-Vars
1. goal-ctx-info	988 (36%)	3	2.99	0.11	1.80
2. op-info	383 (13%)	3	2.95	0.23	1.54
3. state-info	375 (13%)	3	2.88	0.32	1.77
4. space-info	217 (17%)	3	3.00	0.07	1.04
5. order-info	183 (6%)	3	2.99	0.10	1.67
6. preference	157 (5%)	8	5.32	0.78	3.44
7. module-info	87 (3%)	3	2.92	0.27	1.90

Total number of condition element classes is 21

Table 3-6: EP-SOAR: Condition Element Classes

Class Name	# of CEs(%)	Tot-Attr	Avg-Attr	SD-Attr	Avg-Vars
1. goal-ctx-info	278 (44%)	3	2.99	0.10	1.83
2. binding-info	85 (13%)	3	3.00	0.00	1.71
3. state-info	59 (9%)	3	2.90	0.30	1.92
4. eval-info	54 (8%)	3	2.96	0.19	1.83
5. op-info	41 (6%)	3	2.93	0.26	1.54
6. preference	36 (5%)	8	5.47	1.12	3.22
7. space-info	30 (4%)	3	3.00	0.00	1.13

Total number of condition element classes is 10

3.2.11. Action Types

Table 3-7 gives the distribution of actions in the right-hand side into classes *make*, *remove*, *modify*, and *other* for the production-system programs. The only actions that affect the working memory are of type make, remove, or modify. While each make and remove action causes only one change to the working memory, a modify actions causes two changes to the working memory. This data then gives an estimate of the percentage of right-hand side actions that change the working memory. This data can also be combined with data about the number of actions in the right-hand side of productions (given in Section 3.2.2) to determine the average number of changes made to working memory per production firing.

Table 3-7: Action Type Distribution

Action Type	VT	ILOG	MUD	DAA	R1-SOAR	EP-SOAR
1. Make	52%	20%	48%	34%	86%	78%
2. Modify	13%	15%	17%	18%	0%	0%
3. Remove	5%	7%	4%	18%	0%	0%
4. Others	27%	56%	28%	27%	12%	21%

3.2.12. Summary of Surface Measurements

Table 3-8 gives a summary of the surface measurements for the production-system programs. It brings together the average values of the various features for all six programs. The features listed in the table are number of productions in the program, condition elements per production, actions per production, negated condition elements per production, attributes per condition element, variables per condition element, and tests per two-input node.

Table 3-8: Summary of Surface Measurements

Feature	VT	ILOG	MUD	DAA	R1-SOAR	EP-SOAR
1. Prods	1322	1181	872	445	319	62
2. CEs/Prod	3.28	3.92	2.47	3.89	8.60	9.97
3. Actns/Prod	4.80	3.16	3.42	2.42	9.62	4.29
4. nCEs/Prod	0.27	0.35	0.33	0.52	0.24	0.21
5. Attr/CE	2.58	2.87	2.34	2.65	3.10	3.12
6. Vars/CE	1.07	1.97	1.00	2.26	1.77	1.86
7. Tests/2inp	0.37	1.21	0.59	1.27	1.16	1.23

3.3. Measurements on the Rete Network

This section presents results of measurements made on the Rete network constructed by the OPS5 compiler. The measured features include the number of nodes of each type in the network and the amount of sharing that is present in the network.

3.3.1. Number of Nodes in the Rete Network

Table 3-9 presents data on the number of nodes of each type in the network for the various production-system programs. These numbers reflect the complexity of the network that is constructed for the programs. Table 3-10 gives the normalized number of nodes, that is, the number of nodes per production. The normalized numbers are useful for comparing the average complexity of the productions for the various production-system programs.[11]

Table 3-9: Number of Nodes

Node Type	VT	ILOG	MUD	DAA	R1-SOAR	EP-SOAR
1. Const-Test	2849	1884	1743	397	436	118
2. α-mem	1748	1481	878	339	398	96
3. β-mem	1116	1363	358	549	1252	369
4. And	2205	2320	872	847	1542	425
5. Not	332	400	267	144	60	13
6. Terminal	1322	1181	872	445	391	62
7. Total	9572	8629	4990	2721	4079	1083

Table 3-10: Nodes per Production

Node Type	VT	ILOG	MUD	DAA	R1-SOAR	EP-SOAR
1. Const-Test	2.15	1.59	1.99	0.89	1.11	1.90
2. α-mem	1.32	1.25	1.00	0.76	1.01	1.54
3. β-mem	0.84	1.15	0.41	1.23	3.20	5.95
4. And	1.66	1.96	1.00	1.89	3.94	6.85
5. Not	0.25	0.33	0.30	0.32	0.15	0.20
6. Terminal	1.00	1.00	1.00	1.00	1.00	1.00
7. Total	7.22	7.28	5.70	6.09	10.41	17.44

Table 3-11 presents the number of nodes per condition element for the production-system programs. The average number of nodes per condition element over all the systems is 1.86. This number is quite small because many nodes are shared between condition elements. In case no sharing is allowed, this number jumps up two to three fold, as is shown in Table 3-12.

Table 3-11: Nodes per Condition Element (with sharing)

Feature	VT	ILOG	MUD	DAA	R1-SOAR	EP-SOAR
1. Total CEs	4336	4629	2153	1731	2743	618
2. Tot. Nodes	9572	8629	4990	2721	4079	1083
3. Nodes/CE	2.20	1.86	2.31	1.57	1.48	1.75

---

[11]All the numbers listed in Tables 3-9 and 3-10 are for the case where the network compiler is allowed to share nodes.

Table 3-12: Nodes per Condition Element (without sharing)

Feature	VT	ILOG	MUD	DAA	R1-SOAR	EP-SOAR
1. Total CEs	4336	4629	2153	1731	2743	618
2. Tot. Nodes	20950	19717	9953	7006	12024	2532
3. Nodes/CE	4.83	4.25	4.62	4.04	4.38	4.10
4. Sharing	2.19	2.28	2.00	2.57	2.95	2.34

3.3.2. Network Sharing

The OPS5 network compiler exploits similarity in the condition elements of productions to share nodes in the Rete network. Such sharing is not possible in parallel implementations of production systems where each production is placed on a separate processor, although some sharing is possible in parallel implementations that use a shared-memory multiprocessor. To help estimate the extra computation required due to loss of sharing, Table 3-13 gives the ratios of the number of nodes in the unshared Rete network to the number of nodes in the shared Rete network. The ratios do not give the extra computational requirements exactly because they are only a static measure — the exact numbers will depend on the dynamic flow of information (tokens) through the network. Table 3-13 also shows that the sharing is large only for constant-test and α-mem nodes, and small for all other node types.[12]

Table 3-13: Network Sharing (Nodes without sharing/Nodes with sharing)

Node Type	VT	ILOG	MUD	DAA	R1-SOAR	EP-SOAR
1. Const-Test	3.86	4.57	3.21	7.38	10.34	6.90
2. α-mem	2.35	3.04	2.05	4.57	6.85	6.40
3. β-mem	1.35	1.44	1.17	1.44	1.63	1.31
4. And	1.19	1.30	1.12	1.24	1.52	1.27
5. Not	1.08	1.04	1.00	1.61	1.26	1.00

3.4. Run-Time Characteristics of Production Systems

This section presents data on the run-time behavior of production systems. The measurements are useful to identify operations frequently performed by the interpreter and provide some rough bounds on the speed-up that may be achieved by parallel implementations. Although most of the reported measurements are in terms of the Rete network, a number of general conclusions can be drawn from the measurements.

---

[12]Note that the reported ratios correspond to the amount of sharing or similarity exploited by the OPS5 network compiler, which may not be the same as the maximum exploitable similarity available in the production-system program.

3.4.1. Constant-Test Nodes

Table 3-14 presents run-time statistics for constant-test nodes. The first line of the table, labeled "visits/change", refers to the average number of constant-test node visits (activations) per change to working memory.[13] The second line of the table reports the number of constant-test activations as a fraction of the total number of node activations. The third line of the table, labeled "success", reports the percent of constant-test node activations that have their associated test satisfied.

Table 3-14: Constant-Test Nodes

Feature	VT	ILOG	MUD	DAA	R1-SOAR	EP-SOAR
1. visits/change	107.00	231.20	117.79	57.02	48.79	18.93
2. % of total	76.9%	84.6%	70.2%	52.0%	60.0%	35.0%
3. success (%)	15.3%	3.3%	24.5%	8.0%	6.3%	14.1%
4. hash-visits/ch	22.92	24.48	41.96	7.14	5.05	3.97

Although constant-test node activations constitute a large fraction (63% on average) of the total node activations, a relatively small fraction of the total match time is spent in processing them. This is because the processing associated with constant-test nodes is very simple compared with other nodes like α-mem nodes, or and-nodes. In the OPS83 [21] implementation on the VAX-11 architecture, the evaluation of a constant-test node takes only 3 machine instructions. The evaluation of two-input nodes in comparison takes 50-100 instructions.

The numbers on the third line show that only a small fraction (11.9% on average) of the constant-test node activations are successful. This suggests that by using indexing techniques (for example, hashing), many constant-test node activations that do not result in satisfaction of the associated tests may be avoided. The fourth line of the table, labeled "hash-visits/ch", gives the approximate number of constant-test node activations per working-memory change when hashing is used to avoid evaluation of nodes whose tests are bound to fail. Calculations show that approximately 82% of the total constant-test node activations can be avoided by using hashing. The hashing technique is especially helpful for the constant-test nodes immediately below the root node. These nodes check for the class of the working-memory element (see Figure 2-2), and since a working-memory element has only one class, all but one of these constant-test nodes fail their test. Calculations show that by using hashing at the top-level, the total number of constant-test node activations can be reduced by about 43%.

---

[13]The run-time data presented in this chapter corresponds to traces *vto.lin, ilog.lin, mudo.lin, daa.lin, rls.lin,* and *eps.lin.* These traces are described in Section 8.1.

3.4.2. Alpha-Memory Nodes

An α-mem node associated with a condition element stores tokens corresponding to working-memory elements that partially match the condition element, that is, tokens that satisfy all intra-condition tests for the condition element. These nodes are the first significant nodes, in terms of the processing required, that get affected when a change is made to the working memory. It is only later that changes filter through α-mem nodes down to and-nodes, not-nodes, β-mem nodes, and terminal-nodes.

The first line of Table 3-15 gives the number of α-mem node activations per change to working memory. The average number of activations for the six programs is only 5.00. This is quite small because of the large amount of sharing between α-mem nodes. The second line of the table gives the number of α-mem node activations when sharing is eliminated (something that is necessary in many parallel implementations). In this case the average number of α-mem node activations goes up to 26.48, an increase by a factor of 5.30. The third line of the table gives the dynamic sharing factor (line-2/line-1), which may be contrasted to the static sharing factor given in Table 3-13. As can be seen from the data, the dynamic sharing factor is consistently larger than the observed static sharing factor.

Table 3-15: Alpha-Memory Nodes

Feature	VT	ILOG	MUD	DAA	R1-SOAR	EP-SOAR
1. visits/ch(sh)	5.29	6.60	10.73	3.28	2.57	1.55
2. visits/ch(nsh)	29.67	30.06	27.59	37.94	19.17	14.50
3. dyn shar fact	5.60	4.55	2.57	11.56	7.45	9.35
4. avg. tokens	302.76	180.44	64.91	14.91	48.50	7.15
5. max. tokens	1467	572	369	88	197	38

The fourth line of Table 3-15 reports the average number of tokens present in an α-mem node when it is activated. This number indicates the complexity of the processing performed by an α-mem node. When an α-mem node is activated by an incoming token with a − tag, the node must find a corresponding token in its stored set of tokens, and then delete that token. If a linear search is done to find the corresponding token, on average, half of the stored tokens will be looked up. Thus the complexity of deleting a token from an α-mem node is proportional to the average number of tokens. On arrival of a token with a + tag, the α-mem node simply stores the token. This involves allocating memory and linking the token, and takes a constant amount of time. In case hashing is used to locate the token to be deleted, the delete operation can also be done in constant time. However, then we have to pay the overhead associated with maintaining a hash table. Hash tables become more economical as the number of tokens stored in the α-mem increases. The numbers presented in the second line are useful for deciding when hash tables (or other indexing techniques) are appropriate.

The fifth line of Table 3-15 reports the maximum number of tokens found in an α-mem node for the various programs.[14] These numbers are useful for estimating the maximum storage requirements for individual memory nodes. The maximum storage requirements, in turn, are useful in the design of hardware associative memories to hold the tokens.

3.4.3. Beta-Memory Nodes

A β-mem node stores tokens that match a subset of condition elements in the left-hand side of a production. The data for β-mem nodes, presented in Table 3-16, can be interpreted in the same way as that for α-mem nodes. There is, however, one difference that is of relevance. The sharing between β-mem nodes is much less than that between α-mem nodes, so that in parallel implementations the cost of processing β-mem nodes does not increase so much. When no sharing is present, the average number of β-mem node activations goes up from 3.53 to 5.17, an increase by a factor of only 1.46 as compared to a factor of 5.30 for the α-mem nodes.

Table 3-16: Beta-Memory Nodes

Feature	VT	ILOG	MUD	DAA	R1-SOAR	EP-SOAR
1. visits/ch(sh)	0.53	1.57	2.62	4.12	3.89	8.47
2. visits/ch(nsh)	1.29	2.36	4.14	5.44	8.03	9.81
3. dyn shar fact	2.43	1.50	1.58	1.32	2.06	1.15
4. avg. tokens	3.30	3.97	73.10	28.26	7.43	4.95
5. max. tokens	48	50	168	360	85	18

3.4.4. And Nodes

The run-time data for and-nodes are given in Table 3-17. The first line gives the number of and-node activations per change to working memory. The average number of node activations for the six programs is 27.66. The second line gives the average number of and-node activations for which no tokens are found in the opposite memory nodes. For example, for the VT program, the first line in the table shows that there are 25.96 and-node activations. Of these 25.96 activations, 24.48 have an empty opposite memory. Since an and-node activation for which there are no tokens in the opposite memory requires very little processing, evaluating the majority of the and-node activations is very cheap. Most of the processing effort goes into evaluating the small fraction of activations which have non-empty opposite memories. This means that if all and-node activations are evaluated on different processors, then the majority of the processors will finish very early compared to the remaining few. This large variation in the processing requirements of and-nodes (see Tables 8-1 and 8-2 for some actual numbers) reduces the effective speed-up that can be obtained by evaluating each and-node activation on a different processor.

---

[14]It is interesting to note that the value for maximum number of tokens is the same as the value for maximum size of working memory (see Table 3-22) for VT, ILOG, and MUD systems. This implies that there is at least one condition element in each of these three systems that is satisfied by all working-memory elements.

When a token arrives on the left input of an and-node, it must be compared to all tokens stored in the memory node associated with the right input of that and-node. The comparisons may involve tests to check if the values of the variables bound in the two tokens are equal, if one is greater than the other, or other similar tests. The third line of the table gives the percentage of two-input node activations where no equality tests are performed.[15] These numbers indicate the fraction of node activations where hash-table based memory nodes do not help in cutting down the tokens examined in the opposite memory (also see Section 5.2.1).

Table 3-17: And Nodes

Feature	VT	ILOG	MUD	DAA	R1-SOAR	EP-SOAR
1. visits/change	25.96	26.59	25.95	39.41	24.48	23.56
2. null-mem	24.48	23.42	20.26	33.53	16.86	10.81
3. null-tests	13.2%	7.8%	12.8%	8.2%	0.3%	0.0%
4. tokens	17.00	4.39	24.33	27.18	4.87	7.96
5. tests	17.35	5.18	25.94	27.51	5.29	8.45
6. pairs	1.41	0.90	1.06	0.83	0.60	0.71

The fourth line shows the average number of tokens found in the opposite memory for an and-node activation, when the opposite memory is not empty. In case tokens in memory nodes are stored as linked lists, this number represents the average number of tokens against which the incoming token must be matched to determine consistent pairs of tokens. The magnitude of this number can be used to determine if hashing or other indexing techniques ought to be used to limit this search.

The numbers in the fifth line of the table indicate the average number of tests performed by an and-node when a token arrives on its left or right input and its opposite memory is not empty. The number of tests performed is equal to the product of the average number of tokens found in the opposite memory (given in the fourth line) and the number of consistency tests that have to be made to check if the left and right tokens of the and-node are consistent. Thus if the number of tokens that are looked up from the opposite memory is reduced by use of indexing techniques, then this number will also go down.

The numbers in the sixth line of the table show the average number of consistent token-pairs found after matching the incoming token to all tokens in the opposite memory. For example, for the DAA program, on the activation of an and-node, an average of 27.18 tokens are found in the opposite memory node. On average, however, only 0.83 tokens are found to be consistent with the incoming token. This indicates that the opposite memory contains a lot of information, of which only a very small portion is relevant to the current context. The numbers in the sixth line also give a measure of token regeneration taking place within the network. This data may be used to construct probabilistic models of information flow within the Rete network.

---

[15]For reasons too complex to explain here, separate numbers for and-node and not-node activations were not available. That is, the numbers presented in line-3 are for the combined activations of and-nodes and not-nodes.

3.4.5. Not Nodes

Not-nodes are very similar to and-nodes, and the data for them should be interpreted in exactly the same way as that for and-nodes. The data are presented in Table 3-18.

Table 3-18: Not Nodes

Feature	VT	ILOG	MUD	DAA	R1-SOAR	EP-SOAR
1. visits/change	5.01	5.84	5.79	3.97	2.63	0.75
2. null-mem	3.90	4.28	3.89	2.33	1.42	0.27
3. tokens	31.39	5.99	13.94	12.51	9.87	6.43
4. tests	34.95	7.94	14.06	12.53	11.91	7.38
5. pairs	0.25	0.45	0.31	0.43	1.41	0.75

3.4.6. Terminal Nodes

Activations of terminal nodes correspond to insertion of production instantiations into the conflict set and deletion of instantiations from the conflict set. The first line of Table 3-19 gives the number of changes to the conflict set for each working-memory change. The second line gives the average number of changes made to the working memory per production firing, and the third line, the product of the first two lines, gives the average number of changes made to the conflict set per production firing. The data in the third line gives the number of changes that will be transmitted to a central conflict-resolution processor, in an architecture using centralized conflict-resolution. The fourth line gives the size of the conflict-set when averaged over the complete run.

Table 3-19: Terminal Nodes

Feature	VT	ILOG	MUD	DAA	R1-SOAR	EP-SOAR
1. visits/change	1.79	2.06	3.69	1.65	0.55	0.74
2. changes/cycle	3.27	1.70	2.13	2.22	4.55	4.69
3. mods./cycle	5.85	3.50	7.86	3.66	2.50	3.47
4. avg confl-set	35	10	36	22	12	18

3.4.7. Summary of Run-Time Characteristics

Table 3-20 summarizes data for the number of node activations, when a working-memory element is inserted into or deleted from the working memory. The data show that a large percentage (63% on average) of the activations are of constant-test nodes. Constant-test node activations, however, require very little processing compared to other node types, and furthermore, a large number of constant-test activations can be eliminated by suitable indexing techniques (see Section 3.4.1). To eliminate the effect of this large number of relatively cheap constant-test node activations, we subtracted the number of constant-test node activations from the activations of all nodes. These numbers are shown on line-8 of Table 3-20.

The first observation that can be made from the data on line-8 of Table 3-20 is that, the way production-system programs are currently written, changes to working memory do not have global effects, but affect only a very small fraction of the nodes present in the Rete network (see Table 3-9). This also means that the number of productions that are *affected*[16] is very small, as can be seen from line-1 in Table 3-21. Both the small number of affected nodes and the small number of affected productions limit the amount of speed-up that can be obtained from using parallelism, as is discussed in Chapter 4.

The second observation that can be made is that the total number of node activations (excluding constant-test node activations) per change is quite independent of the number of productions in the production-system program. This, in turn, implies that the number of productions that are affected is quite independent of the total number of productions present in the system, as can be seen from Table 3-21. There are several implications of the above observations. First, we should not expect smaller production systems (in terms of number of productions) to run faster than larger ones. Second, it appears that allocating one processor to each node in the Rete network or allocating one processor to each production is not a good idea. Finally, there is no reason to expect that larger production systems will necessarily exhibit more speed-up from parallelism.

Table 3-20: Summary of Node Activations per Change

Node Type	VT	ILOG	MUD	DAA	R1-SOAR	EP-SOAR
1. Const-Test	107.00	231.20	117.79	57.02	48.79	18.93
2. α-mem	5.29	6.60	10.73	3.28	2.57	1.55
3. β-mem	0.53	1.57	2.62	4.12	3.89	8.47
4. And	25.96	26.59	25.95	39.41	24.48	23.56
5. Not	5.01	5.84	5.79	3.97	2.63	0.75
6. Terminal	1.79	2.06	3.69	1.65	0.55	0.74
7. Total	145.58	273.92	166.57	109.45	82.91	54.00
8. Line7 – Line1	38.58	42.72	48.78	52.43	34.12	35.07

Table 3-21: Number of Affected Productions

Feature	VT	ILOG	MUD	DAA	R1-SOAR	EP-SOAR
1. p-aff/change	31.22	34.19	27.01	28.54	34.57	12.07
2. SD[17] for Line1	19.55	38.53	25.39	27.77	60.16	14.69
3. changes/cycle	3.27	1.70	2.13	2.22	4.55	4.69
4. p-aff/firing	40.14	36.49	32.05	40.04	63.04	20.45
5. SD for Line4	31.59	52.70	28.69	32.55	93.67	20.12

Table 3-22 gives general information about the runs of the production-system programs from

---

[16] A production is said to be *affected* by a change to working memory, if the working-memory element satisfies at least one of its condition elements.

[17] SD stands for Standard Deviation.

which data is presented in this chapter.[18] The first two lines of the table give the average and maximum sizes of the working memory. The third and the fourth lines give the average and maximum values for the sizes of the conflict set. The fifth and the sixth lines give the average and maximum sizes of the token memory when memory nodes may be shared. (The size of the token memory at any instant is the total number of tokens stored in all memory nodes at that instant.) The seventh and the eighth line give the average and the maximum sizes of the token memory when memory nodes may not be shared. The last line in the table gives the total number of changes made to the working memory in the production system run from which the statistics are gathered.

Table 3-22: General Run-Time Data

Feature	VT	ILOG	MUD	DAA	R1-SOAR	EP-SOAR
1. avg work-mem	1134	486	241	250	543	199
2. max work-mem	1467	572	369	308	786	258
3. avg confl-set	35	10	36	22	12	18
4. max confl-set	131	38	648	88	36	31
5. avg tokm(sh)	5485	3506	3176	1182	1515	555
6. max tokm(sh)	7416	4204	4576	2624	2716	856
7. avg tokm(nsh)	13366	5363	4717	18343	3892	2546
8. max tokm(nsh)	22640	8346	7583	23213	7402	3480
9. WM changes	1767	2191	2074	3200	2220	924

Finally, it is important to point out that, the results of measurements presented for the six systems in this chapter are very similar to the results obtained for another set of systems (R1 [58], XSEL [57], PTRANS [35], HAUNT, DAA [43], and EP-SOAR [46]) analyzed in [30]. Consequently, there is a good reason to believe that the results about parallelism (presented later in the thesis) apply not only to the six systems discussed here, but also to most other systems that have been written in the OPS5 and Soar languages.

---

[18]The numbers presented in this chapter and in later chapters of the thesis are based on one run per production system program. Detailed simulation-based analysis (results presented in Chapter 8) was not done for multiple runs of programs because of the large amount of data involved and because of the large processing requirements. However, we did gather statistics, like the ones presented in this chapter, for multiple runs of programs. The variation in the numbers obtained from the multiple runs was small.

4 Parallelism in Production Systems

On the surface, production systems appear to be capable of exploiting large amounts of parallelism. For example, it is possible to perform match for all productions in parallel. This chapter identifies some obvious and other not-so-obvious sources of parallelism in production systems, and discusses the feasibility of exploiting them. It draws upon performance results reported in Chapter 8 of the thesis to motivate the utilization of some of the sources. Note that for reasons stated in Section 2.4, most of the discussion focuses on the parallelism that may be used within the context of the Rete algorithm.

4.1. The Structure of a Parallel Production-System Interpreter

As discussed in Section 2.1, there are three steps that are repeatedly performed to execute an OPS5 production-system program: match, conflict-resolution, and act. Figure 4-1 shows the flow of information between these three stages of the interpreter. It is possible to use parallelism while performing each of these three steps. It is further possible to overlap the processing performed within the match step and the conflict-resolution step of the same recognize-act cycle, and that within the act step of one cycle and the match step of the next cycle. However, it is not possible to overlap the processing within the conflict-resolution step and the subsequent act step. This is because the conflict-resolution must finish completely before the next production to fire can be determined and its right-hand side evaluated. Thus, in an OPS5 programming environment, the possible sources of speed-up are (1) parallelism within the match step, (2) parallelism within the conflict-resolution step, (3) parallelism within the act step, (4) overlap between the match step and the conflict-resolution step of the same cycle, and (5) overlap between the act step of one cycle and the match step of the next cycle.

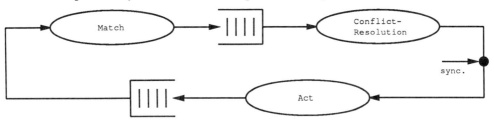

Figure 4-1: OPS5 interpreter cycle.

As pointed out in Section 2.2, Soar programs do not execute the standard match — conflict-resolution — act cycle executed by OPS5 programs. A simplified diagram of the information flow in the Soar cycle is shown in Figure 4-2. The match step and the act step are the same as in OPS5, but the conflict-resolution step is not present. Instead, the computation is divided into an *elaboration* phase and a *decision* phase. Within each phase all productions that are satisfied may be fired concurrently, and the productions that become satisfied as a result of such firings may also be fired concurrently with the originally satisfied productions. Such concurrency increases the speed-up that may be obtained from using parallelism, as will be discussed later in this chapter. There are, however, synchronization points between the elaboration phase and the decision phase; the elaboration phase must finish completely before the processing may proceed to the decision phase, and vice versa. The serializing affect of these two synchronization points in Soar is not as bad as that of the synchronization point between the conflict-resolution and the act step in OPS5. This is because Soar systems usually go through a few loops internally within the elaboration phase and within the decision phase, with no synchronization points to produce any serialization.

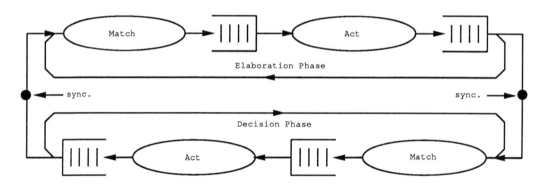

Figure 4-2: Soar interpreter cycle.

4.2. Parallelism in Match

Current production-system interpreters spend almost 90% of their time in the match step, and only around 10% of the time in the conflict-resolution and the act steps. The reason for this is the inherent complexity of the match step, as was discussed in Section 2.3. This makes it imperative that we speed up the match step as much as possible. The following discussion presents several ways in which parallelism may be used to speed up the match step.

The processing done within the match step can be divided into two parts: the *selection* phase and the *state-update* phase [69]. During the selection phase, the match algorithm determines those condition elements that are satisfied by the new change to working memory, that is, it determines those condition elements for which all the intra-condition tests are satisfied by the newly inserted working-memory element. During the state-update phase, the match algorithm updates the state (stores a token in the memory nodes) associated with the condition elements determined in the selection phase. In addition, this new state is matched with previously stored state to determine new instantiations of satisfied productions. In the context of the Rete algorithm, the processing done during the selection phase corresponds to the evaluation of the top-part of the Rete network, the part consisting of constant-test nodes. The processing done during the state-update phase corresponds to the evaluation of α-mem nodes, β-mem nodes, and-nodes, not-nodes, and terminal nodes.

Figure 4-3: Selection and state-update phases in match.

Although the beginning of selection phase must precede the state-update phase, the processing for the two phases may overlap. As soon as the selection phase determines the first satisfied condition element the state-update phase can begin. In case many changes to working memory are to be processed concurrently, it is also possible to overlap the processing of the selection phase for one change to working memory with the state-update phase for another change.

Comparing the selection phase and the state-update phase, about 75%-95% of the processing time is spent in performing the state-update phase. The main reason for this, as stated in Section 3.4.1, is that the activations of constant-test nodes are much cheaper than the activations of memory nodes and two-input nodes. This disparity in the computational requirements between the two phases makes it necessary to speed up the state-update phase much more than the selection phase to attain balance. Since the state-update phase is more critical to the overall performance of the match algorithm, the following subsections focus primarily on the parallelization of the state-update phase.[19]

4.2.1. Production Parallelism

To use *production parallelism*, the productions in a program are divided into several partitions and the match for each of the partitions is performed in parallel. In the extreme case, the number of partitions equals the number of productions in the program, so that the match for each production in the program is performed in parallel. Figure 4-4 shows the case where a production system is split into N partitions. The main advantage of using production parallelism is that no communication is required between the processes performing match for different productions or different partitions.

---

[19]Kemal Oflazer has developed a special algorithm, which uses the information in both the left-hand sides and right-hand sides of productions to speed up the selection phase. So far we have not felt the necessity to use this more complex selection algorithm, because even with the standard selection/discrimination network used by Rete, the state-update phase is still the bottleneck.

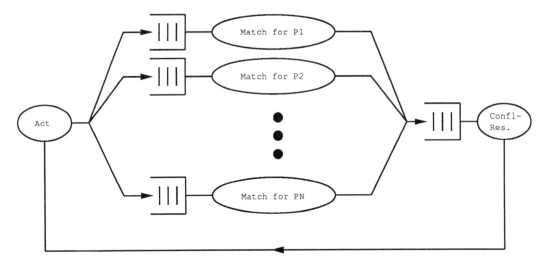

Figure 4-4: Production parallelism.

Before going into the implementation issues related to exploiting production parallelism, it is useful to examine the approximate speed-up that may be obtained from using production parallelism. For example, do we expect 10-fold speed-up, do we expect 100-fold speed-up, or do we expect 1000-fold speed-up provided that enough processors are present. Our studies for OPS5 and Soar programs show that the true speed-up expected from production parallelism is really quite small, only about 2-fold. Some of the reasons for this are given below:

- Simulations show that the average number of productions affected[20] per change to working memory is only 26. This implies that if there is a separate processor performing match for each production in the program, only 26 processors will be performing useful work and the rest will have no work to do. Thus the maximum speed-up from production parallelism is limited to 26.[21] For reasons stated below, however, the expected speed-up is even smaller.

- The speed-up obtainable from production parallelism is further reduced by the variance in the processing time required by the affected productions. The maximum speed-up that can be obtained is proportional to the ratio t_{avg}/t_{max}, where t_{avg} is the average time taken by an affected production to finish match and t_{max} is the maximum time taken by any affected production to finish match. The parallelism is inversely proportional to t_{max} because the next recognize-act cycle cannot begin until all productions have finished match. Simulations for OPS5 and Soar programs

---

[20]Recall that a production is said to be *affected* by a change to working memory, if the new working-memory element matches at least one of the condition elements of that production. Updating the state associated with the affected productions (the state-update phase computation) takes about 75%-95% of the total time taken by the match phase.

[21]Note that in the above discussion we have only been concerned with the state-update phase computation. This is possible because we already have parallel algorithms to execute the selection phase very fast.

show that because of this variance the maximum *nominal* speed-up[22] that is obtainable using production parallelism is 5.1-fold, a factor of 5.1 less than the average number of affected productions.[23]

- The third factor that influences the speed-up is the loss of sharing in the Rete network when production parallelism is used. The loss of sharing happens because operations which would have been performed only once for similar productions are now performed independently for such productions, since the productions are evaluated on different processors. Simulations show that the loss of sharing increases the average processing cost by a factor of 1.63. Thus if there are 16 processors that are active all the time, the speed-up as compared to a uniprocessor implementation (with no loss in sharing) will still be less than 10.

- The fourth factor that influences the speed-up is the overhead of mapping the decomposition of the algorithm onto a parallel hardware architecture. The overheads may take the form of memory-contention costs, synchronization costs, or task-scheduling costs. Simulations done for an implementation of the parallel Rete algorithm on a shared-memory multiprocessor show that such overheads increase the processing cost by a factor of 1.61.

The combined sharing, synchronization, and scheduling overheads account for loss in performance by a factor of 2.62 (1.61×1.63). As a result of the combined losses the true speed-up from using production parallelism is only 1.9-fold (down from the nominal speed-up of 5.1-fold).

Some implementation issues associated with using production-level parallelism are now discussed. The first point that emerges from the previous discussion is that it is not advisable to allocate one processor per production for performing match. If this is done most of the processors will be idle most of the time and the hardware utilization will be poor [22, 31].[24] If only a small number of processors are to be used, there are two alternative strategies. The first strategy is to divide the production-system program into several partitions so that the processing required by productions in each partition is almost the same, and then allocate one processor for each partition. The second strategy is to have a task queue shared by all processors in which entries for all productions requiring processing are placed. Whenever a processor finishes processing one production, it gets the next production that needs processing from the task queue. Some advantages and disadvantages of these two strategies are given below.

---

[22]*Nominal* speed-up (or *concurrency*) refers to the average number of processors that are kept busy in the parallel implementation. Nominal speed-up is to be contrasted against *true* speed-up which refers to the speed-up with respect to the highest performance uniprocessor implementation, assuming that the uniprocessor is as powerful as the individual nodes of the parallel processor. True speed-up is usually less than the nominal speed-up because some of the resources in a parallel implementation are devoted to synchronizing the parallel processes, scheduling the parallel processes, recomputing some data which is too expensive to be communicated, etc.

[23]Note that the numbers given in this section and the following sections correspond to the simulation results for production-system traces listed in Section 8.1.

[24]Low utilization is not justifiable, no matter how inexpensive the hardware, for it indicates that some alternative design can be found that can attain more performance at the same cost.

The first strategy is suitable for both shared-memory multiprocessors and non-shared-memory multicomputers. It is possible for each processor to work from its local memory and little or no communication between processors is required. The main difficulty, however, is to find partitions of the production system that require the same amount of processing. Note that it is not sufficient to find partitions with only one affected production per partition, because the variance in the cost of processing the affected productions still destroys most of the speed-up.[25] The task of partitioning is also difficult because good models are not available for estimating the processing required by productions, and also because the processing required by productions varies over time. A discussion of the various issues involved in the partitioning task is presented in [69, 70].

The second strategy is suitable only for shared-memory architectures, because it requires that each processor have access to the code and state of all productions in the program.[26] Since the tasks are allocated dynamically to the processors, this strategy has the advantage that no load-distribution problems are present. Another advantage of this strategy is that it extends very well to lower granularities of parallelism. However, this strategy loses some performance due to the synchronization, scheduling, and memory contention overheads present in a multiprocessor.

. In conclusion, the maximum speed-up that can be obtained from production-level parallelism is equal to the average number of productions affected per change to working memory (average of 26 for the production systems studied). However, in practice, the nominal speed-up that is obtained is only 5.1-fold. This is due to the variance in the processing times required by the affected productions. The true speed-up that can be obtained is even less, only 1.9-fold. This is due to the loss of sharing in parallel decompositions (a factor of 1.63), and the overheads of mapping the decompositions onto hardware architectures (a factor of 1.61).

4.2.2. Node Parallelism

Unlike production parallelism, *node parallelism* is specific to the Rete algorithm. When node parallelism is used, activations of different two-input nodes in the Rete network are evaluated in parallel.[27] Node parallelism is graphically depicted in Figure 4-5. It is important to note that node parallelism subsumes production parallelism, in that node parallelism has a finer grain than production parallelism. Thus, using node parallelism, both activations of two-input nodes

---

[25]Kemal Oflazer in his thesis [70] evaluates a scheme where more than one processor is allocated to each partition to offset the effect of the variance.

[26]While it is possible to replicate the code (that is, the Rete network) in the local memories of all the processors, it is not possible to do so for the dynamically changing data.

[27]Note that in the context of node parallelism, the activation of a two-input node corresponds to the processing required by both the two-input node (the and-node or the not-node) and the associated memory node. Lumping the memory node together with the two-input node is necessary when using hash-table based memory nodes, and is discussed in detail later in Section 5.2.2.

belonging to different productions (corresponding to production parallelism), and activations of two-input nodes belonging to the same production (resulting in the extra parallelism) are processed in parallel.

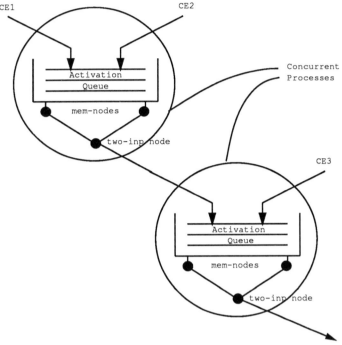

Figure 4-5: Node parallelism.

The main reason for going to this finer granularity of parallelism is to reduce the value of t_{max}, the maximum time taken by any affected production to finish match. This decreased granularity of parallelism, however, leads to increased communication requirements between the processes evaluating the nodes in parallel. In node parallelism a process must communicate the results of a successful match to its successor two-input nodes. No communication is necessary if the match fails. To evaluate the usefulness of exploiting node parallelism, it is necessary to weigh the advantages of reducing t_{max} against the cost of increased communication and the associated limitations on feasible architectures.

Another advantage of using node parallelism is that some of the sharing lost in the Rete network when using production parallelism is recovered. If two productions need a node with the same functionality, it is possible to keep only one copy of the node and it is possible to evaluate it only once, since it is no longer necessary to have separate nodes for different productions. The gain due to the increased amount of sharing is a factor of 1.33, which is quite significant.

The extra speed-up available from node parallelism over that obtained from production parallelism is bounded by the number of two-input nodes present in a production. The reason for this is that the extra speed-up comes only from the parallel evaluation of nodes belonging to the same production. Since the average number of two-input nodes (one less than the average number of condition elements) in the production systems considered in this thesis is quite small, the maximum extra speed-up expected from node parallelism is also small. The results of simulations indicate that using node parallelism results in a nominal speed-up of 5.8-fold and true speed-up of 2.9-fold. Thus it is possible to get about 1.50 times more true speed-up than that could be obtained if production parallelism alone was used.[28]. The increase in speed-up is significantly lower than the number of two-input nodes per production (around 4), because most of the time all two-input nodes associated with a production do not have to be evaluated.

The implementation considerations for node parallelism are very similar to those for production parallelism described in the previous subsection. However, since the communication required between the parallel processes is more, shared-memory architectures are preferable. The size of the tasks when node parallelism is used is smaller than when production parallelism is used. Simulations indicate that the average time to process a two-input node activation is around 50-100 computer instructions. This number is significant in that it limits the amount of synchronization and scheduling overhead that can be tolerated in an implementation.

4.2.3. Intra-Node Parallelism

The previous two subsections expressed the desirability of reducing the value of t_{max}, the maximum time taken by any affected production to finish the match phase. Looking at simulation traces of production systems using node parallelism, a major cause for the large value of t_{max} was found to be the *cross-product* effect. As shown in Figure 4-6,[29] the cross-product effect refers to the case where a single token flowing into a two-input node finds a large number of tokens with consistent bindings in the opposite memory. This results in the generation of a large number of new tokens, all of which have to be processed by the successor node. Since node parallelism does not permit multiple activations of the *same* two-input node to be processed in parallel, they are processed sequentially and a large value of t_{max} results.

Intra-node parallelism is designed to reduce the impact of the cross-product effect and some other problems that arise when multiple changes to working memory are processed in parallel. When intra-node parallelism is used, not only are multiple activations of *different* two-input nodes evaluated in parallel (as in node parallelism), but also multiple activations of the *same* two-input node are evaluated in parallel.[30]

---

[28]This factor of 1.50 includes the factor of 1.33 that was gained because of reduced loss of sharing, as stated in the previous paragraph

[29]In Figure 4-6, the arrows represent the flow of tokens in the Rete network for the production.

[30]Just as node parallelism subsumes production parallelism, intra-node parallelism subsumes node parallelism.

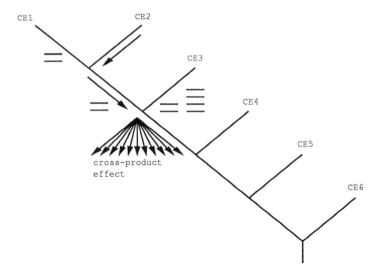

Figure 4-6: The cross-product effect.

Because of its finer granularity, intra-node parallelism requires some extra synchronization over that required by node parallelism, but its impact is relatively insignificant. Simulations show that using intra-node parallelism results in a nominal speed-up of 7.6-fold and a true speed-up of 3.9-fold. Thus it is possible to get an extra factor of 1.30 over the speed-up that can be obtained from using node parallelism alone. This factor is larger when many changes are processed in parallel, as is discussed in the next subsection.

4.2.4. Action Parallelism

Usually, when a production fires, it makes several changes to the working memory. Measurements show that the average number of changes made to the working memory per execution cycle is 7.34.[31] Processing these changes concurrently, instead of sequentially, leads to increased speed-up from production, node, and intra-node parallelism.

The reasons for the increased speed-up from production parallelism when used with action parallelism are the following. In Section 4.2.1, it was observed that the speed-up available from production parallelism is proportional to the average number of affected productions. The set of productions which is affected as a result of processing many changes concurrently is the union of the sets of affected productions for the individual changes to the working memory. Since this combined set of affected productions is larger than that affected by any individual change, more

---

[31]The average number of changes that are processed in parallel for the four OPS5 traces is 2.44 and the average for the four Soar traces is 12.25. Note that the number of changes that may be processed in parallel for the Soar systems is the sum of changes made by all the productions that fire in parallel.

speed-up can be obtained. For example, consider the case where a production firing results in two changes to working memory, such that change-1 affects productions p1, p2, and p3, and change-2 affects productions p4, p5, and p6. If change-1 and change-2 are processed sequentially, it is best to use three processors. Assuming that each affected production takes the same amount of processing time, each change takes one cycle and the total cost is two cycles. However, if change-1 and change-2 are processed concurrently, they can be processed in one instead of two cycles using six processors. Simulations indicate that processing multiple changes in parallel the average size of the affect sets goes up from 26.3 to 59.5 (a factor of 2.26) and the speed-up obtainable from production parallelism alone goes up by a factor of 1.5. Thus using both production and action parallelism results in a nominal speed-up of 7.6-fold, as compared to a nominal speed-up of 5.1-fold when only production parallelism is used. The extra speed-up is less than the average number of working-memory changes per cycle, because the sets of productions affected by the multiple changes are not distinct but have considerable overlap (see line-1 and line-4 of Table 3-21).

Analysis shows that often two successive changes to working memory affect two distinct condition elements of the same production, as a result causing two distinct two-input node activations. It is then possible, using node parallelism, to process these node activations in parallel, thus increasing the available parallelism. For example, consider the case where both change-1 and change-2 affect productions p1, p2, and p3. If the activations correspond to distinct two-input nodes, it is possible to process both the changes in parallel, in one instead of two cycles. Simulations indicate that the use of action parallelism increases the speed-up obtainable from node parallelism alone by a factor of around 1.85, resulting in a nominal speed-up of 10.7-fold.

In a manner similar to node parallelism, when successive changes to working memory cause multiple activations of the same two-input node, then using intra-node parallelism it is possible to process them in parallel. Simulations indicate that the use of action parallelism increases the speed-up obtainable from intra-node parallelism alone by a factor of around 2.54, resulting in a nominal speed-up of 19.3-fold. The average increase in performance for the OPS5 programs is a factor of 1.84 and that for the Soar programs is a factor of 3.30. The increase in speed-up is larger for Soar programs because, on average, 12.25 working-memory changes are processed in parallel for Soar programs, while only 2.44 changes are processed in parallel for OPS5 programs.

It is interesting to note that the factor by which the speed-up improves when using action parallelism increases as we go from production parallelism (factor of 1.50) to node parallelism (factor of 1.85) to intra-node parallelism (factor of 2.54). The reason for this is that node parallelism subsumes production parallelism and intra-node parallelism subsumes node parallelism. Thus node parallelism gets the extra speed-up from action parallelism that production parallelism can get. In addition node parallelism gets extra speed-up from parallelism that production parallelism could not obtain, for example, when the multiple changes affect different two-input nodes belonging to the same production. The reasoning between node parallelism and intra-node parallelism is similar.

4.3. Parallelism in Conflict-Resolution

The thesis does not evaluate the parallelism within the conflict-resolution phase in detail. This is partly because the conflict-resolution phase is not present in new production systems like Soar, and partly because the conflict-resolution phase is not expected to be a bottleneck in the near future. The reasons why conflict-resolution is not expected to become a bottleneck are:

- Current production-system interpreters spend only about 5% of their execution time on conflict-resolution. Thus the match step has to be speeded up considerably before conflict-resolution becomes a bottleneck.

- In production, node, and intra-node parallelism discussed earlier, the match for the affected productions finishes at different times because of the variation in the processing required by the affected productions. Thus many changes to the conflict set are available to the conflict-resolution process, while some productions are still performing match. Thus much of the conflict-resolution time can be overlapped with the match time, reducing the chances of conflict-resolution becoming a bottleneck.

- If the conflict-resolution does becomes a bottleneck, there are several strategies for avoiding it. For example, to begin the next execution cycle, it is not necessary to perform conflict-resolution for the current changes to completion. It is only necessary to compare each current change to the highest priority production instantiation so far. Once the highest priority instantiation is selected the next execution cycle can begin. The complete sorting of the production instantiations can be overlapped with the match phase for the next cycle. Hardware priority queues provide another strategy.

4.4. Parallelism in RHS Evaluation

The rhs-evaluation step like the conflict-resolution step takes only about 5% of the total time for the current production systems. When many productions are allowed to fire in parallel, as in Soar, it is quite straight forward to evaluate their right-hand sides in parallel. Even when the right-hand side of only a single production is to be evaluated, it is possible to overlap some of the input/output with the match for the next execution cycle. Also when the right-hand side results in several changes to the working memory, the match phase can begin as soon as the first change to working memory is determined.

In the beginning of Section 4.1, we had stated that the conflict-resolution step must finish completely before the right-hand side can be evaluated (until that time we can not be sure which rule will fire next). However, if one takes the approach of speculative parallelism, it is possible to overlap the conflict-resolution and the RHS evaluation step. The solution is to make an intelligent guess about which production is going to fire next. For example, we may guess that the second-best instantiation from the previous conflict-resolution step is going to fire next. After making the guess, we can go ahead and evaluate the right-hand side of the associated production, that is, determine what changes are going to be made to the working memory. (Note, we actually do not modify the working memory at this point.) At the end of conflict-resolution step when we find out the winning rule, if our guess was correct, we are already done with the RHS evaluation step. If our guess was wrong, then we have only wasted some processing resources, which is not too bad. For the above reasons the RHS-evaluation step is not expected to be a bottleneck in speeding up the execution of production systems. The thesis does not evaluate the parallelism in the RHS-evaluation in any greater detail.

4.5. Application Parallelism

There is substantial speed-up to be gained from *application parallelism*, where a number of cooperating but loosely coupled production-system tasks execute in parallel [29, 90]. The cooperating tasks may arise in the context of search, where there are a number of paths to be explored, and it is possible to explore each of the paths in parallel (similar to *or-parallelism* in logic programs [94]). Alternatively, the cooperating tasks may arise in the context where there are a number of semi-independent tasks, all of which have to be performed, and they can be performed in parallel (similar to *and-parallelism* in logic programs). It is also possible to have cooperating tasks that have a producer-consumer relationship among them (similar to *stream-parallelism* in logic programs). The maximum speed-up that can be obtained from application parallelism is equal to the number of cooperating tasks, which can be significant. Unfortunately, most current production systems do not exploit such parallelism, because (1) the production-system programs were expected to run on a uniprocessor, where no advantage is to be had from having several parallel tasks, and (2) current production-system languages do not provide the features to write multiple cooperating production tasks easily.

Although not currently exploited by OPS5 programs, it is possible to use a simple form of application parallelism in Soar programs. In Soar all problem-solving is done as heuristic search within a problem-space, and Soar permits exploring several paths in the problem-space concurrently. The use of application parallelism within the two Soar programs studied in this thesis increases the nominal speed-up obtained using intra-node and action parallelism from 17.9-fold to 30.4-fold, an extra factor of 1.7. It is interesting to note that to the implementor, the use of application parallelism in Soar appears simply as several productions firing in parallel. This results in a large number of working-memory changes that may be processed in parallel. No special mechanisms are required to make use of application parallelism, since the mechanisms developed for exploiting action parallelism suffice.

4.6. Summary

In summary, the following observations can be made about the parallelism in production systems:

- Contrary to initial expectations, the speed-up obtainable from parallelism is quite limited, of the order of few tens rather than hundreds or thousands.

- The match step takes the most time in the recognize-act cycle, and for that reason the match needs to be speeded up most.

- The first important source of parallelism for the match step is production parallelism. Using production parallelism it is possible to get an average nominal speed-
up of 5.1-fold and average true speed-up of 1.9-fold. The speed-up is limited by the
small number (approx. 26) of productions affected per change to working memory.
The speed-up is further limited by the large variance in the amount of processing
required by the affected productions (factor of 5.10), by the loss of sharing in the
Rete network (factor of 1.63), and by the overheads of mapping the parallel algorithm onto a multiprocessor (factor of 1.61).

- To reduce the variance in the processing requirements of the affected productions, it
is necessary to exploit parallelism at a much finer granularity than production parallelism. The two schemes proposed for this are node parallelism and intra-node
parallelism. Exploiting the parallelism at a finer granularity increases the communication requirements between the parallel processes, and restricts the class of
suitable architectures to shared-memory multiprocessors.

- When using node parallelism, it is possible to process activations of distinct two-
input nodes in parallel. This results in average nominal speed-up of 5.8-fold and
average true speed-up of 2.8-fold (an extra factor of 1.50 over the speed-up that can
be obtained by using production parallelism alone).

- Intra-node parallelism is even finer grain that node parallelism, and it permits the
processing of multiple activations of the same two-input node in parallel. This
results in average nominal speed-up of 7.6-fold and average true speed-up of 3.9-
fold (an extra factor of 1.30 over the speed-up that can be obtained by using node
parallelism alone).

- Processing many changes to working memory in parallel (action parallelism) en-
hances the speed-up obtainable from production, node, and intra-node parallelism.
The nominal speed-up obtainable from production parallelism increases to 7.6-fold
(a factor of 1.50 over when action parallelism is not used), that from node parallelism increases to 10.7-fold (an extra factor of 1.85), and that from intra-node
parallelism increases to 19.3-fold (an extra factor of 2.54).

- The conflict-resolution step and the RHS-evaluation step take only a small fraction
(5% each) of the processing time required by the recognize-act cycle. Much of the
processing required by the conflict-resolution step can be overlapped with the
match step. These two steps are not expected to become a bottleneck in the near
future.

- Significant speed-up can be obtained by letting several loosely coupled threads of
computation to proceed in parallel (application parallelism). Simulation results for
two Soar systems show that the speed-up obtainable from intra-node parallelism
increases by a factor of 1.7 when application parallelism is used.

4.7. Discussion

The results presented earlier in this chapter indicate the performance of only one model (that of
OPS5-like production systems using a Rete-like match algorithm) for parallel interpretation of
production systems. It is therefore essential to ask whether it is possible to change the parallel
interpreter design — or even the production systems being interpreted — in such a way so as to

increase the speed-up obtainable from parallelism. Of course, one is not likely to be able to give universal answers to questions like this. It is surely the case that there are applications and associated implementation techniques that permit quite high degrees of parallelism to be used, and that there are other applications that do not permit much parallelism at all to be used. However, by examining the basic factors affecting the speed-up obtained from parallelism, one can develop fairly general evaluations about the speed-up that is obtainable from parallelism, independent of the design decisions made in any particular parallel implementation. The following paragraphs give reasons why the three main factors responsible for the limited speed-up, namely (1) the small number of productions affected per change to working memory, (2) the small number of changes made to working memory per cycle, and (3) the large variation in the processing requirements of the affected productions, are not likely to change significantly in the near future, and consequently, why it is not reasonable to expect significantly larger speed-ups from parallelism.

Let us first examine the reasons for the observations that the affect-sets (the set of affected productions) are small and that the size of the affect-sets is independent of the total number of rules in the program (see Table 3-21). One possible way to explain these observations is to note that to perform most interesting tasks, the rule-base must contain knowledge about many different types of objects and many diverse situations. The number of rules associated with any specific object-type or any situation is expected to be small [59]. Since most working-memory elements describe aspects of only a single object or situation, then clearly most working-memory elements cannot be of interest to more than a few of the rules.

Another way that one might explain the small and independent size of the affect-sets is the conjecture that programmers recursively divide problems into subproblems when writing the programs. The final size of the subproblems at the end of the recursive division of problems into subproblems (which is correlated to the number of productions associated with the subproblems) is independent of the size of the original problem and primarily depends on (1) the complexity of the subproblems, and (2) the complexity that the programmer can deal with at the same time (see [59] for a discussion of this hypothesis). Since, at any given time, the program execution corresponds to solving only one of these subproblems, the number of productions that are affected (relevant to the subproblem) is small and independent of the overall program size.[32]

Yet another way to look at the size of the affect-sets is in terms of the organization of knowledge in programs. If the knowledge about a given situation is small (the number of as-

---

[32]The above discussion only addresses the case where application parallelism is not exploited. In case application parallelism is used, it is possible for a program to be working on several subproblems simultaneously, thus having a larger set of affected productions. Also note, it is not argued that the size of affect-sets will be the same in future systems as has been measured for existing systems. It is, of course, possible to construct systems that have more knowledge applicable to each given situation, thus increasing the number of affected productions by some small factor. It is, however, argued that the probability that the number of affected productions will increase by 50-fold, 100-fold, or more in the future is small.

sociated rules are small), the affect-sets would also be small. If the amount of knowledge about the given situation is very large, it is possible that the affect-sets are large. However, whenever the amount of knowledge is large, we tend to structure it hierarchically or impose some other structure on the knowledge, so that it is easily comprehensible to us and so that it is easy to reason about [85]. For example, the structure of knowledge in classification tasks is not flat but usually hierarchical. Consequently, when classifying an object we do it in several sequential steps, each with a small branching factor, rather than in one step with a very large branching factor. Thus if there was one rule associated with each branch of the decision tree, the total number of rules relevant at any node in the decision tree would be small.

We now give reasons why the number of working-memory changes per recognize-act cycle is not likely to become significantly larger in future production-system programs. The reason for using production systems is to permit a style of programming in which substantial amounts of knowledge can affect each action that the program takes. If individual rules are permitted to do much more processing (which would correspond to making a large number of changes to working memory), then the advantages of this programming style begin to be lost. Knowledge is brought to bear only during the match phase of the cycle, and the less frequently match phases occur, the less chance other rules have to affect the outcome of the processing. Certainly there are many applications in which it is possible to perform substantial amounts of processing without stepping back and reevaluating the state of the system, but those are not the kinds of tasks for which one should choose the production-system paradigm.

Alternatively, the argument may be made as follows. As stated in Chapter 1, an intelligent agent must perform knowledge search after each *small* step to avoid the combinatorial explosion resulting from uncontrolled problem-space search. Since most often, a small step in the problem space also corresponds to a small change in the state/environment of the agent, the number of changes made between consecutive knowledge-search steps is expected to be small. It is possible to envision situations when there are local spurts in the number of changes made to the working memory per cycle (for example, when an intelligent agent returns from solving a subgoal, it may want to delete much of the local state associated with that subgoal [49]), but the average rate of change to working memory per cycle is expected to remain small.

Before leaving this point, it should be observed that there is one way to increase the rate of working-memory turnover — using parallelism in the production system itself. If a system has multiple threads, each one could be performing only the usual small number of working-memory changes per cycle, but since there would be several threads, the total number of changes per cycle would be several times higher. Thus application-level parallelism will certainly help when it can be used. However, it may not be actually used in very many cases for two reasons: First, obviously, it can only be used in tasks that have parallel decompositions, and not all interesting tasks will. Second, using application-level parallelism places additional burdens on the developers of the applications. They must find the parallel decompositions and then implement them in such a way that the program is both correct and efficient.

The final factor, the large variation in the processing required by the affected productions, may change somewhat because researchers are actively working on techniques to reduce this. Even here, however, it is not likely that much improvement is possible. The obvious way to handle the problem is to divide the match process into a large number of small tasks (for example, as done in going from production parallelism to node parallelism to intra-node parallelism). This is effective, but it cannot be carried too far because the amount of overhead time (for scheduling, for synchronization, etc.) goes up as we go to finer granularity and the number of processes increases.

5 Parallel Implementation of Production Systems

In the previous chapter, we discussed the various sources of parallelism that may be exploited in the context of the Rete algorithm — production parallelism, node parallelism, intra-node parallelism, and action parallelism. We also observed that intra-node and action parallelism when combined together provided the most speed-up. This chapter discusses the hardware and software structures necessary for efficiently exploiting these sources of parallelism. Section 5.1 discusses the architecture of the multiprocessor proposed to execute the parallel version of the Rete algorithm. Section 5.2 presents the data representations and constraints necessary for the parallel processing of the state-update phase, that is, while processing activations of memory nodes, two-input nodes, and terminal nodes. Section 5.3 presents the data structures and constraints necessary for the parallel processing of the selection phase, that is, while processing activations of constant-test nodes. This section also discusses issues that arise at the boundary between the selection phase and the state-update phase.

5.1. Architecture of the Production-System Machine

This section describes the architecture of the *production-system machine* (PSM), the hardware structure suitable for executing the parallel version of the Rete algorithm. We begin with a description of the proposed machine (see Figure 5-1), and later provide justifications for each of the design decisions. The major characteristics of the machine are:

1. The production-system machine should be a *shared-memory multiprocessor* with about 32-64 processors.

2. The individual processors should be high performance computers, each with a small amount of private memory and a cache.

3. The processors should be connected to the shared memory via one or more *shared buses*.

4. The multiprocessor should support a *hardware task scheduler* to help enqueue node activations that need to be evaluated on the task queue and to help assign pending node activations to idle processors.

To execute the parallel Rete algorithm on the PSM we propose the following mapping. There will be one process that is responsible for performing conflict-resolution and right-hand side evaluation. This process will be locked on to one of the processors. The remaining processors

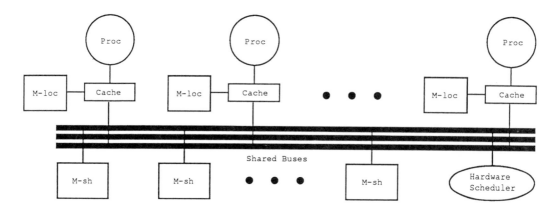

Figure 5-1: Architecture of the production-system machine.

will be used for evaluating node activations in the Rete network. At any given point in time, there will be some processors evaluating node activations and some processors waiting on the hardware task scheduler looking for new node activations to process. As soon as the processors evaluating node activations generate new successor activations, these will be assigned to the waiting idle processors. If there are no idle processors, the new activations will be stored in the scheduler until some processor becomes idle.

Returning to the requirements we proposed for the PSM, the first requirement is that it should be a shared-memory multiprocessor with 32-64 processors. The main reason for using a shared-memory architecture stems from the fact that to achieve a high degree of speed-up from parallelism, the parallel Rete algorithm exploits parallelism at a very fine grain. For example, in the parallel Rete algorithm multiple activations of the same node may be evaluated in parallel. This requires thàt multiple processors have access to the state corresponding to that node, which strongly suggests a shared-memory architecture. It is not possible to replicate the state, since keeping all copies of the state up to date is extremely expensive.

Another important reason for using a shared-memory architecture relates to the load distribution problem. In case processors do not share memory, the processor on which the activations of a given node in the Rete network are evaluated must be decided at the time the network is loaded into the parallel machine. Since the number of node activations is much smaller than the total number of nodes in the Rete network [30], it is necessary to assign several nodes in the network to a single processor. This partitioning of nodes amongst the processors is a very difficult problem, and in its full generality is shown to be NP-complete [70]. Using a shared-memory architecture the partitioning problem is bypassed since all processors are capable of processing all node activations, and it is possible to assign processors to node activations at run-time.

The suggestion of 32-64 processors for the multiprocessor is derived as a result of measurements and simulations done for many large production-system programs [40, 44, 56, 57]. Because of the small number of productions affected per change to working memory and because of the variance in the processing required by the affected productions, simulations for most production-system programs show that using more than 32 processors does not yield any additional speed-up. There are some production systems which can use up to 64 processors, but the number of such systems is small. The fact that only about 32 processors are needed is also consonant with our use of a shared-memory architecture — it is quite difficult to build shared-memory multiprocessors with very large number of processors. In case it does become useful to use a larger number of processors (say 256) for some programs, the use of hierarchical multiprocessors is proposed for the parallel Rete algorithm, where the latency for accessing information in another multiprocessor cluster is longer than the latency for accessing information in the local cluster. The reasons for using eight clusters of 32-processor multiprocessors instead of a single 256-processor multicomputer are: (1) it is easier to partition a production-system program into 8 parts than it is to partition it into 256 parts; (2) within each 32-processor multiprocessor it is possible to exploit very fine-grain parallelism (for example, intra-node parallelism) to reduce the maximum time taken by any single production to finish match.

The second requirement for the proposed production-system machine is that the individual processors should be high-performance computers, each with a cache and a small amount of private memory. Since simulations show that the number of processors required for the proposed production-system machine is small, there is no reason not to use the processors with the highest performance — processors having wide datapaths and which use the fastest technology available.[33] It is interesting to note that the code sequences used to execute production-system programs do not include complex instructions. The instructions used most often are simple loads, compares, and branches without any complex addressing modes (see Appendix B and [22, 72]). As a result, the reduced instruction set computers (RISCs) [37, 71, 73] form good candidates for the individual processors in the production-system machine.

The reason for associating a small amount of private memory with each processor is to reduce the amount of traffic to the shared memory, since the traffic to shared memory results in both bus contention and memory contention. The data structures stored in the private memory would be those that do not change very often or those that change at well defined points, an example being the data structure storing the contents of the working memory. It is possible to replicate such data structures in the private memories of processors and to keep them updated, thus saving repeated references to shared memory. Some of the frequently used code to process node activations can also be replicated in the private memories of the processors.

---

[33]The suggestion for using a small number (32-64) of *high-performance* processors may be contrasted with suggestions for using a very large number (1000-100,000) of *weak* processors, as originally suggested for DADO and NON-VON [82, 87]. While the schemes using a small number of processors can use expensive very high performance processors, schemes using a very large number of processors cannot afford to have the fast processors for each of the processing nodes. In [31] we show that the performance lost as a result of weak individual processing nodes is difficult to recover by simply using a large number of them.

The third requirement for the proposed production-system machine is that the processors should be connected to the shared memory via shared buses. The reasons for suggesting a shared-bus scheme, instead of a crossbar switch or other communication networks (such as an Omega network or a Shuffle Exchange network [9]), are: (1) it is much easier to construct sophisticated multi-cache coherency solutions when shared buses are used [79], and (2) simulation results show that a single high-speed bus should be able to handle the load put on it by about 32 processors, provided that reasonable cache-hit ratios are obtained (see Section 8.8 for assumptions). The reason why caches must be able to hold shared data objects is that a large number of memory accesses in the parallel Rete algorithm are expected to be to such shared objects. If the processor suffers a cache miss for all shared-memory references, the performance penalty will be significant. When shared objects can be stored in cache, it is also possible to implement short synchronization structures, like spin-locks [54], very efficiently. It is possible for the processor to loop out of the cache when the synchronization structure is busy, thus causing no additional bus traffic.

The fourth and final requirement for the proposed production-system machine is that it should be able to support a hardware task scheduler, that is, a hardware mechanism to enqueue node activations into a task queue and to help assign node activations in the task queue to idle processors. The hardware scheduler for the nodes is needed because it is often necessary to schedule several node activations for the same node in parallel. In order to do this, several tests must be made before scheduling each activation to ensure that it cannot interfere with other activations of the same node that are being processed at that time. While the amount of checking that must be done is small, it is nonetheless of great importance to the efficiency of the production-system machine, since the scheduling must be done serially. The hardware task scheduler is expected to sit on the shared bus, and the time to schedule an activation using such a scheduler is expected to be one bus cycle. The details for the necessity and structure of such a scheduler are given in Chapter 6.

5.2. The State-Update Phase Processing

This section discusses various issues regarding the parallel implementation of the state-update phase of the Rete algorithm on a multiprocessor.

5.2.1. Hash-Table Based vs. List Based Memory Nodes

Line 2 in Tables 3-15 and 3-16 (see Chapter 3) gives the average number of tokens found when a memory node is activated. Similarly, Line 3 in Tables 3-17 and 3-18 gives the number of tokens in the opposite memory when a two-input node is activated. The significance of these numbers is that they indicate the complexity of processing memory-nodes and two-input nodes respectively.

Existing OPS5 and Soar interpreters store the contents of the memory nodes as a linear list of tokens. Thus when a token with a − tag arrives at a memory node, a corresponding token must be found and deleted from the memory node. If a linear search is done, then on average, half of the tokens in that memory node will be looked up. Similarly, for an activation of a two-input node, all tokens in the opposite memory must be looked up to find the set of matching tokens.

It is proposed that, instead of storing tokens in a memory node as a linear list, it is better to store them in a hash table. The hash function used for storing the tokens corresponding to a memory node is based on (1) the tests associated with the two-input node below the memory node, and (2) the distinct node-id associated with the two-input node. (Recall that the memory nodes always feed into some two-input node, and that two-input nodes have tests associated with them to determine those sets of tokens that have consistent variable bindings.) For example, consider the Rete network shown in Figure 5-2. The hash function used for a token entering the left memory node is based on the value of **attr2** field of the associated working-memory element and the node-id of the and-node below. The hash function for a token entering the right memory node is based on the value of **attr1** field and the node-id of the and-node below.

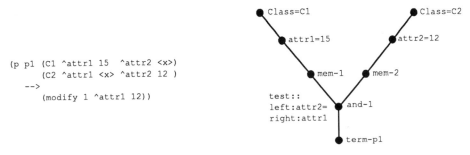

```
(p p1 (C1 ^attr1 15   ^attr2 <x>)
      (C2 ^attr1 <x> ^attr2 12 )
   -->
      (modify 1 ^attr1 12))
```

Figure 5-2: A production and the associated Rete network.

There are two main advantages of storing tokens in a hash table. First, the cost of deleting a token from a memory node is now a constant, instead of being proportional to half the number of tokens in that memory node. Similarly, the cost of finding matching tokens in the opposite memory is now proportional to the number of successful matches, instead of being proportional to the number of tokens in the opposite memory.[34] Second, hashing cuts down the variance in the processing time required by the various memory node and two-input node activations, which is especially important for parallel implementations. The main disadvantage of using hashing is the overhead of computing the value of the hash function for each node activation. However, because of the fact that hashing reduces the variance, even if the cost with hashing is greater than the cost when linear lists are used, hash-table based memory nodes may still be advantageous for parallel implementations.

---

[34]However, in case of two-input nodes with no equality tests, hashing does not provide any discriminating effect. The processing times, in such cases, are the same as when linear lists are used. Fortunately, the number of such nodes is quite small.

As far as the implementation of the hash table-based node memories is concerned, there are two options. The hash table may be shared between all the memory nodes in the Rete network, or there may be separate hash tables for each memory node. Since there are a large fraction of memory nodes that do not have any tokens at all (or have very few tokens), it would be waste of space to have a separate hash table for each node.[35] Also, since there is a large variation in the number of tokens that are present in the various memory nodes, a hash table of a single size for each memory node would not be appropriate. In the implementation suggested in the thesis, two hash tables are used for all memory nodes in the network. One hash table for all memory nodes that form the left input of a two-input node, and another hash table for all memory nodes that form the right input of a two-input node.

5.2.2. Memory Nodes Need to be Lumped with Two-Input Nodes

Uniprocessor implementations of the Rete algorithm save significant processing by sharing nodes between similar productions (see Table 3-13). This section discusses reasons why in the parallel implementation proposed in this thesis, it is not possible to share a memory node between multiple two-input nodes.[36] Simulations show that the loss of such sharing increases the total cost of performing match by about 25%.

The main problem with the straightforward sharing of memory nodes is that it violates some of the assumptions made by the Rete algorithm. The Rete algorithm assumes that (1) the processing of the memory node and the associated two-input node is an atomic operation and (2) while the two-input node is being processed the contents of the opposite memory do not change. The problem can be explained with the help of the Rete network shown in Figure 5-3. The network shows a memory node shared between the two condition elements of a production. When working-memory element "wme-1" (shown at the bottom-left of Figure 5-3) is added to the working memory, it passes the constant-test "Class = C1", and is then added to the memory node. This causes both a left activation of the and-node and a right activation of the and-node. When the left activation is processed, the and-node finds a matching token in the right memory node (it is the same as the left memory node), and outputs a token to the terminal node. Similarly, when the right activation of the and-node is processed, another token is output to the terminal node. This is incorrect, because if the memory nodes were not shared there would have been only one token sent to the terminal node.

The problem as described above would occur in both sequential and parallel implementations.

---

[35]One reason why a large fraction of memory nodes have no tokens or very few tokens is that, like programs in many other programming languages, only a small fraction of the total productions are responsible for most of the action in a run.

[36]The run-time data presented in Table 3-20 shows that the number of memory node activations is about a third of the two-input node activations. This indicates that, on average at run-time, each memory node is shared between three two-input nodes.

```
(p p1 (C1 ^attr1 <x> ^attr2 <y>)
      (C1 ^attr1 <y> ^attr2 <x>)
   -->
      (remove 1))


wme1: (C1 ^attr1 7  ^attr2 7)
```

Figure 5-3: Problems with memory-node sharing.

There are techniques, however, which permit the problem to be avoided for sequential implementations, but they do not work well for the parallel case. For example, in current
uniprocessor implementations of Rete, a memory node keeps two lists of successor nodes — the
left successors and the right successors. The left successors correspond to those two-input
nodes for which this memory node forms the left input, and the right successors correspond to
those two-input nodes for which the memory node forms the right input. The uniprocessor algorithm processes all the left successors (including the activations caused by the processing of the
immediate left successors) before actually adding the new token into the memory node (a
pointer to the token to be added is passed as a parameter), then the token is added to the memory
node, and then all the right successors are processed. Thus for the network shown in Figure 5-3,
no token is sent to the terminal node for the left activation of the and-node, and one token is sent
for the right activation, as desired.

The above scheme is not suitable for parallel implementations because it is too constraining. It
requires that all left successors (including all successors of the immediate left successors) be
processed before the right successors are processed, and this defeats the whole purpose of the
parallel implementation. Other more complex schemes, for example, associating a marker array
with each newly added token that keeps track of the successor two-input nodes that have really
seen and processed the token added to the memory node, impose too much overhead to be useful. In some simple-minded parallel implementations, sharing of memory nodes can also cause
deadlocks, for example, when two processes try to ensure that the shared memory node does not
get modified while the two-input nodes are being processed.

For the implementation proposed in this thesis, there is one other reason why memory nodes
need to be lumped with the two-input nodes. This reason is the use of hash-table based memory
nodes. As suggested in the previous section, to enable finding matching tokens in the opposite
memory efficiently, the hash function uses the values of the tests present in the associated two-
input node. Thus if the tests associated with the successor two-input nodes are different, then it
is not possible to share the memory nodes feeding into those two-input nodes. In all subsequent
sections of this thesis, it is assumed that memory nodes are not shared (that is, there are two

separate memory nodes for each two-input node), and that the processing associated with a two-input node refers to the processing required by the and-node or the not-node and the associated memory nodes. However, note that it is still possible to share two-input nodes (and-nodes and the not-nodes) in the Rete network, and if the two-input nodes are shared then the associated memory nodes are automatically shared too.

5.2.3. Problems with Processing Conjugate Pairs of Tokens

Sometimes when performing match for a single change or multiple changes to working memory, it is possible that the same token is first added to and then deleted from a memory node. Such a pair of tokens is called a *conjugate* pair of tokens [17]. For example, consider the productions and the corresponding Rete network shown in Figure 2-2 (see Chapter 2). Let the initial condition of the network correspond to the state when working-memory elements wme1 and wme2 (shown at the bottom-left of Figure 2-2) have been added to the working memory. Now consider a production firing that inserts wme3 to working memory and deletes wme1 from working memory. If wme3 is processed before wme1, the token t-w1w3 will first be added to the memory node at the bottom-left of the Rete network, and subsequently when deletion of wme1 is processed, the token t-w1w3 will be deleted from the memory node. Although conjugate pairs are not generated very often, their occurrence poses problems for parallel implementations, as explained below.

Consider the case when the insertion of wme3 and deletion of wme1 are processed concurrently. In this case, as before, requests for both the addition of t-w1w3 and the deletion of t-w1w3 to the memory node are generated. Now it is quite possible, that the scheduler used in the parallel implementation assigns the processing of the deletion of t-w1w3 to a processor before it assigns the processing of the addition of t-w1w3.[37] When the delete t-w1w3 request is processed, the token to be deleted would not be found, since it has not been added so far.[38] There are two alternatives. First, the request for the deletion of the token can simply be aborted, and no more action taken. Second, the fact that the token to be deleted was not found should be recorded somewhere. This way when the add t-w1w3 request is processed, it is possible to determine that an extra delete operation had been performed on the memory node and appropriate action can be taken.

The first alternative suggested above is not reasonable, since it would lead to incorrect results

---

[37]There are a number of reasons why this may happen. For example, although the request for the addition of t-w1w3 is generated before the request for the deletion, because of arbitrary delays in the communication process, the request for the deletion may reach the scheduler before the request for addition. Also there is no simple way for the scheduler to realize that the delete request it has just received is part of a conjugate pair.

[38]Note that there are no such problems in uniprocessor implementations of the Rete algorithm. The reason is that, in uniprocessor implementations, it is possible to ensure that the sequence in which the requests for insertions and deletions of tokens are processed is the same as the sequence in which these requests were generated.

from the match. The second alternative is what this thesis proposes. In the proposed implementation, extra tokens from early deletes are stored in a special *extra-deletes-list* associated with each two-input node. Whenever a token is to be inserted into a memory node, the extra-deletes-list associated with the corresponding two-input node is first checked to see if the token to be inserted cancels out an early delete. Most of the time this list is expected to be empty, so the overhead of such a check should not be too much.

5.2.4. Concurrently Processable Activations of Two-Input Nodes

In Section 4.2.3 on intra-node parallelism, it was proposed that multiple activations of the same two-input node should be evaluated in parallel to obtain additional speed-up. This section discusses some of the restrictions that need to be put on processing multiple activations of the same node in parallel. These restrictions are necessary to reduce the amount of synchronization needed to ensure correct operation of the algorithm.

Figure 5-4 shows the various kinds of situations that may arise when multiple activation of the same two-input happen. For example, case-1 in the figure refers to multiple insert-requests from the left side, case-4 refers to multiple delete-requests from the right side, case-5 refers to both insert and delete requests from the left side, and case-7 refers to multiple insert-requests, some of which are from the left side of the two-input node and the some of which are from the right side. We propose that only the multiple activations depicted in cases 1-6 should be processed in parallel, and that multiple activations depicted in the cases 7-10 (or their combinations) should not be processed in parallel. To justify these restrictions, the various cases are divided into three groups. Cases 1-4 are grouped together, and represent the case when multiple inserts or multiple deletes from the same side are to be processed. Cases 5-6 are grouped together, and represent the case when both insert and delete requests from the same side are to be processed. Cases 7-10 are grouped together, and represent the case when activations from both sides are to be processed concurrently.

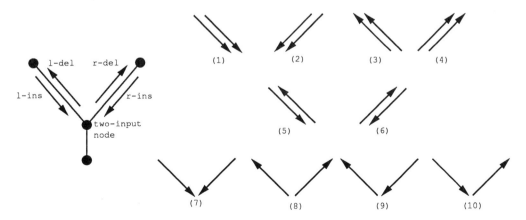

Figure 5-4: Concurrent activations of two-input nodes.

The reason for not processing cases 7-10 in parallel is related to the assumption of Rete algorithm that, while a two-input node is being processed the opposite memory should not be modified. The effect of violating this assumption was also shown in Section 5.2.2. To illustrate the problems with processing such activations in parallel, consider case-7 where an insert request from the left and an insert request from the right are processed concurrently. Also assume that the tokens corresponding to these requests satisfy the tests associated with the two-input node. It is possible to have the following sequence of operations: (1) The token corresponding to left insert-request is added to left memory-node. (2) The token corresponding to the right insert-request is added to the right memory-node. (3) The left activation of the two-input node finds the newly inserted right-token and results in the generation of a successor token. (4) Similarly, the right activation of the two-input node results in the generation of another successor token. This is incorrect, since only one successor token should have been generated. The cost of detection and deletion of duplicates at the successor nodes is too expensive a solution. Similarly, there is no simple way of ensuring that the relevant portion of the opposite memory does not get modified while the two-input node is being processed.[39] The reasons for not permitting cases 8-10 to be processed in parallel are along the same lines as above.

Whether cases 5-6 are permitted to be processed in parallel, depends on some subtle implementation decisions. For example, when the extra-deletes-list is associated with each two-input node in the Rete network (as proposed in Section 5.2.3), it is not possible to process activations corresponding to cases 5-6 in parallel. The reasons are related to the conjugate-pair problem discussed in the previous subsection. Consider the case when both an insert request and a delete request for a token are to be processed. It is possible that the following sequence of operations takes place: (1) The delete request begins first, it locks the memory node (the lock associated with the appropriate bucket of the hash table storing the tokens), it does not find the token to be deleted, it releases the lock on the memory node. It then attempts to get a second lock, the lock necessary to insert the extra delete into the special extra-deletes-list associated with the corresponding two-input node. (2) Before the delete request can get hold of the second lock, the insert request gets hold of that lock to check if any extra deletes have been done. It finds no extra deletes, it releases this lock, and then goes on to insert the token into the memory node. (3) The delete request gets hold of the second lock, and inserts the token into the extra-deletes-list. The result of the above sequence is obviously incorrect, since the correct result should have been no token in the memory node and no token in the extra-deletes-list.

A solution to the above problem, so that activations corresponding to cases 5-6 may be processed in parallel, is to use only a single lock to check/change the contents of the memory

---

[39]In the current implementation, the relevant portion of the opposite memory is identified by the tokens in the corresponding bucket of the opposite hash table. Thus if it is ensured that this specific opposite bucket is not being modified, the rest of the opposite memory may be modified in any way. Although this idea has not been developed any further, it should be possible to work out a solution along these lines, so that multiple activation of the same two-input node from different directions can be processed in parallel.

node and to check/change the contents of the extra-deletes-list. This can be achieved by associating an extra-deletes-list with each bucket of the hash table and using a common lock, rather than associating an extra-deletes-list with each two-input node (as proposed in Section 5.2.3). Because of the late discovery of this solution, the simulation results presented in Chapter 8 represent the case when node activations corresponding to cases 5-6 are not processed in parallel. Some simulations done to test the new solution show an overall performance improvement of about 5%. The increase in performance is not very significant because multiple insert and delete requests for a two-input node from the same side are rare.

The reason why cases 1-4 can be processed easily in parallel is that, while the multiple activations of the two-input nodes are being processed, the opposite memory stays stable and does not change, unlike in cases 7-10. There is also no potential for race conditions, where the same token is being inserted and deleted from a memory node at the same time, as in cases 5-6. The parallel processing of cases 1-4 results in the most increase in speed-up as it eliminates the cross-product bottleneck mentioned in Section 4.2.3.

5.2.5. Locks for Memory Nodes

As proposed in Section 5.2.1, the tokens associated with all memory nodes in the Rete network are stored in two global hash tables — one for the tokens belonging to the left memory-nodes and one for tokens belonging to the right memory-nodes. Since multiple node activations may be processed in parallel, it is necessary to control access to the individual buckets of the hash tables. It is proposed that there should be a lock associated with each bucket of the two hash tables. Furthermore, the locks should be of *multiple-reader/single-writer* type, that is, the lock associated with a bucket should permit multiple readers at the same time, but it should permit only a single writer at the same time, and it should exclude readers and writers from entering the bucket at the same time.

The use of the read and write locks is expected to be as follows. For the left activation of a two-input node, a write-lock is used to insert/delete the token from the chosen bucket in the left hash table. The read-lock is used to look at the contents of the corresponding bucket in the right hash table to find tokens in the right memory node that have consistent variable bindings with the left token. Thus a multiple-reader/single-writer lock permits several node activations that wish to look at a bucket in read-mode to proceed in parallel. Such a scheme is expected to help in handling the hash table accesses generated during the processing of cross-products.

5.2.6. Linear vs. Binary Rete Networks

In Section 2.4.2 it was pointed out that there is a large variability possible in the amount of state that a match algorithm stores. For example, on the low side, the TREAT algorithm [61] stores information only about matches between individual condition elements and individual working-memory elements. On the high side, the algorithm proposed by Kemal

Oflazer [70] stores information about matches between all possible combinations of condition elements that occur in the left-hand side of a production and the sequences of working-memory elements that satisfy them. The state stored by the Rete-class of algorithms falls in between the above two schemes. The Rete-class of algorithms, in addition to storing information about matches between individual condition elements and working-memory elements, store information about matches between some fixed combinations of condition elements occurring in the left-hand sides of productions and working-memory element tuples. The combinations for which is stored are decided at the time when the network is compiled. This section discusses some of the factors that influence the selection of the combinations of condition elements for which state is stored.

To study the state stored for a production by the *standard* Rete algorithm,[40] the algorithm used in existing OPS5 interpreters, consider the following production with k condition elements: $C_1 \& C_2 \& \ldots \& C_k \rightarrow A_1.A_2 \ldots A_l$. The state stored consists of working-memory elements matching the individual condition elements (stored in the α-memory nodes of the Rete network), working-memory element pairs jointly matching the condition elements $C_1 \& C_2$, working-memory element triples matching $C_1 \& C_2 \& C_3$, and so on (stored in the β-memory nodes of the Rete network), and finally working-memory element k-tuples matching $C_1 \& C_2 \& \ldots \& C_k$ (stored in the conflict-set). The algorithm does not store state for any other combinations of condition elements, for example, working-memory element pairs matching the combination $C_2 \& C_3$ are neither computed nor stored.

To make the discussion of the advantages and disadvantages of the scheme used by the standard Rete algorithm easier, it helps to consider the state of a production in terms of relational database concepts [93]. In relational database terminology, the sets of working-memory elements matching the individual condition elements $C_1, \ldots, C_k$ can be considered as relations $R_1, \ldots, R_k$. The relation specifying the working-memory element k-tuples matching the complete production is denoted by $R_1 \otimes R_2 \otimes \ldots \otimes R_k$, and is computed by the join of the relations $R_1, \ldots, R_k$, where the join conditions correspond to those tests that ensure the consistency of variable bindings between the various condition elements. The state stored by the standard Rete algorithm corresponds to the tuples in the relations:

- $R_1, \ldots, R_k$. This is the state stored in the α-memory nodes of the Rete network.
- $R_1 \otimes R_2, R_1 \otimes R_2 \otimes R_3, \ldots, R_1 \otimes R_2 \otimes \ldots \otimes R_k$. This is the state stored in the β-memory nodes of the Rete network and the conflict-set.

The processing required when a working-memory element is either inserted or deleted corresponds to keeping all these relations updated. In this process, the algorithm makes use of the smaller joins that have been computed earlier to compute the larger joins. For example, to compute the join $R_1 \otimes R_2 \otimes R_3$, the algorithm uses the join $R_1 \otimes R_2$ and the relation R_3 that have been

---

[40]Also called the *linear* Rete, because of the linear chain of two-input nodes constructed by it.

computed earlier. Similarly, the addition of a new working-memory element to the relation R_k requires that the relation $R_1 \otimes R_2 \otimes \ldots \otimes R_k$ be updated. This is done by computing the join $(R_1 \otimes R_2 \otimes \ldots \otimes R_{k-1}) \otimes \{new\text{-}wme\}$, where the join of $R_1, \ldots, R_{k-1}$ already exists.

The *goodness* of the state-saving strategy used by a match algorithm is determined by the amount of work needed to compute the conflict-set, that is, the relation $R_1 \otimes R_2 \otimes \ldots \otimes R_k$ for all the productions, and of course, any other intermediate relations used in the process.[41] Empirical studies show that by the above criteria, the standard Rete algorithm does quite well. The work required to keep the relations $R_1 \otimes R_2, R_1 \otimes R_2 \otimes R_3, \ldots$, updated is quite small (as shown by the small number of β-memory node activations per change to working memory in Section 3.4.3). The reasons for this are:

- The way productions are currently written, the initial condition element of a production is very constraining, which makes the cardinality of the relations $R_1, R_1 \otimes R_2, \ldots$, quite small, which in turn implies that the processing required to keep the state updated is small. For example, the first condition element of a large fraction of productions is of the type *context*, and since normally only one context is active at any given time, the relation R_1 is empty for all productions that do not belong to the active context, and they do not require any state processing for the β-memory nodes.[42]

- Relations corresponding to a large number of condition elements, that is, relations of the form $R_1 \otimes \ldots \otimes R_p$, where p is 3 or more, are naturally restrictive (do not grow too large) because of the large number conditions involved and the associated tests.[43]

While the scheme used by the standard Rete algorithm works fine for uniprocessor implementations, some problems are present for parallel implementations. This is because the criteria for goodness for parallel implementations are slightly different from that for uniprocessor implementations. In a uniprocessor implementation the aim is to minimize the total processing required in the state-update process, and it is not important if the state-update phase for some productions takes much longer than that for other productions. In a parallel implementation, while it is important to keep the sum of the state-update costs for the affected productions down, it is equally important to reduce the variation in the costs of the affected productions. The standard Rete algorithm keeps the total cost of the state-update phase well under control, but it is not so good at keeping the variation down. Some of the reasons are discussed below.

---

[41] This criterion of goodness is appropriate primarily for uniprocessor implementations.

[42] In case the first condition element of a production is not very constraining, it is often possible to reorder the condition elements so that the first condition element is restrictive. Such transformations may either be done by machine [49] or by a person.

[43] Again, the ordering of condition elements can help to reduce the amount of state that has to be updated on each cycle.

Simulation studies for parallel implementations using the state-saving strategy of standard Rete show that a common reason for the large value of t_{max}/t_{avg} is a long chain of dependent node activations, that is, often a node activation causes an activation of a successor node, which in turn causes an activation of its successor node, and so on. This is called the *long-chain* effect (see Figure 5-5), and it is especially important in programs that have productions with a large number of condition elements. It is possible to reduce the length of these long sequences of dependent node activations by shortening the maximum length of chains that is possible — by changing the intermediate state that is computed by the algorithm and the way it is combined to get the final changes to the conflict-set.

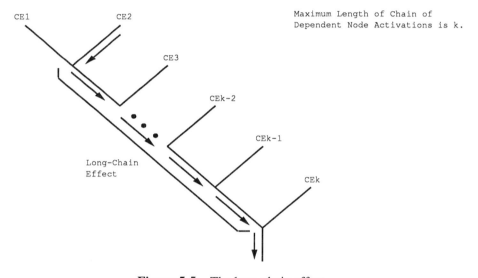

Figure 5-5: The long-chain effect.

One way to reduce the length of the long chains is to construct the Rete network as a binary network (see Figure 5-6) instead of as a linear network. This way the maximum length of a chain of dependent node activations is cut down from k to $\lceil \log_2 k \rceil + 1$. In such a scheme the stored state corresponds to tuples in the relations:

- $R_1, \ldots, R_k,$
- $R_1 \otimes R_2, R_3 \otimes R_4, \ldots, R_{k-1} \otimes R_k,$
- $R_1 \otimes R_2 \otimes R_3 \otimes R_4, \ldots, R_{k-3} \otimes R_{k-2} \otimes R_{k-1} \otimes R_k,$
- and so on.

Simulations for Soar programs show that the binary network scheme reduces the variation in the processing costs of productions significantly, thus increasing the number of processors that can be effectively used in a parallel implementation. For example, for the eight-puzzle program

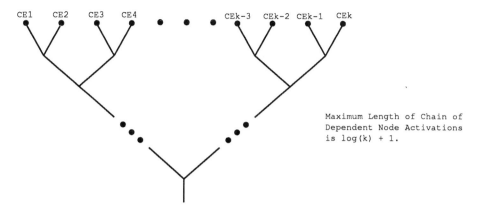

CE1　CE2　CE3　CE4　　●　●　●　　CEk-3　CEk-2　CEk-1　CEk

Maximum Length of Chain of
Dependent Node Activations
is log(k) + 1.

Figure 5-6: A binary Rete network.

in Soar, using the binary network increases the speed-up from 9-fold to 15-fold. The speed-up obtained for normal OPS5 programs is not as good, in fact, in most cases the speed-up is reduced.

The reasons for the reduction in speed-up in OPS5 programs are the following. First, the average number of condition elements per production in OPS5 programs is quite small, 3.4 for OPS5 programs as compared to 6.8 for the Soar programs. Since the number of condition elements is small, the difference between the length of chains in the linear and the binary networks is not significant, and thus not much improvement can be expected. Second, the total cost of the state-update phase when using the binary network scheme is often much larger than the total cost when using the linear network scheme. As an example, consider the following production:

```
(p free-all-hands
            (robot     ^hand1 <x>     ^hand2 <y>     ^hand3 <z>)
            (object    ^name    <x>)
            (object    ^name    <y>)
            (object    ^name    <z>)
   -->
            (modify 1 ^hand1 free ^hand2 free ^hand3 free)
```

The above production consists of four condition elements and the joins stored by the linear Rete are $R_1 \otimes R_2$, $(R_1 \otimes R_2) \otimes R_3$, $(R_1 \otimes R_2 \otimes R_3) \otimes R_4$. The joins stored by the binary Rete are $R_1 \otimes R_2$, $R_3 \otimes R_4$, $(R_1 \otimes R_2) \otimes (R_3 \otimes R_4)$. Note that the relations in parentheses indicate the way a larger relation is computed. Thus the relation $(R_1 \otimes R_2) \otimes R_3$ implies that it is computed as the join of $R_1 \otimes R_2$ and R_3, and not as the join of R_1 and $R_2 \otimes R_3$.

Now consider the scenario where there is one working-memory element of type *robot* (corresponding to a single robot in the environment) and there are 100 working-memory elements of type *object* (corresponding to 100 different objects in the environment). In such a case the cardinality of the relations R_1, R_2, R_3, and R_4 will be 1, 100, 100, and 100 respectively. Then in the case of the linear network all β-memory nodes will have a cardinality of 1, that is, they will contain only one token. This is because of the constraining effect of the first condition element, and the fact that the variables x, y and z are all bound by the time the join operation moves to the second, third, and the fourth condition elements. In case of the binary Rete network, however, the β-memory node corresponding to the relation $R_3 \otimes R_4$ will have 10,000 tokens in it, since there are no common variables between the third and the fourth condition elements. So whenever a working-memory element of type *object* is inserted about 100 tokens have to be added to that memory node, in contrast to only a single addition if the linear network is used.

As the above discussion shows, the use of a binary network can often result in a large number of node activations that would not have occurred in the linear network.[44] This increase in the basic cost of the state-update phase often offsets the extra advantage given by the smaller value of t_{max}/t_{avg} found in binary networks. In fact, in all systems studied, there were at least a few productions where the state grew enormously when the binary networks were used. The networks for these few productions had to be changed back to the linear form (or some mixture of binary and linear forms) before the production-system programs could be run to completion.

As a result of the various studies and simulation done for this thesis, it appears that there is no single state-storage strategy that is good for all production systems. There is no reason, however, to have the restriction that all productions in a program should use the linear network, the binary network, or any other fixed network form. We propose that the compiler should be built so that the network form to be used with each production can be specified independently, and that this network form should be individually tailored to each production. The form of the network may be provided by the programmer at the time of writing a production. This strategy has the advantage that the programmer often has semantic information that permits him to determine the sizes of the various relations; information that a machine may not have. Alternatively, the form of the network may be provided by another program that uses various heuristics and analysis techniques [86]. Such a program may also use data gathered about relation sizes from earlier runs of the program to optimize the network form.[45]

---

[44]Note that it is also possible to construct examples where the state-update phase for the linear network is much more expensive than that for the binary network. However, in practice, such cases are not encountered as often.

[45]The network compiler may also provide some default network forms that may be used with the productions, as is the case currently in standard Rete.

5.3. The Selection Phase Processing

Given a working-memory element, the selection phase identifies those condition elements that are satisfied by that working-memory element. The processing done during the selection phase primarily involves evaluating the constant-test nodes found in the upper part of the Rete network. This section discusses some of the issues that arise when the selection phase is performed on a multiprocessor.

5.3.1. Sharing of Constant-Test Nodes

A production-system program often has different productions to deal with variants of the same situation, and as a result the condition elements of these productions are also similar. The Rete network compiler shares constant-test nodes whenever such similar condition elements are compiled, and the uniprocessor implementations of the Rete algorithm rely greatly on the sharing of constant-test nodes to save processing time in the selection phase (see Section 3.3.2). For example, the constant-test nodes immediately below the root-node consist of tests that check the type of the condition element, since that is the first field of all condition elements. For the VT production system [52], the total number of condition element types is 48, thus with sharing only 48 constant-test nodes are needed at the top-level, each checking for one of the 48 types. If no sharing is present, however, a separate node would be needed to check the type of each condition element, and since the system consists of approximately 4500 condition elements, that many nodes will be required at the top-level.

In a non-shared memory multicomputer implementation of production systems, where each production is allocated to a separate processor, it is not possible to exploit the sharing mentioned above. This is because each processor must independently determine which of the condition elements of the production allocated to it are satisfied. There is no reason, however, not to use such sharing in a shared-memory multiprocessor implementation of production systems. One of the consequences of the sharing of constant-test nodes is that often a constant-test node may have a large number of successors. These successors may either be other constant-test nodes or they may be α-memory nodes. Some implementation issues related to how these successors ought to be evaluated are discussed below.

5.3.2. Constant-Test Node Successors

Consider the cost of evaluating a constant-test node. The cost consists of: (1) In case the activation is picked up from the centralized task queue, the cost of removing the activation from the task queue and the cost of setting up the registers so that the processing may begin. (2) The cost of evaluating the test associated with the constant-test node. (3) In case the associated test succeeds, the cost of pushing the successor nodes onto a local stack (for activations to be processed on the same processor) or to the centralized task queue (for activations to be picked up by any idle processor). In the proposed implementation using a hardware task scheduler, the cost of the first step is about 10 instructions, the cost of the second step about 5-8 instructions, and the cost of the third step is about 2 instructions for a local push and about 5 instructions for a global push.

Since the cost of evaluating the test associated with a node (cost of step-2) is small compared to the costs of pushing and popping an activation from the task queue (costs of step-1 and step-3), it is not advisable to schedule each constant-test node activation through the global task queue. Instead, it is suggested that only bunches of constant-test node activations should be scheduled through the global task queue, and that all nodes within a bunch should be processed on the same processor (thus saving the cost of step-1). One way to achieve this is to schedule node activations close to the top-level through the global task scheduler, and have the activations in the subtrees of these globally scheduled nodes processed locally (see Figure 5-7). Another alternative is for the network compiler to use heuristics to decide which nodes are to be scheduled globally and which nodes are to be scheduled locally.

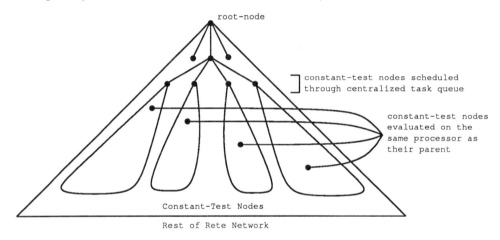

Figure 5-7: Scheduling activations of constant-test nodes.

It was observed in Section 3.4.1 that only about 12% of the constant-test node activations have their associated test satisfied. The reason for the large number of activations with failed tests is that the standard Rete algorithm does not use any indexing techniques (for example, hashing) to filter out node activations that are bound to fail their tests. For example, consider a node whose four successor nodes test if the value of some attribute is 1, 2, 3, or 4 respectively. The standard Rete algorithm would evaluate all these nodes, even though 3 of them are bound to fail. The choice whether or not to use indexing is, however, not always so clear. This is because using a hash function imposes the overhead of computing the hash value, and because the constant-test node activations are very cheap to evaluate (the OPS83 implementation evaluates a constant-test node in three machine instructions). Since the constant-test nodes are not as cheap to evaluate in a multiprocessor implementation, it is proposed that indexing be used in most places, especially in places where the branching factor is large.

5.3.3. Alpha-Memory Node Successors

At the interface between the selection phase and the state-update phase are the α-memory nodes (recall that the constant-test nodes feed directly into the α-memory nodes). Normally, when a constant-test node succeeds, the associated processor builds tokens for the activations of its successor α-memory nodes. These tokens are then given to the task scheduler so that they may be processed by other idle processors. A problem, however, occurs when a constant-test node having a large number (10-30) of α-memory successors is satisfied. Since preparing a token for the scheduler requires the execution of several instructions by the processor, around 5 in the proposed implementation (see Appendix B for details), it implies that by the time the last successor node is scheduled, 100 instructions worth of time has already elapsed (assuming 20 successor nodes).

The time taken by 100 instructions is quite large considering the fact that processing a constant-test node activation takes only around 5-20 instructions (only 3 instructions in the uniprocessor implementation) and that processing a two-input node activation takes only 50-100 instructions. (See Tables 8-3 and 8-4 for the relative costs of processing different node activations.) For this reason, it is proposed that in case a constant-test node has a large number of α-memory successors, it is advisable to replicate that constant-test node, such that each of the replicated nodes has a small number of successors, as shown in Figure 5-8. Thus when the multiple copies of the original constant-test node are evaluated in parallel, the successors would get scheduled in parallel. The number of times that a node ought to be replicated is a function of (1) the number of successor nodes, and (2) the relative costs of processing a constant-test node activation, of processing a two-input node activation, and of preparing and scheduling a successor node. An alternative to replicating the constant-test node is to use a new node type which does not perform the test made by the constant-test node but simply helps in scheduling the α-memory successors in parallel.

5.3.4. Processing Multiple Changes to Working Memory in Parallel

As in the case of the state-update phase, it is possible to process the selection phase for multiple changes to working memory in parallel. Since the constant-test nodes do not store any state, there are no restrictions placed on the constant-test node activations that may be evaluated in parallel.

5.4. Summary

In this chapter various software and hardware issues dealing with the parallel implementation of production systems have been studied. The discussion may be summarized as follows:

- The hardware architecture suitable for implementing production systems is a shared-memory multiprocessor consisting of 32-64 high-performance processors. Each processor should have a small amount of private memory and a cache that is capable of storing both private and shared data. The multiprocessor should support

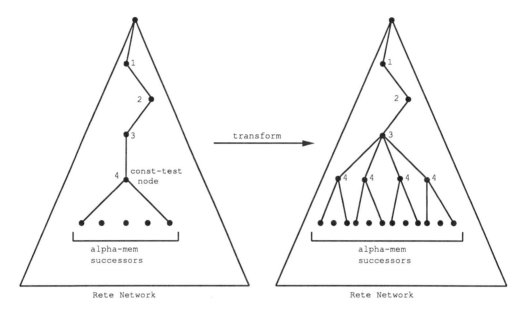

Figure 5-8: Possible solution when too many alpha-memory successors.

a hardware task scheduler to help in the task of assigning pending node activations to idle processors.

- The following points list some of the problems and issues that arise when implementing the state-update phase on a multiprocessor:

  - The tokens associated with the memory nodes should be stored in global hash tables instead of in linear lists, as is done in existing implementations. This helps in reducing the variance in processing required by insertion and deletion of tokens. It is further suggested that a multiple-reader/single-writer lock be associated with each bucket of the hash tables to enable correct access by concurrent node activations.

  - Section 5.2.2 gives reasons why it is not possible to share a memory node between multiple two-input nodes, as is done in uniprocessor implementations of Rete. The reasons have to do with synchronization constraints and the use of hash tables for storing tokens.

  - A solution is given to the problem of processing conjugate pairs of tokens. The solution consists of associating an extra-deletes-list with each memory node. This way whenever a delete-token request is processed before the corresponding add-token request, it can be put on the extra-deletes-list and processed appropriately later.

  - In the proposed parallel implementation it is not possible to process all activations of a two-input node in parallel. Section 5.2.4 gives reasons why multiple activations from one side of a two-input node can be processed concurrently, but why multiple activations from both the left and the right side should not be processed concurrently.

- Within the Rete-class of match algorithms many different state-saving strategies can be used. Section 5.2.6 discusses the relative merits of the linear-network strategy used by the standard Rete algorithm and the alternative binary-network strategy. While the binary-network strategy is found to be much more suitable for Soar programs (programs having productions with a large number of condition elements), the linear-network strategy is found to be more suitable for the OPS5 programs. In general, even within a single program, no single strategy is found to be suitable for all the productions, and it is suggested that tailoring the networks to individual productions can lead to significant speed-ups.

- The following points list some of the problems and issues that arise when implementing the selection phase:

  - Measurements show that only 12% of constant-test node activations have their associated tests satisfied. To avoid evaluating node activations which fail their tests, it is proposed that indexing/hashing techniques should be used. This can result in significant savings.

  - The cost of evaluating the test associated with a constant-test node activation is significantly less compared to the cost of enqueueing and dequeueing a node activation from the centralized task queue. For this reason instead of scheduling individual constant-test node activations through the centralized task queue, it is suggested that only bunches of constant-test node activations should be scheduled through the centralized task queue.

  - Often a constant-test node may have a large number of α-memory node successors. Scheduling these successors serially results in a significant delay by the time the last successor node is scheduled. A solution using replicated constant-test nodes and another solution using a new node type are proposed for scheduling the successors in parallel.

6 The Problem of Scheduling Node Activations

The model for parallel execution of production systems proposed in the previous chapter consists of two components: (1) a number of node processors connected to a shared memory, where each node processor is capable of processing any given node activation; and (2) a centralized task scheduler, where all node node activations requiring processing may be placed and subsequently extracted by idle processors. This chapter explores the implementation issues that arise in the construction of such a centralized task scheduler.

The first difficulty in implementing a centralized task scheduling mechanism stems from the fine granularity of the node activations that are processed. For example, in the current implementation, the average processing required by a node activation is only 50-100 instructions and processing a change to working memory results in about 50 node activations. In a centralized task scheduler, even if enqueueing and dequeueing an activation took only 10 instructions, by the time the last activation is enqueued and finally picked-up for processing, 500 instructions worth of time would have elapsed.[46] This time is significantly larger than that to process individual node activations, and if the scheduler is not to be a bottleneck, the processing required for enqueueing and dequeueing activations must be made much smaller.

The second difficulty associated with implementing a centralized task scheduling mechanism for the parallel Rete algorithm is that the functionality required of it is much more than that of a simple queue. This is because all node activations present in the task queue are not processable all of the time. To be concrete, consider the example shown in Figure 6-1. The figure shows a two-input node for which four activations $a1, a2, a3$, and $a4$ are waiting to be processed. However, because of synchronization constraints given in Section 5.2.4, left activations may not be processed concurrently with right activations. Thus, while node activations $a1$ and $a2$ may be processed concurrently and node activations $a3$ and $a4$ may be processed concurrently, node activations $a1$ and $a3$ may not be processed concurrently. As a result, as soon as the node activation $a1$ is assigned to an idle processor for evaluation, the activations $a3$ and $a4$ become unprocessable for the duration that $a1$ is being processed. Similar restrictions would apply if

---

[46]We do not assume a memory structure of the form proposed for the NYU Ultracomputer [28], where enqueues and dequeues can be done in parallel. Because of the additional complexities in the enqueue and dequeue required for production systems, the standard structure proposed for the Ultracomputer would not work.

activation *a3* had been picked up first for processing. This dynamically changing set of process-able node activations in the task queue makes the scheduler much more complex, and consequently much more difficult to implement.

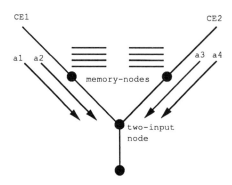

Figure 6-1: Problem of dynamically changing set of processable node activations.

The following sections discuss two solutions for solving the scheduling problem. The first solution involves the construction of a *hardware task scheduler* (HTS) and the second solution involves the construction of *multiple software task schedulers* (STSs).

6.1. The Hardware Task Scheduler

6.1.1. How Fast Need the Scheduler be?

To get a rough estimate of the performance that is required of the hardware task scheduler, consider the following simple model for parallel execution of production systems. Let the total number of independently schedulable tasks generated during a recognize-act cycle be n. Let the average cost of processing one such task be c. Let the cost of enqueueing and dequeueing a task from the scheduler be s. Note that s corresponds only to that part of the scheduling cost during which the scheduler is locked, for example, when the task queue is being modified. Let the cost when the scheduler is not locked, for example, the time taken for preparing a token to be inserted into the task queue, be t. Now the cost of performing the recognize-act cycle on a single processor is $C_{uni} = n \cdot c$. If there are k processors, then assuming perfect division of work between the k processors, the cost of performing the match on a multiprocessor with a centralized scheduler is $C_{mul} = \lceil n/k \rceil (c+t) + n \cdot s$, and the maximum speed-up obtainable on the multiprocessor is given by $S = C_{uni}/C_{mul}$.

Figure 6-2 shows the maximum speed-up that can be obtained when $n=128$ tasks/cycle, $c=100$ instructions, $t=10$ instructions, and for varying values of s and k. As the figure shows, the effect of the duration for which the scheduler is locked is very pronounced. For large values of s, the saturation speed-up is reached with a relatively small number of processors, irrespective of the inherent parallelism in the problem. In terms of the parameters described above, the saturation speed-up as $k \to \infty$ is given by $S = n \cdot c/(c+t+n \cdot s)$, and then as $n \to \infty$, the expression for speed-up reduces to $S = c/s$. Thus it is extremely important to maximize c/s, but it is not easy to increase c (the only reasonable way to increase c is to increase the granularity of the tasks, which then reduces the value of n, which has other adverse effects). Hence, the value of s must be reduced as much as possible. In fact, as seen from the graph in Figure 6-2, if 20-40 fold speed-up is to be obtained, then the time for which the scheduler is locked to process an activation must not be much longer than the time taken by a processor to execute a single instruction. It is possible to construct such a scheduler in hardware, as is discussed next.

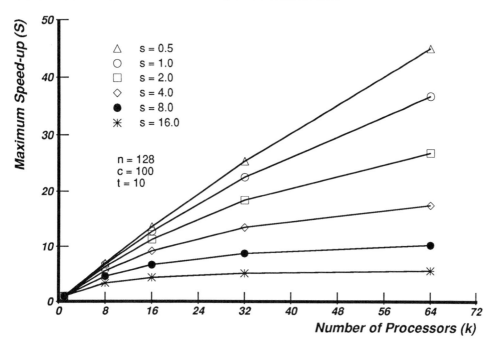

Figure 6-2: Effect of scheduler performance on maximum speed-up.

6.1.2. The Interface to the Hardware Task Scheduler

In the proposed production-system machine (see Section 5.1), the hardware task scheduler sits on the main bus along with the processors and the shared memory in the multiprocessor. The scheduler is mapped onto the shared address-space of the multiprocessor, and the synchronization (locking of the scheduler) is achieved simply from the serialization that occurs over the bus on which the requests for enqueueing and dequeueing activations are sent to the hardware task scheduler. The scheduler is assumed to be fast enough that it can process a request in a single bus cycle.

There are three types of messages that are exchanged between the processors and the hardware task scheduler. (1) *Push-Task*: The processor sends a message to the scheduler when it wants to enqueue a new node activation. (2) *Pop-Task*: The scheduler sends a message to the processor when it wants an idle processor to evaluate a pending node activation (the scheduler keeps track of the idle processors in the system). (3) *Done-Task*: The processor sends a message to the scheduler when it is done with evaluating a node activation.

The *Push-Task(flag-dir-nid, tokenPtr)* command sent to the scheduler by the processor takes two arguments. The first argument, *flag-dir-nid*, encodes three pieces of information: (1) the flag associated with the activation (insert or delete token request), which takes one bit, (2) the direction (dir) of the node activation (left or right), which takes one bit, and (3) the node-id (nid) of the activation, which is allocated the remaining 30 bits of the first word. The second argument, *tokenPtr*, is a pointer to the token that is causing the activation (the token is stored in shared memory), which takes all 32 bits of the second word. The combined size of all this information is 64 bits or 8 bytes. It is assumed that the bus connecting the processors to the scheduler can deliver this information without any extra synchronization. This may be easily achieved if the bus is 64 bits wide (in this case the synchronization is achieved through the bus arbiter, which permits only one processor to use the bus at a time). This can also be achieved if the bus is only 32 bits wide, but if it is possible for a processor to obtain its use for two consecutive cycles. As stated earlier, the scheduler is mapped onto the shared address-space of the multiprocessor. The addresses to which the hardware task scheduler is mapped, however, are different for each of the processors (the low order 10 bits correspond to the identity of the processor). This enables the scheduler to determine the identity of the processor making a request, even though that information is not explicitly sent with the request.

There are two distinct locations in shared memory (8 bytes) associated with each processor where the scheduler puts information about the node activations to be processed by that processor. Thus, to inform an idle processor to begin processing a pending node activation, the scheduler executes a *Pop-Task(flag-dir-nid, tokenPtr)* command, and transfers the flag, direction, node-id, and token-pointer information to the two locations assigned to that processor. Before the command is executed, the idle processor keeps executing a loop checking for the second location to have a non-null token pointer. The processor is expected to be looping out of its cache, so that it does not cause any load on the shared bus. When the hardware scheduler writes to the two locations, the cache of the processor gets invalidated, it gets the new information destined for it, and it can begin processing the new node activation.

When a processor is finished with evaluating a node activation, it first sets the value of the second of the two locations assigned to it for receiving node activations to null (this is the location on which the processor will subsequently be looping, waiting for it to be set to a non-null value by the scheduler). It then executes the *Done-Task(proc-id, node-id)* command and transfers the node-id to the scheduler, informing the scheduler that it is finished with processing that node activation. This information is very important, because using it the scheduler can determine: (1) the set of processors that are idle, and (2) the set of node activations in the task queue that are processable (recall that all activations in the task queue are not necessarily processable).

For all of the above commands, the hardware task scheduler is locked only for the bus cycles during which data is being written into or written by the scheduler. For example, if the bus is 64 bits wide and the bus cycle is 100ns (corresponding to a bus bandwidth of 80 MegaBytes/sec), then the total duration for which the scheduler is locked for the Push-Task, Pop-Task, and Done-Task commands for a node activation is only 300ns.

6.1.3. Structure of the Hardware Task Scheduler

The hardware task scheduler consists of three main components: (1) the *proc-state array*, (2) the *task queue*, and (3) the *controller*, as shown in Figure 6-3. Both the proc-state array and the task queue are built out of content-addressable memory. The proc-state array keeps track of the node activations being processed by each of the k processors in the multiprocessor. The task queue keeps track of all node activations that are pending processing or are currently being processed, up to a maximum of n.[47] The *enable-array* associated with the task queue keeps track of all pending node activations that are processable given the contents of the proc-state array (the node activations being currently processed). The controller consists of microcode to control both the proc-state array and the task queue.

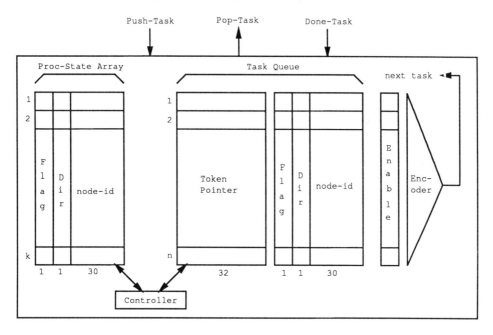

Figure 6-3: Structure of the hardware task scheduler.

---

[47]Simulations show that the average number of activations present in the task queue is around 90. The maximum number of activations, however, can be as high as 2000.

To get some insight into the internal functioning of the hardware task queue, consider the processing required by the various commands:

- *Push-Task(flag-dir-nid,tokenPtr):* (1) Find empty slot in task queue, and insert entry (the 64 bits of information associated with the command) there. (2) If there is no entry in the proc-state array with the same node-id as that in the command or if the xxxx-dir-nid[48] of some entry in the proc-state array matches the xxxx-dir-nid given in the command, then set the enable bit for the new entry to true otherwise set the enable bit to false.

- *Pop-Task(flag-dir-nid,tokenPtr):* (1) The encoder on the extreme right of Figure 6-3 gives the next node activation to be processed. (2) Put this entry (the information corresponding to the node activation) in the appropriate slot in the proc-state array, that is, in the slot corresponding to the processor to which this node activation is being assigned. (3) For all entries in the task queue for which the node-id matches that of the assigned entry, if the direction field also matches then set enable bit to true. Otherwise if the node-id matches but the direction field does not match, then set enable bit to false.

- *Done-Task(proc-id, nid):* (1) Clear the slot in proc-state array corresponding to processor-id (proc-id). Furthermore, let *count* be the number of activations in the proc-state array that have the same node-id as the node activation that has just finished. (2) If *count* > 0 then do nothing, otherwise for all entries in the task queue for which the node-id matches set enable to true.

The above steps ensure that only those node activations that are considered concurrently processable by the criteria given in Section 5.2.4 are permitted to be processed in parallel.

The hardware task scheduler is expected to be able to process the required commands (push-task, pop-task, done-task) in one bus cycle, about 100ns. It is estimated that each of the commands can be executed within two μ-instructions from the controller and for that reason the controller and the associative arrays must be capable of operating on a clock of 50ns or less. Current high-speed technologies like TTL, ECL, high-speed CMOS should be able to support the kinds of speeds that are required.

6.1.4. Multiple Hardware Task Schedulers

While the speed of a single hardware task scheduler may be able to support 32-64 parallel processors, what if the parallelism is much more and the number of processors is much larger? This section discusses some issues regarding the use of multiple hardware task schedulers; cases where a single task scheduler is not powerful enough. The multiple schedulers may appear on a single bus (where it is possible for each scheduler to observe the commands being processed by the other schedulers), or they may appear on multiple buses (where it is not possible for a given scheduler to watch the commands being processed by the other schedulers).

---

[48]The xxxx in xxxx-dir-nid indicates that we do not care about the value of the flag field.

A basic assumption made in the design of the scheduler described in the previous section is that it is possible for the scheduler to determine from its local state (the contents of the proc-state array) the subset of node activations in the task queue that are processable (using the criteria given in Section 5.2.4). This is easily possible when there is only one scheduler, since the proc-state array keeps track of all node activations being processed at any given time, and that is enough to determine which other activations are processable. However, when there are multiple schedulers, each scheduler cannot observe the activity of all other schedulers, and the proc-state array of a scheduler cannot keep track of all node activations being processed at any given time.

There are two solutions to the above problem. The first is to have the schedulers communicate with each other or with some other centralized resource to determine which node activations are processable. This solution does not look very attractive because the overhead of communication will probably nullify any advantage gained from the extra schedulers. The second solution, which is more reasonable, is to partition the node activations between the multiple schedulers. For example, if there are two schedulers, then one scheduler could be responsible for all node activations that have an even node-id and the other scheduler for all node activations that have an odd node-id. Since activations which have a different node-id do not interact with each other, they may always be processed concurrently (see Section 5.2.4), the activations assigned to processors by one scheduler will not affect the processability of activations in the task queue of the other scheduler. Thus the local proc-state array of each scheduler[49] contains sufficient information for deciding the processability of nodes in its task queue.

There is still one problem that remains in using multiple schedulers, especially if each scheduler is to be capable of scheduling a task on any processor. In the previous section, there was a single scheduler that knew the state of all the processors — it knew which of them were idle and could automatically schedule activations on such processors. When there are multiple schedulers, none of the schedulers has knowledge of the state of all the processors. Furthermore, even if a scheduler knows that a processor is idle in the current bus cycle, say because it executed the Done-Task command in the current bus cycle, there is no way for it to know the state of that processor in the next bus cycle, since in the next bus cycle some other scheduler may have assigned a task to that processor.[50] The suggested solution to the problem is to have the processors poll the schedulers for processable tasks, instead of the schedulers assigning tasks to idle processors of their own accord. By having each scheduler set a flag in the shared memory indicating the presence of processable tasks, it is possible to make the idle processors

---

[49]Note that the local proc-state array stores information only about those node activations that were assigned by the associated scheduler for processing. It does not keep track of the node activations assigned for processing by the other task schedulers.

[50]A scheduler may know when a processor is idle in case the processors are also partitioned amongst the schedulers, just as the nodes are partitioned amongst the schedulers. However, such a partitioning would violate the initial idea that each scheduler is to be capable of scheduling activations on all processors.

loop out of cache (instead of causing traffic on the bus) when no processable tasks are available in the schedulers.

6.2. Software Task Schedulers

While it would be nice to have hardware task schedulers for the production-system machine, there are two main problems associated with them: (1) hardware task schedulers are not flexible, in that they are not easy to change as the algorithms evolve, and (2) the resources needed to build hardware task schedulers and to interface them to the rest of the system are more than that required by software task schedulers. However, as worked out in Section 6.1.1, if a single task scheduler is not to be a bottleneck, then it must be able to schedule a task within the period of about one instruction. While it is not feasible to achieve such performance out of a single software task scheduler, it is possible to use *multiple* software task schedulers to achieve reasonable performance. This section discusses some of the issues involved in the design of such software task schedulers.

The main reason for going to multiple software task schedulers is to avoid the serial bottleneck caused by a single task scheduler through which all activations must be scheduled. In terms of the model described in Section 6.1.1, the multiple schedulers modify the equation for maximum speed-up as follows. Recall that n is the number of tasks that need to be scheduled per cycle, c is the average cost of processing a task, s is the average serial cost of enqueueing and dequeueing a task, t is the average non-serial cost of enqueueing and dequeueing a task, and k is the number of processors in the multiprocessor. Let l be the number of schedulers (software task queues) in the system. The cost per cycle on a uniprocessor is $C_{uni}=n\cdot c$. The cost per cycle on the multiprocessor (assuming that the load is uniformly distributed amongst the k processors and the l task queues) is given by $C_{mul}=\lceil n/k \rceil(c+t)+\lceil n/l \rceil\cdot s$, and the speed-up is given by $S=C_{uni}/C_{mul}$. The graph for the maximum speed-up when $n=128, c=100, t=10$, and varying values of k, l, and s is shown in Figure 6-4.[51] It shows that even if the serial cost of enqueueing and dequeueing a task is only 16 instructions, the maximum speed-up obtainable with 64 processors and 32 schedulers is only 45-fold — almost a quarter of the processing power is wasted while waiting for the schedulers.

A software task scheduler may either be passive or active. A *passive* scheduler, or preferably a task queue, corresponds to an abstract data structure where node activations may be stored or retrieved using predefined operations like push-task and pop-task. On the other hand, an *active* scheduler corresponds to an independent process to which messages for pushing and popping tasks may be sent. Once the processor has issued the request, it may proceed with what it was doing earlier. The requesting processor does not have to wait while its request is being processed.

---

[51] Although the curves in the graph are shown to be continuous, the actual plot of the equation for S would have discontinuities in it because of the ceiling function used in C_{mul}. The curves in the graph are an approximation to the actual curves for the equations.

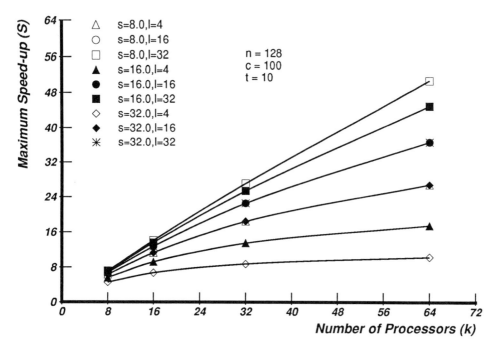

Figure 6-4: Effect of multiple schedulers on speed-up.

In this thesis only passive software schedulers (*software task queues*) are studied, The main reason is that there are a number of overheads associated with the active schedulers which are not present in the passive schedulers. For example, in an active scheduler, scheduling a task involves the sending of a message to the active scheduler, and then the processing of this request by the scheduler. It is quite possible that the cost of sending the message is more than the cost of scheduling on the passive scheduler. Similarly, it is quite possible that when a message is sent to an active scheduler, the scheduler process is not running and it has to be swapped in before the message can be processed. This could cause a significant delay in the message getting processed. The main advantage of active schedulers occurs when the cost of scheduling a task is significantly larger than the cost of sending the message to the scheduler. In that case the task sending the message can continue without waiting for the processing required by the scheduler to complete.

Figure 6-5 shows an overview of the structure proposed for using multiple software task queues. To schedule tasks there exist several task queues, all of which can be accessed by each of the processors. There is a lock associated with each task queue, and this lock must be obtained by a processor before it can put or extract any tasks from the task queue. To obtain a task an idle processor first checks if the task queue is empty. If it is empty, the processor goes on to check the next task queue to see if it has any processable tasks.[52] If it is not empty, the match process obtains the lock for the task queue, extracts a processable task (if any is present) from the task queue, and then releases the lock. By having a dynamic cache coherence strategy [79], it is possible to arrange the locks so that idle processors looking for a task (when none are available) spin on their cache without causing a large traffic on the shared bus.

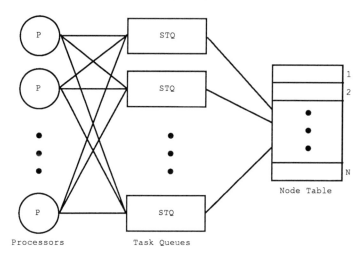

Figure 6-5: Multiple software task queues.

To determine whether a node activation in the task queue is processable, the match processes access the *node table*. For each node in the Rete network, the node table keeps track of information about its activations that are being currently processed. This information is sufficient to determine whether a node is processable or not. There is a separate lock associated with each entry of the node table, and this lock must be obtained before the related information is modified or checked. Since there is a separate lock associated with each entry in the node table, the multiple schedulers looking for the processability of different node activations do not clash with each other.

The processing required when a new task is to be put in a task queue or when the match process finishes processing a node activation is also quite simple. To push a new node activation into a task queue, the match process selects a random task queue from the several that are available. If the lock associated with that task queue is busy, the match process simply goes on and tries another task queue. Otherwise it obtains the lock and enters the new node activation

---

[52]Note, the match process checks whether a task queue is empty or not without obtaining the lock. Of course, this information can be inaccurate since it is checked without obtaining the lock, but since it is only used as a hint it does not matter. If one match process misses a task that was just being enqueued when it checked the task queue, another match process at some later time will find it.

into the task queue. When a match process finishes processing a node activation, it modifies the corresponding entry in the node table to indicate that there is one less activation of that node being processed.

Simulations done for the above scheme using multiple software task queues show that approximately a factor of 2 is lost in performance compared to when a hardware task scheduler is used (detailed results are presented in Chapter 8). We are currently experimenting with variations of the above scheme. For example, one possible variation is that instead of putting both processable and non-processable node activations in the task queue, one may put only processable node activations in the task queue. The non-processable node activations would be attached to the associated slots in the node table, and whenever the last processable activation of a node finishes, the additional processable entries would be put into the task queues. Such a scheme would reduce the cost of extracting a node activation from a task queue, since no checks have to be made about the processability of the node activation. However, this would also increase the time to enqueue a node activation, since now it is necessary to first determine whether the given activation is processable or not. Another variation is to use some kind of a priority scheme for ordering pending node activations. For example, node activations that can potentially result in long chains of activations should be processed before activations that cannot result in long chains of activations. We are also experimenting with the use of multiple active software task schedulers.

7 The Simulator

Most of the earlier studies exploring parallelism in production systems were done using simulators with very simple cost models [22, 32, 69], or were done using average-case data as presented in Chapter 3 [30, 38, 61]. The simulators did not take many of the overheads into account, and often variations in the cost of processing productions were not taken into account. This chapter presents details about a second generation simulator that has been constructed to evaluate the potential of using parallelism to speed up the execution of production systems. The aims of the simulator are: (1) to study the speed-up obtainable from the various sources of parallelism and to determine the associated overheads, (2) to determine the bottlenecks that reduce the speed-up obtainable from parallelism and the effects of eliminating these bottlenecks, (3) to study the advantages and disadvantages of using the hardware and software task schedulers, and (4) to study the effects of different data structures and algorithms on the amount of speed-up that is obtainable. The reasons for using a simulator instead of an actual implementation on a multiprocessor are the following:

- An implementation on a multiprocessor which incorporates all the planned optimizations would have taken a very long time to do. An implementation which does not include the optimizations leads to significantly different results from one that includes them, and for that reason it is not very useful.

- An implementation corresponds to the case where most of the design decisions are already frozen. There is not as much scope for trying out various alternatives, which is what our aim is at this moment.

- A multiprocessor consisting of 32-64 processors, that has a smart cache-coherence strategy, and that supports other features mentioned in Section 5.1 is not currently available to us. Although such a multiprocessor may be available in the near future, until then we have to rely on a simulator to obtain results. To test some of our ideas about using parallelism, we are currently implementing OPS5 on the VAX-11/784, a four processor multiprocessor from Digital Equipment Corporation. However, the implementation is still in its early stages and the results are not available at this time.

7.1. Structure of the Simulator

The simulator that we have constructed is an event-driven simulator. The inputs to the simulator consist of: (1) a detailed trace of node activations in the Rete network corresponding to an actual production-system run; (2) a specification of the parallel computational model on which the production system is to be run; and (3) a cost model that can be used to determine the cost of any given node activation. The output of the simulator consists of various statistics for the overall run and for the individual cycles of the run.

7.1.1. Inputs to the Simulator

7.1.1.1. The Input Trace

Figure 7-1 shows a small fragment of a trace that is fed to the input simulator. The trace is obtained by actually running a production system and recording the activations of nodes in the Rete network in a file. The trace contains information about the dependencies between the node activations. The simulator, depending on the granularity of parallelism being used, can lump several activations into one task, and knows which activations can be and which activations can not be processed in parallel. Information about nodes that remains fixed over the complete run, for example, the tests associated with a node and the type of a node, are presented to the simulator in a static table, as shown in Figure 7-2. The combined information available to the simulator from the input trace and the static table is sufficient to provide fairly accurate estimates of the cost of processing a given node activation.

7.1.1.2. The Computational Model

The computational model specifies the hardware and software structure of the parallel processor on which the production-system traces are to be evaluated. The computational model specifies:

- The sources of parallelism (production, node, intra-node, action parallelism, etc.) that are to be used in executing the production-system trace. For example, when only production parallelism is to be used, the simulator lumps all node activations belonging to the same production together, and processes them as one task. Also activations of nodes that are shared between several productions are replicated (once for each production), since nodes cannot be shared between different productions when using production parallelism.

- Whether a hardware task scheduler or software task queues are to be used. In case several software task queues are to be used, then the number of such task queues.

- The hardware organization of the parallel processor. For example, the number of processors in the parallel machine, the speed of the individual processors, etc.

- Whether the effects of memory contention are to be taken into account. If they are to be taken into account, then it is possible to specify the expected cache-hit ratio, the bus bandwidth, etc. Details on how the effects of memory contention are handled are given in Section 7.1.1.4.

```
(pfire uwm-no-operator-retry)
(wme-change 914)
((prev 914) (cur 13630) (type bus) (lev 1))
((prev 13630) (cur 13631) (type teqa) (lev 2))
((prev 13631) (cur 1022389) (node-id 541) (side right) (flag insert) (num-left 4) (num-right 20))
((prev 13631) (cur 13632) (type teqa) (lev 3))
((prev 13632) (cur 13633) (type tnea) (lev 4))
((prev 13633) (cur 13634) (type tnea) (lev 5))
((prev 13632) (cur 13635) (type teqa) (lev 4))
((prev 13635) (cur 1022390) (node-id 576) (side right) (flag insert) (num-left 1) (num-right 4))
((prev 1022390) (cur 1022391) (node-id 577) (flag insert))
((prev 13635) (cur 1022392) (node-id 201) (side right) (flag insert) (num-left 4) (num-right 4))
((prev 1022392) (cur 1022393) (node-id 202) (side left) (flag delete) (num-left 3) (num-right 36))

(pfire eight-copy-unchanged)
(wme-change 915)
((prev 915) (cur 13636) (type bus) (lev 1))
((prev 13636) (cur 13637) (type teqa) (lev 2))
((prev 13637) (cur 13638) (type teqa) (lev 3))
((prev 13638) (cur 1022394) (node-id 207) (side right) (flag insert) (num-left 1) (num-right 21))
((prev 13638) (cur 1022395) (node-id 197) (side right) (flag insert) (num-left 1) (num-right 21))
((prev 13638) (cur 1022396) (node-id 193) (side right) (flag insert) (num-left 1) (num-right 21))
```

;;; pfire: The name of the production that fired at this point in the trace.
;;; wme-change: The number of changes made to working memory so far.
;;; prev: The activation-number of the predecessor of this node activation.
;;; cur: The unique activation-number associated with a node activation.
;;; type: The type of a constant-test node activation.
;;; lev: The distance between the root-node and the associated constant-test node.
;;; node-id: The unique id associated with each node in the Rete network.
;;; side: Whether a left-activation or a right-activation (only for and-nodes and not-nodes).
;;; flag: Whether the token is being inserted or deleted.
;;; num-left/num-right: The number of tokens in the left-memory/right-memory node.

Figure 7-1: A sample trace fragment.

- The cost model to be used in evaluating the cost of the individual node activations. Different cost models permit experimentation with different algorithms, data structures, and processor architectures. However, different cost models cannot account for major changes in the algorithms or data structures.

7.1.1.3. The Cost Model

The simulator relies on an accurate cost model for determining the time required to (1) process node activations (given the information in the input trace), (2) push node activations (tasks) into the task queue, (3) pop tasks from the task queue, etc. The cost model reflects the effects of:

- The algorithms and data structures used to process the node activations.

- The code used to push/pop node activations from the task schedulers.

```
((node-id 193) (type and) (prods (p8)) (lev 10) (lces 6) (rces 1) (tests (teqb 10001 1)))
((node-id 197) (type and) (prods (p8)) (lev 6) (lces 10) (rces 1) (tests (teqb 30001 1)))
((node-id 201) (type not) (prods (p8)) (lev 2) (lces 14) (rces 1) (tests (teqb 3 1 teqb 100001 5 teqb 1 6)))
((node-id 202) (type and) (prods (p8)) (lev 1) (lces 14) (rces 1) (tests (teqb 10003 1 teqb 3 2 teqb 10001 3)))
((node-id 207) (type and) (prods (p9)) (lev 6) (lces 4) (rces 1) (tests (teqb 3 1)))
((node-id 541) (type not) (prods (p45)) (lev 1) (lces 2) (rces 1) (tests (teqb 3 1)))
((node-id 576) (type and) (prods (p51)) (lev 1) (lces 2) (rces 1) (tests (teqb 1 5 teqb 10003 6 teqb 3 7)))
((node-id 577) (type term) (prods (p51)) (lev 3) (lces -) (rces -))

;;; node-id: The unique id associated with each node in the Rete network.
;;; type: Type of the node (and-node, not-node, or term-node).
;;; prods: The production or productions (in case the node is shared) to which the node belongs.
;;; lev: The number of intervening nodes to get to the terminal node.
;;; lces: The size of the tokens (number of wme pointers needed) in the left-memory node.
;;; rces: The size of the tokens (number of wme pointers needed) in the right-memory node.
;;; tests: The tests associated with the two-input nodes to ensure consistent variable bindings.
```

Figure 7-2: Static node information.

- The instruction set architecture of the individual processing elements (this determines the number of machine instructions required to implement the proposed algorithms).

- The time taken by different instructions in the architecture, for example, synchronization instructions may take much longer than register-register instructions.

- The structure of the multiprocessor, the presence of memory contention, etc.

The basic cost models used in the simulations have been obtained by writing parametrized assembly code for various primitive operations required in processing node activations. For example, code sequences are written for computing the hash value corresponding to a token, for deleting a token from a memory node, and so on. These code sequences can then be combined to obtain the code for processing a complete node activation. For example, the code to process the left activation of an and-node is shown in Figure 7-3 (details of data structures and code are presented in Appendix B).

In the code in Figure 7-3, the operations listed in capitals refer to macros that would be expanded at a later point in time. The register allocation for the code for processing node activations is done manually, since the total amount of code is small and it is used very often.[53]

Given the code for the primitive operations involved in executing a node activation, the next

---

[53]The cost models used in the simulator assume that no overheads are caused by the operating system of the production-system machine. This is a reasonable assumption to make because all synchronization code and scheduling code is a part of the production-system implementation code. The production-system machine is also expected to have enough main memory so that the operating system intervention to handle page faults is minimal.

```
           HASH-TOKEN-LEFT                 ! compute hash value for left token
           cb_eq    Delete,R-flg,L_del     ! if (flag = Delete) goto L_del
L10:       MAKE-TOKEN                       ! Allocate storage and make token
           INSERT-LTOKEN                    ! Insert token in left hash table
           br       L11                     ! Goto L11
L_del:     DELETE-LTOKEN                    ! Delete token from left hash table
L11:       ldal     (R-rtokHT)R-hIndex,r5  ! Get address of relevant bucket in
                                            ! right hash table (opposite memory)
           cmp      NULL,(r5)tList          ! Check if the hash bucket is empty
           br_eq    L_exit                  ! If so, then goto L_exit
           LOCK-RTOKEN-HT                   ! Obtain lock for the hash bucket
           ldl      (r5)tList,R-state       ! Load pointer to first token in opp.
                                            ! memory into register R-state
L_loop:    NEXT-MATCHING-RTOKEN             ! Find first matching token in opp mem
           SCHEDULE-SUCCESSORS              ! Schedule activations of successor nodes
           br       L_loop                  ! Goto L_loop
L12:       RELEASE-RTOKEN-HT                ! Free lock for the hash bucket
L_exit:    RELEASE-NODE-LOCK                ! Inform scheduler that processing for
                                            ! this node activation is finished
```

Figure 7-3:   Code for left activation of an and-node.

step is to calculate the time taken to execute these pieces of code. To achieve this, the instructions in a code sequence are divided into groups, such that the instructions in the same group take the same amount of time. Thus *register-register* instructions are grouped together, *branch* instructions are grouped together, *memory-register* instructions are grouped together, and *synchronization* instructions are grouped together.[54]   Once the instructions have been divided into groups, the cost of executing an operation can simply be found by adding the time of executing instructions in each group. The cost of a node activation can then be computed by adding the cost of the primitive operations involved. Note that processing different node activations requires a different combination of the primitive operations. The set of primitive operations required is determined by the parameters associated with the node activation in the input trace, for example, the number of tokens in the opposite memory, the set of tests associated with the node, and so on.

7.1.1.4. The Memory Contention Model

Modeling the overhead due to memory contention accurately is an extremely difficult problem [5, 6, 39, 53]. Since actual measurements are not possible until the multiprocessor system and the algorithms have actually been designed and implemented, one has to rely on analytical and simulation techniques. The analytical models are more difficult to discover and usually require

---

[54]Note that the instruction set [3] of the processors (described in Appendix A) has been chosen so that the number of such groups is very small. For example, almost all instructions make either 0 or 1 memory references. There are very few instructions that make 2 memory references, and they are treated specially when computing the cost models for the simulator. Table 7-1 shows the instruction categories and their relative costs as used in the simulator. The relative costs can be changed in the simulator just by changing some constant definitions.

Table 7-1: Relative Costs of Various Instruction Types

Instruction Type	Relative Cost
register-register	1.0
memory-register	1.0
memory-memory-register	2.0
synchronization/interlocked	3.0
compare-and-branch	1.5
branch	1.5

more assumptions than the simulation models. However, once they have been built, they permit the exploration of the design space very quickly. The simulation models are easier to come up with, but to get each data point can require a lot of computing time. To model the effects of memory contention on the parallel execution of production systems, our simulator uses a mixture of analytical and simulation techniques.

As the first step, the simulator generates a table which gives degradation in processing power due to memory contention as a function of:

- Number of active processors in the multiprocessor. At any given time many processors may be idle; it is assumed that these processors will be looping out of cache and will not cause any load on the memory system.

- The number of memory modules. This determines the contention when requests are sent to the same memory module.

- The characteristics of the bus (bandwidth, synchronous/asynchronous, etc.) interconnecting the processors to the memory modules. This information is used to determine the contention for the bus.

- The cache-hit ratio. It is assumed that the processors communicate with the external memory system through a cache which captures most of the requests.

Once such a table has been generated, then the memory contention overhead is included in the simulations as follows. The simulator keeps track of the number of active processors while processing the trace. Whenever the cost for processing a node activation is required, instead of using the basic cost for the node activation (the cost computed by the method described in Section 7.1.1.3), the basic cost is multiplied by the appropriate contention-factor ($1/processor\_efficiency$) from the table and then used.

The tables for the contention-factor used in the simulator are computed using an analytical model for memory contention proposed in [39]. The proposed model deals with multiple-bus multiprocessor systems and makes the following assumptions:

- When a processor accesses the shared memory, a connection is immediately established between the processor and the referenced memory module, provided the referenced memory module is not being accessed by another processor and a bus is available for connection.

- A processor cannot make another request if its present request has not been granted.

- The duration between the completion of a request and the generation of the next request to the shared memory is an independent exponentially distributed random variable with the same mean value $1/\lambda$ for all the processors.

- The duration of an access by a processor to the common memory is an independent exponentially distributed variable with the same mean value $1/\mu$ for all the memory modules.

- The probability of a request from a processor to a memory module is independent of the module and is equal to $1/m$, where m is the number of shared-memory modules.

A problem with the above model is that it deals with *multiple-bus* multiprocessors with *non-time-multiplexed* buses, while we are interested in evaluating a multiprocessor with a *single* *time-multiplexed* bus (such a bus makes it simple to implement cache-coherence strategies).[55] However, we have found a way of approximating a single time-multiplexed bus with multiple non-time-multiplexed buses. We assume that the number of non-time-multiplexed buses is equal to the degree of time multiplexing of the single time-multiplexed bus. Thus if the time-multiplexed bus delivers a word of data 1μs after the request (has a latency of 1μs), but it can deliver a word of data every 100ns (throughput of 10 requests per latency period), then it is assumed that there are 10 non-time-multiplexed buses, each with a latency of 1μs. It can be shown that using this approximation, the inaccuracy in the results can be at most a factor of 2. In other words, if the approximate model predicts that the processing power lost due to contention is 10%, then in the accurate model with a single time-multiplexed bus, not more than 20% of the processing power would be lost due to contention. The situation where the results are off by a factor of 2 is quite pathological, when all requests come to the time-multiplexed bus at exactly the same time.[56] In actual operation it is hoped that the error due to the approximation would be significantly less.

Figure 7-4 shows the degradation in performance due to memory contention as predicted by the analytical model given in [39]. To compute the curves, it is assumed that $\lambda=3.0 MACS$ (million accesses per second), $\mu=1.0 MACS$, the number of memory modules $m=32$, and the number of non-time-multiplexed buses $b=1000ns/100ns=10$. The curves show the processor efficiency as a function of the number of active processors k, and the cache-hit ratio c. It can be observed that the degradation in processor efficiency is significant if the cache-hit ratio is not high.

---

[55]We could not find an analytical model dealing with contention for time-multiplexed buses in the literature.

[56]Let the latency for the time-multiplexed bus be l and the degree of time-multiplexing be k. Then in the approximate model we use k non-time-multiplexed buses, each with latency l. The worst case occurs when k requests are presented to the buses at the same time. In the time-multiplexed bus the last request is satisfied by time $(k \times l/k)+l$, which simplifies to $2l$. In the case of k non-time-multiplexed buses, the last request is satisfied by time l, thus resulting in a factor of 2 loss in performance. Note that if $k+1$ requests had arrived at the same time, then the time for the time-multiplexed bus would have been $2l+l/k$, the time for the non-time-multiplexed buses would have been $2l$, and the loss factor would have been only $1+(1/2k)$, which is less than 2. In case $k-1$ requests had arrived at the same time, then the time for the time-multiplexed bus would have been $2l-(l/k)$, the time for the non-time-multiplexed buses would have been l, and the loss factor would have been $2-(1/k)$, which is less than 2.

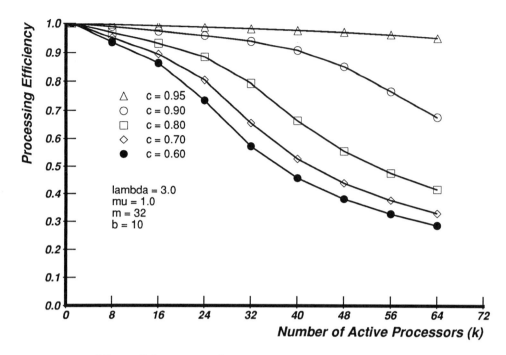

Figure 7-4: Degradation in performance due to memory contention.

7.1.2. Outputs of the Simulator

The statistics output by the simulator consist of both per-cycle information and overall-run information. The statistics that are output for each match-execute cycle of the production system are:

- $S_{max-i} = n_i \cdot t_{avg-i} / t_{max-i}$, where S_{max-i} is the maximum speed-up that can be achieved in the ith cycle assuming no limit on the number of processors used, n_i is the number of tasks[57] in the ith cycle, t_{avg-i} is the average cost for tasks in the ith cycle, and t_{max-i} is the maximum cost of any task in the ith cycle as determined by the simulator. Note that $n_i \cdot t_{avg-i}$ represents the cost of executing the ith cycle on a uniprocessor.

- $S_{nom-i} = n_i \cdot t_{avg-i} / t_{cyc-i}$, where S_{nom-i} is the nominal speed-up (or concurrency) that is achieved in the ith cycle using the number of processors specified in the computational model, and t_{cyc-i} is the cost of the ith cycle as computed by the simulator. Note that it follows from the definitions of t_{max-i} and t_{cyc-i} that $t_{cyc-i} \geq t_{max-i}$.

- $PU_i = S_{nom-i} / k$, where PU_i is the processor utilization in the ith cycle and k is the number of processors specified in the computation model.

---

[57] A task here corresponds to an independently schedulable piece of work that can be executed in parallel. Thus when using production-level parallelism, a task corresponds to all node activations belonging to a production. When using node-level parallelism a task becomes more complex, corresponding approximately to a sequence of dependent-node activations, i.e., a set of node activations no two of which could have been processed in parallel.

The same set of statistics can also be computed at the level of the complete run. The overall statistics are:

- $S_{max} = \sum_{i=1}^{N} n_i \cdot t_{avg-i} / \sum_{i=1}^{N} t_{max-i}$, where S_{max} is the maximum speed-up that can be achieved over the complete program run assuming no limit on the number of processors used.

- $S_{nom} = \sum_{i=1}^{N} n_i \cdot t_{avg-i} / \sum_{i=1}^{N} t_{cyc-i}$, where S_{nom} is the nominal speed-up over the complete run using the number of processors specified in the computation model.

- $PU = S_{nom}/k$, where PU is the processor utilization over the complete run and k is the number of processors specified in the computation model.

The results presented in Chapter 8 mainly refer to the overall statistics. The following equations show the relationship between the overall statistics and the per-cycle statistics:

$$S_{max} = \sum_{i=1}^{N} S_{max-i} \cdot (t_{max-i} / \sum_{j=1}^{N} t_{max-j}).$$

$$S_{nom} = \sum_{i=1}^{N} S_{nom-i} \cdot (t_{cyc-i} / \sum_{j=1}^{N} t_{cyc-j}).$$

The above equations state that the overall speed-up is not a simple average of the per-cycle speed-ups but a weighted average of the per-cycle speed-ups. The weight for the ith cycle is $t_{max-i}/\sum t_{max}$ in the first equation and $t_{cyc-i}/\sum t_{cyc}$ in the second equation. Thus the per-cycle statistic is weighted by its fraction of the total cost in the parallel implementation (not the total cost in the uniprocessor implementation). As a result, a few long cycles with low speed-ups can destroy the overall speed-up for a run.

In addition to statistics about the obtainable speed-up, the simulator also outputs statistics about individual node activations. For example, for each type of node activations (constant-test nodes, and-nodes, not-nodes, terminal-nodes) it outputs the (1) number of node activations of that type per-cycle, (2) the average cost of such node activations, and (3) the variance in the cost of evaluating such activations. This information can then be used to modify the algorithms and data structures so as to reduce the cost and variance of evaluating node activations.

7.2. Limitations of the Simulation Model

The simulator, although obviously not as accurate as an actual implementation, provides considerable flexibility in evaluating different algorithms and architectures for the parallel implementation of production systems. The main inaccuracies in the simulator come from:

- The simulator models the execution of production system at an abstract level, in the sense that each instruction in the code is not actually executed but only the combined cost is taken into account. Thus low-level effects, such as locality of memory references, bursts of cache misses when processing for a new node activation is begun, are not taken into account.

101

- The simulator ignores contention for certain kinds of resources. For example, contention for the locks associated with the buckets of the token hash-table is ignored. The reason for making such approximations is to make the simulator simple and fast, especially since the traces are quite long (each trace is about 5-10 MBytes long). It was also felt that the errors due to such approximations would be small. For example, if in an actual implementation it is observed that many clashes are occurring, it is easily possible to increase the size of the hash table.

- The cost model makes certain simplifying assumptions as well. For example, if a token is to be searched in a list, then the cost model assumes that half of that list would have to be searched before the token is found. Such an assumption masks the effects of the variations that would occur in an actual implementation. One way to take such variations into account would be to build a new version of the Rete interpreter with the same processing model as that of the proposed parallel implementation, and extract traces from that interpreter. Due to various time constraints this was not done.

- As cited in the previous section on memory contention, there are also a number of approximations that have been made in the memory contention model.

As mentioned in the above points, a number of approximations have been made in building the simulation model. Some of the approximations were made for reasons of efficiency of the simulator, some were made because it would have been too time consuming to fix them, and some were made because we did not know any reasonable way of handling them. On the whole, however, we believe that most of the important sources of cost in processing node activations and the variations therein are taken into account by the simulator.

7.3. Validity of the Simulator

In any simulation based study it is essential to somehow establish the validity of the simulator, that is, to establish that the simulator gives results according to the prescribed model and assumptions. One way to validate a simulator is to compare its results to an actual implementation for some limited set of sample cases, and then make only high-level checks for the other cases. This method is not possible in this thesis, since there is no actual parallel implementation corresponding to the model used in the simulator. However, for the following reasons we believe that the results of the simulator are correct:

- Before implementing the simulator, we implemented a parallel version of the Rete interpreter on the VAX-11/784, a four processor multiprocessor. The interpreter was not optimized for performance, but it included all the synchronization code necessary to be able to process node activations in parallel. The assembly code written for the parallel Rete algorithm in the thesis (from which the cost models used in the simulator are derived) uses data structures and algorithms similar to those used in the working VAX-11/784 implementation. Thus there is good reason to believe that the algorithms and the code from which the cost models for the simulator are derived are correct (see Appendix B for the code).

- The performance predicted by the simulator for production-system execution on a uniprocessor is close to the performance predicted independently for an optimized uniprocessor implementation of OPS5.[58] Both the simulator and the independent study predict a performance of 400-800 wme-changes/sec on a 1 MIPS uniprocessor. This again indicates that there are no major costs that are being ignored by the simulator.

- Finally, the simulation results have been hand verified for small runs, and local checks made on portions of large runs to check the correct operation of the simulator.

Because of reasons given above, we believe that the simulator is giving the correct results (of course, while keeping the limitations mentioned in the previous section in mind). Based on these simulation results, an optimized parallel implementation is currently being done on the VAX-11/784 and on an Encore Multimax computer. Once these implementations are running, it will be possible to validate the simulator more completely.

---

[58]Independent estimate for OPS5.provided by Charles Forgy of Carnegie-Mellon University.

8 Simulation Results and Analysis

This chapter presents simulation results for the parallel execution of production systems. The chapter is organized as follows. The traces used in the simulations are presented first. Next results are presented for the execution of production systems on uniprocessor systems. This section also discusses the overheads due to loss of sharing of nodes, synchronization, and scheduling in parallel implementations. Subsequently, Sections 8.3, 8.4, and 8.5 discuss the speed-up obtainable from production parallelism, node parallelism, and intra-node parallelism when a hardware task scheduler is used. Section 8.6 discusses the effect of using binary Rete networks (instead of linear Rete networks) on the amount of speed-up obtainable. Section 8.7 discusses the execution speeds when multiple software task queues are used instead of hardware task schedulers. Finally, Section 8.8 discusses the effects of memory contention on the execution speed of production systems. The results are summarized in Section 8.9.

8.1. Traces Used in the Simulations

The simulation results presented in this chapter correspond to traces obtained from six production-system programs. The following are the six production systems and the traces associated with them (the names given to traces below are used consistently through the rest of the chapter):

- VT: An expert system that selects components for a traction elevator system [52]. The associated traces were obtained from a run involving 1767 changes to working memory and they are named as follows:

  - *vto.lin*: This trace corresponds to the case when the interpreter constructs linear networks (see Section 5.2.6) for the productions.

  - *vto.bin*: This trace corresponds to the case when the interpreter constructs binary networks for the productions.

  - *vt.lin* and *vt.bin*: These traces correspond to the linear and binary network versions of the VT system from which seven productions have been removed.[59] These productions were removed since the node activations as-

---

[59]The names of the productions that have been removed are (1) *detail::create-item-from-input*, (2) *detail::insert-value-from-input*, (3) *detail::ladder-duct-1-car-so*, (4) *build-why-answer-for-item-without-dependency*, (5) *build-why-answer-for-attribute*, (6) *save-cleanup::remove-wmes*, and (7) *save-current-job::remove*.

sociated with them had very large costs, which increased the variance of processing node activations and consequently decreased the speed-up available from parallelism. It was felt that these productions could be modified or coded in another way so as to reduce the large costs associated with the node activations.

- ILOG: An expert system to maintain inventories and production schedules for factories [59].[60] The associated traces were obtained from a run involving 2191 changes to working memory. The traces are:
  - *ilog.lin* and *ilog.bin*: These traces correspond to the linear network and binary network versions of the ILOG system.

- MUD: An expert system to analyze the mud-lubricant used in drilling operations [40]. The associated traces were obtained from a run involving 2074 changes to working memory. The traces are:
  - *mudo.lin* and *mudo.bin*: These traces correspond to the linear and binary network versions of the MUD system.

  - *mud.lin* and *mud.bin*: These traces correspond to the linear and binary network versions of the MUD system from which two productions have been removed.[61] The reasons for removing the two productions are the same as that for VT.

- DAA: An expert system that designs computer systems from a high-level specification of the system [44]. The associated traces were obtained from a run involving 3200 working-memory changes. The traces are:
  - *daa.lin* and *daa.bin*: These traces correspond to the linear and binary network versions of the DAA system.

- R1-SOAR: A Soar expert system that configures the UNIBUS for Digital Equipment Corporation's VAX-11 computer systems [77]. The associated traces are:
  - *rls.lin* and *rls.bin*: These traces correspond to the *sequential* version of the R1-Soar program, that is, a version in which the problem-space is searched sequentially. The traces were obtained from a run involving 2220 changes to working memory.

  - *rlp.lin* and *rlp.bin*: These traces correspond to the *parallel* version of the R1-Soar program, that is, a version in which some of the problem-space search is done in parallel. The traces were obtained from a run involving 3231 changes to working memory.

- EP-SOAR: A Soar expert system that solves the Eight Puzzle [48]. The associated traces are:
  - *eps.lin* and *eps.bin*: These traces correspond to the *sequential* version of the EP-Soar program. The traces were obtained from a run involving 924 changes to working memory.

---

[60]ILOG is referred to as PTRANS in the cited work.

[61]The names of the productions that have been removed are (1) *cleanup::* and (2) *undo-analysis::1*.

• *epp.lin* and *epp.bin*: These traces correspond to the *parallel* version of the EP-Soar program. The traces were obtained from a run involving 948 changes to working memory.

8.2. Simulation Results for Uniprocessors

When production systems are implemented on a multiprocessor there are a number of over-heads that are encountered, for example, memory contention, loss of node sharing, synchronization, and scheduling overheads. This section discusses the speed of production systems on a uniprocessor when such overheads are not present and also when such overheads are present. These results then form the basis for the speed-up numbers given in the subsequent sections. For example, consider a production system that without overheads of a parallel implementation runs at a speed of 400 wme-changes/sec on a uniprocessor, and that with the overheads runs at a speed of 200 wme-changes/sec on a uniprocessor. Now if a parallel implementation using eight processors runs at a speed of 1200 wme-changes/sec, then the *nominal* speed-up (the average number of processors that are busy or the speed-up with respect to the parallel implementation on a uniprocessor) is 6-fold, while the *true* speed-up (speed-up with respect to the base serial implementation with no overheads) is only 3-fold. The nominal speed-up (sometimes called *concurrency*) is an indicator of the average processor utilization in the parallel implementation, while the true speed-up is an indicator of the performance improvement over the best known sequential implementation.

Tables 8-1 and 8-2 present the data for the uniprocessor execution of production systems when the synchronization and scheduling overheads are not present.[62] The cost models for these simulations were derived by removing all the synchronization and scheduling code from the code for the parallel implementation (given in Appendix B). Adjustments were also made to compensate for the loss of sharing of memory nodes in the parallel implementation. The costs listed for the various node activations and the cost per wme-change are in milliseconds, and correspond to a machine that executes one million register-register instructions per second (the relative costs of other instructions are shown in Table 7-1).

Table 8-1: Uniprocessor Execution With No Overheads: Part-A

Feature	vto.lin	vt.lin	ilog.lin	mudo.lin	mud.lin
1. root-per-ch, avg cost, sd	1.0, .010, .000	1.0, .010, .000	1.0, .010, .000	1.0, .010, .000	1.0, .010, .000
2. ctst-per-ch, avg cost, sd	22.92, .014, .025	22.92, .014, .024	24.48, .011, .029	41.96, .011, .017	41.96, .011, .017
3. and-per-ch, avg cost, sd	25.96, .086, .357	24.02, .046, .025	26.59, .050, .039	25.95, .076, .150	24.62, .058, .051
4. not-per-ch, avg cost, sd	5.01, .049, .039	4.65, .049, .038	5.84, .051, .033	5.79, .059, .044	5.79, .059, .044
5. term-per-ch, avg cost, sd	1.79, .028, .000	1.03, .028, .000	2.06, .028, .000	3.69, .028, .000	3.69, .028, .000
6. cost per wme-ch (ms)	1.656	1.346	1.646	2.255	2.019
7. speed (wme-ch/sec)	603.9	742.9	607.5	443.5	495.3

---

[62]The corresponding data for traces using binary Rete networks are presented in Section 8.6.

Table 8-2: Uniprocessor Execution With No Overheads: Part-B

Feature	daa.lin	r1s.lin	r1p.lin	eps.lin	epp.lin
1. root-per-ch, avg cost, sd	1.0, .010, .000	1.0, .010, .000	1.0, .010, .000	1.0, .010, .000	1.0, .010, .000
2. ctst-per-ch, avg cost, sd	7.14, .034, .092	5.05, .026, .059	5.07, .026, .059	3.97, .025, .042	3.99, .025, .041
3. and-per-ch, avg cost, sd	39.41, .052, .054	24.58, .059, .048	24.68, .060, .049	23.56, .071, .054	34.56, .088, .079
4. not-per-ch, avg cost, sd	3.97, .057, .037	2.63, .067, .016	2.85, .068, .015	0.75, .062, .022	0.76, .062, .022
5. term-per-ch, avg cost, sd	1.65, .028, .000	0.55, .028, .000	0.55, .028, .000	0.74, .028, .000	0.78, .028, .000
6. cost per wme-ch (ms)	1.911	1.420	1.458	1.616	2.985
7. speed (wme-ch/sec)	523.3	704.2	685.9	618.8	335.0

The data in Tables 8-1 and 8-2 may be interpreted as follows. Lines 1-5 give the average number of node activations of each type per change to working memory, and the mean and standard deviation of cost per node activation of that type.[63] Line 6 gives the average cost of processing a working-memory change, and line 7 gives the execution speed of production systems on a 1 MIPS uniprocessor.[64] Using the data the following observations may be made: (1) The average speed of production systems on a uniprocessor is 589.1 wme-changes/sec, where the average is computed over vt.lin, ilog.lin, mud.lin, daa.lin, r1s.lin, r1p.lin, eps.lin, and epp.lin traces.[65] (Note all data in the following sections of this chapter is also averaged over the this set of traces). (2) The performance of vt.lin is better than that of vto.lin by 23%, which implies that the seven productions removed from vto.lin were taking almost a quarter of the total processing time. (3) Similarly, the performance of mud.lin is better than that of mudo.lin by 12%, indicating that the two productions removed from mudo.lin were taking an eighth of the total processing time. (4) However, the more important effect of removing the seven productions from vto.lin and the two productions from mudo.lin is the large reduction in the standard deviation of the cost of processing and-node activations for the two systems. The standard deviation drops down from 0.357 ms for vto.lin to 0.025 ms for vt.lin. Similarly, the standard deviation drops down from 0.150 ms for mudo.lin to 0.051 ms for mud.lin. As a result, although the improvements in the uniprocessor speed are just 23% and 12% for vt.lin and mud.lin respectively, the improvements in the multiprocessor speed are much more significant, close to 200%-300% (see Section 8.5).

Other interesting numbers that may be extracted from the tables are the average costs of

---

[63]The standard deviation for the cost of processing root-node activations and terminal-node activations is zero because these nodes do not perform any data dependent action. For more details about the actual code executed by these node activations, see Appendices B and C.

[64]Note that for each of the traces, the sum of the product of the first two entries in each of lines 1-5 is greater than the number given in line-6. This is not an error. The sum computed from lines 1-5 does not take into account the sharing of memory nodes that takes place in an actual uniprocessor implementation. The savings in cost due to memory-node sharing are subtracted from the sum computed from lines 1-5 to obtain the cost listed in line-6.

[65]The traces vto.lin and mudo.lin have been excluded, because otherwise the VT and MUD systems would have had too much weight.

processing various types of node activations. The average cost for processing constant-test node activations is .021 ms (equivalent to 21 register-register instructions[66]); for and-node activations is .060 ms; for not-node activations is .059 ms; and for terminal node activations is .028 ms. These numbers are indicative of the kinds of scheduling and synchronization overheads that may be tolerated in processing these activations on a parallel computer.

Tables 8-3 and 8-4 present the data for the uniprocessor execution of production systems when the synchronization and scheduling overheads that occur in parallel implementations are taken into account.[67] The tables give the data for overheads corresponding to the use of node parallelism and intra-node parallelism. The data when production parallelism is used are given later. Lines 1-7 are to be interpreted in the same way as that for Tables 8-1 and 8-2. Line 8 gives the overhead in parallel implementations because of loss of sharing of memory nodes (see Section 5.2.2). Line 9 gives the loss in performance due to the synchronization and scheduling overhead, and line 10 gives the combined loss in performance due to all the overheads. The data shows that the average execution speed including all the overheads is 296.8 wme-changes/sec, that is a factor of 1.98 less than the speed when the overheads are not present. Thus a parallel implementation must recover this factor before it would perform better than a uniprocessor implementation. Another way of looking at it is that the maximum speed-up using k processors is not going to be better than $k/1.98$. The factor of 1.98 is composed of (1) a factor of 1.22 from loss of sharing of nodes and (2) a factor of 1.62 from the synchronization and scheduling overheads.

With the inclusion of overheads, the cost of processing individual node activations also goes up. The average cost of processing constant-test nodes goes up from .021 ms to .029 ms (increase of 38%), of and-nodes goes up from .060 ms to .098 ms (increase of 63%), of not-nodes goes up from .059 ms to .096 ms (increase of 63%), and of terminal nodes goes up from .028 ms to .043 ms (increase of 54%). Although the increases are significant they are not too bad, since much of the performance loss can be recovered using a larger number of processors. More critical than the cost of individual node activations is the cost of the longest chain of activations from the root-node down, since that is what determines the final processing speed.

Unlike when node parallelism or intra-node parallelism is used, when production parallelism is used, two-input nodes that were shared between distinct productions in the Rete network can no longer be shared. This loss in performance due to lack of sharing of two-input nodes is over and above the loss due to lack of sharing of memory nodes, a loss that is also encountered when using node parallelism and intra-node parallelism. Tables 8-5 and 8-6 give some of the data for systems executing on a uniprocessor when the overheads for using production parallelism are

---

[66]The cost is much higher than that for constant-test nodes in the OPS83 implementation because of the hashing techniques being used.

[67]The memory contention overheads are not included here, but are considered in Section 8.8.

Table 8-3: Uniprocessor Execution With Overheads: Part-A
Node Parallelism and Intra-Node Parallelism

Feature	vto.lin	vt.lin	ilog.lin	mudo.lin	mud.lin
1. root-per-ch, avg cost, sd	1.0, .019, .000	1.0, .019, .000	1.0, .019, .000	1.0, .019, .000	1.0, .019, .000
2. ctst-per-ch, avg cost, sd	22.92, .021, .029	22.92, .020, .028	24.48, .019, .034	41.96, .019, .026	41.96, .019, .026
3. and-per-ch, avg cost, sd	25.96, .121, .358	24.02, .081, .029	26.59, .087, .045	25.95, .113, .152	24.62, .095, .058
4. not-per-ch, avg cost, sd	5.01, .086, .043	4.65, .085, .043	5.84, .089, .039	5.79, .096, .049	5.79, .096, .049
5. term-per-ch, avg cost, sd	1.79, .043, .000	1.03, .043, .000	2.06, .043, .000	3.69, .043, .000	3.69, .043, .000
6. cost per wme-ch (ms)	4.158	2.887	3.404	4.490	3.895
7. speed (wme-ch/sec)	240.5	346.4	293.8	222.7	256.7
8. sharing overhead	1.73	1.26	1.24	1.28	1.16
9. (sync+sched) overhead	1.45	1.70	1.67	1.56	1.66
10. (sync+sched+shar) ovrhd	2.51	2.14	2.07	1.99	1.93

Table 8-4: Uniprocessor Execution With Overheads: Part-B
Node Parallelism and Intra-Node Parallelism

Feature	daa.lin	r1s.lin	r1p.lin	eps.lin	epp.lin
1. root-per-ch, avg cost, sd	1.0, .019, .000	1.0, .019, .000	1.0, .019, .000	1.0, .019, .000	1.0, .019, .000
2. ctst-per-ch, avg cost, sd	7.14, .044, .097	5.05, .034, .062	5.07, .034, .062	3.97, .030, .043	3.99, .030, .042
3. and-per-ch, avg cost, sd	39.41, .088, .058	24.58, .098, .055	24.68, .098, .057	23.56, .112, .064	34.56, .129, .087
4. not-per-ch, avg cost, sd	3.97, .098, .043	2.63, .103, .019	2.85, .103, .019	0.75, .099, .028	0.76, .098, .028
5. term-per-ch, avg cost, sd	1.65, .043, .000	0.55, .043, .000	0.55, .043, .000	0.74, .043, .000	0.78, .043, .000
6. cost per wme-ch (ms)	4.272	2.893	2.943	2.888	4.722
7. speed (wme-ch/sec)	234.1	345.7	339.8	346.3	211.8
8. sharing overhead	1.36	1.27	1.25	1.15	1.08
9. (sync+sched) overhead	1.65	1.61	1.61	1.56	1.46
10. (sync+sched+shar) ovrhd	2.24	2.04	2.02	1.79	1.58

included. Lines 1 and 2 give the cost of processing a working-memory change and the overall speed of execution on a 1 MIPS processor. Line 3 gives the sharing overhead factor over a uniprocessor implementation with no sharing losses. Line 4 gives the extra loss due to sharing when using production parallelism over the loss due to sharing when using node parallelism (basically, line 3 of Tables 8-5 and 8-6 divided by corresponding entries in line 8 of Tables 8-3 and 8-4). The data shows that the average extra loss due to sharing when using production parallelism is a factor 1.33. Line 5 gives the total loss factor over an uniprocessor implementation with no overheads. The average value of this loss factor for production parallelism is 2.64 as compared to 1.98 for node and intra-node parallelism.

8.3. Production Parallelism

In this section simulation results about the speed-up obtained using production parallelism on a multiprocessor are presented. It is assumed that the multiprocessor has a hardware task scheduler associated with it. The results for the case when multiple software task queues are used are presented in Section 8.7.

Table 8-5: Uniprocessor Execution With Overheads: Part-A
Production Parallelism

Feature	vto.lin	vt.lin	ilog.lin	mudo.lin	mud.lin
1. cost per wme-ch (ms)	4.51	3.23	3.74	4.58	3.99
2. speed (wme-ch/sec)	221.7	309.6	267.4	218.3	250.6
3. sharing overhead	1.878	1.407	1.363	1.307	1.185
4. extra sharing ovrhd	1.086	1.117	1.099	1.021	1.025
5. (sync+sched+shar) ovrhd	2.72	2.40	2.27	2.03	1.98

Table 8-6: Uniprocessor Execution With Overheads: Part-B
Production Parallelism

Feature	daa.lin	r1s.lin	r1p.lin	eps.lin	epp.lin
1. cost per wme-ch (ms)	5.80	5.30	5.36	3.62	5.43
2. speed (wme-ch/sec)	172.4	188.7	186.6	276.2	184.2
3. sharing overhead	1.845	2.328	2.278	1.442	1.241
4. extra sharing ovrhd	1.357	1.833	1.822	1.254	1.149
5. (sync+sched+shar) ovrhd	3.04	3.73	3.68	2.24	1.82

Figures 8-1, 8-2, and 8-3 show the graphs for speed-up when production parallelism is used without action parallelism, that is, when each change to working memory is processed to completion before the processing for the next change is begun. Figure 8-1 shows the *nominal* speed-up, Figure 8-2 shows the *true* speed-up, and Figure 8-3 gives the actual execution speed of the parallel implementation (in working-memory changes processed per second), assuming that the individual nodes in the multiprocessor work at a speed of 2 MIPS.[68] (We choose 2 MIPS as the processor speed to roughly match the current operating region of technology. Within limits set by the operating regions of other components of the multiprocessor system, the results can simply be scaled for other processor speeds.) To explain the nature of the graphs it is convenient to divide the curves into two regions. The first region, the *active* region, of the curve is where the overall speed-up is increasing significantly with an increase in the number of processors (say up to the 16 processor mark). The second region, the *saturation* region, corresponds to the portion where the curve is almost flat (beyond the 16 processor mark).

The saturation speed-up, or the maximum speed-up, available from production parallelism is primarily affected by the following factors: (1) It is limited by the number of productions *affected* per change to working memory, that is, the number of productions whose state changes as a result of a working-memory change. For the traces under consideration the average size of the affect-sets is 26.3. The two curves at the bottom of Figure 8-1 representing eps.lin and epp.lin have an affect-set size of 12.1 and 11.9 respectively. The curve at the top representing vt.lin has an affect-set size of 31.2. (2) The saturation speed-up is proportional to the ratio t_{avg}/t_{max}, where t_{avg} is the average cost of processing an affected production and t_{max} is the cost

---

[68]The terms *nominal* speed-up and *true* speed-up were defined in the beginning of Section 8.2.

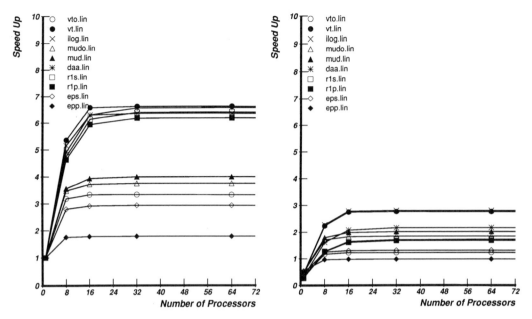

Figure 8-1: Production parallelism (nominal speed-up).

Figure 8-2: Production parallelism (true speed-up).

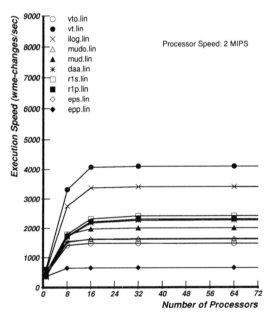

Figure 8-3: Production parallelism (execution speed).

of processing the production requiring the most time in that cycle (also see Section 7.1.2). For the curves shown in Figure 8-1, the average saturation nominal speed-up is 5.1, which is much smaller than the average size of the affect-sets. A large factor of almost 5 is lost due to the variation in the cost of processing affected productions. (3) The effect of loss of sharing in the Rete network on the saturation speed-up is as follows. In the saturation region, when as many processors as needed are available, multiple activations corresponding to a single shared node in the original network are all processed in parallel. While this makes the nominal speed-up higher than it would have been if nodes were still shared, the true speed-up remains the same. This is because the true speed-up in the saturation region is primarily dependent on the longest chain (most expensive chain) of node activations, and loss of sharing only affects the branching factor of nodes in the chain, but not the length of the longest chain.[69] (4) The effect of the synchronization and scheduling overheads on the saturation speed-up is very complex. The portion of these overheads that simply increases the cost of the individual node activations does not effect the saturation nominal speed-up much, but it does effect the saturation true speed-up significantly. The portion of these overheads that requires serial processing (for example, the processing required for each node to be scheduled through a serial scheduler) can, however, significantly effect both the saturation nominal and saturation true speed-ups.

The speed-up in the active region of the curves, in addition to being limited by the factors affecting the saturation speed-up, is dependent on the following factors: (1) The speed-up is obviously bounded by the number of processors in the system. (2) The speed-up is reduced by the variation in the size of the affect-sets. The variation results in a loss of processor utilization because, within the same run, for some cycles there are too many processors (the excess processors remaining idle) and for some cycles there are too few processors (some processors have to process more than one production activation, while other processors are waiting for these to finish). (3) The loss of sharing of nodes in the parallel implementations also affects the active region of the true speed-up curves. Since the maximum nominal speed-up is bounded by the number of processors, if the loss due to sharing is high, then the maximum true speed-up is correspondingly reduced. Thus if the loss of sharing increases the cumulative cost of processing all the node activations by a factor of 2, then using eight processors, no better than 4-fold true speed-up can be obtained. (4) In the case of non-shared memory multicomputers, the speed-up is greatly dependent on the quality of the partitioning, that is, the uniformity with which the work is distributed amongst the processors. The work in this thesis, however, does not address the issues in implementation of production systems on non-shared memory multicomputers. Some discussion can be found in [32, 69, 70].

There are several other observations that can be made from the curves in Figures 8-1, 8-2, and

---

[69]The change in the branching factor does have second order effects on the saturation speed-up. For example, if the branching factor is large, then by the time the node corresponding to the longest chain gets scheduled for parallel execution, a significant amount of time may have elapsed.

8-3: (1) The average nominal saturation speed-up is 5.1.[70] (2) The average true saturation speed-up is only 1.9. In fact for the epp.lin trace, the true speed-up never goes over 1.0, that is, the parallel implementation cannot even overcome the losses due to the overheads in the parallel implementation. (3) The average saturation execution speed using 2 MIPS processors is around 2350 wme-changes/sec or about 1000 prod-firings/sec. (4) The saturation region of the speed-up curves is reached while using 16 processors or less. In fact for most systems, using more than 8 processors does not seem to be advisable. (5) The average loss of speed-up due to the overheads of the parallel implementation is a factor of 2.65. This suggests that if only production parallelism is to be used, then it may be better to use the partitioning approach (divide the production system into several parts and perform match for each part in parallel) rather than the centralized task queue approach suggested in this thesis. The advantage of the partitioning approach is that the synchronization and scheduling overheads are not present, although the sharing overheads are still present. (6) Although the production-system programs considered have very different complexity and size, the larger programs do not appear to gain more from parallelism than the smaller systems. This is a consequence of the fact that the sizes of the affect-sets are quite independent of the sizes of the production-system programs.

At the level of individual production-system programs the following observations can be made: (1) The Soar Eight-Puzzle program traces (eps.lin and epp.lin) are not doing well at all. The reasons for the low speed-up are the small size of the affect-sets (12.1 and 11.8 respectively) and the large variance in processing times. The large variance is a result of the long-chain effect and the cross-product effect discussed in Sections 5.2.6 and 4.2.3. (2) The difference in the speed-ups obtained by the vt.lin and vto.lin systems is quite large, about a factor of 2. Since the size of the affect-sets for vt.lin and vto.lin are about the same, this shows that the removal of the 7 productions from vto.lin significantly reduces the variation in the processing times. The difference in the speed-ups achieved by the mud.lin and the mudo.lin systems is, however, not very large. This is because the productions that were removed did not have a very high cost compared to the processing required by the rest of the affected productions. The difference in the speed-up obtained by mud.lin and mudo.lin becomes more significant when intra-node parallelism is used (see Figure 8-13), which suggests that the two removed productions contained node activations that could not be processed in parallel using production parallelism or node parallelism but that could be processed in parallel using intra-node parallelism.

---

[70]Note that all average numbers reported in this Section (unless otherwise stated) are computed over the traces vt.lin, ilog.lin, mud.lin, daa.lin, r1s.lin, r1p.lin, eps.lin, and epp.lin. The traces vto.lin and mudo.lin are excluded because that would have resulted in excess weight for the vt and mud production systems.

8.3.1. Effects of Action Parallelism on Production Parallelism

Figures 8-4, 8-5, and 8-6 present speed-up data for the case when both production and action parallelism are used. Figure 8-4 presents data about nominal speed-up, Figure 8-5 presents data about true speed-up, and Figure 8-6 presents data about the execution speed. Comparing the graphs for speed-up with action parallelism with those without action parallelism the following observations can be made: (1) Some systems (vt.lin, r1s.lin, r1p.lin, and eps.lin) show a significant increase in the speed-up with the use of action parallelism, while other systems (vto.lin, ilog.lin, mud.lin, mudo.lin, daa.lin, and epp.lin) show very little extra speed-up. The main reason why some of the systems show little extra speed-up is that the affect-sets corresponding to the multiple changes have large amounts of overlap. For example, if the production taking the longest time to process is affected by each of the changes to the working memory, then no extra speed-up is obtained from processing such changes in parallel. (This is exactly what happens in the case of the epp.lin trace.) The second limitation is imposed by the number of changes made to working memory per production firing (per phase for Soar systems). This number itself is quite small for the OPS5 systems. (2) For the systems that show significant improvement, the number of processors needed to get to the saturation point goes up from 8-16 processors to 16-32 processors. (3) The average nominal saturation speed-up goes up from 5.1 to 7.6, an improvement by a factor of 1.50. (4) The average saturation execution speed correspondingly goes up from 2350 to 3550 wme-changes/sec.

115

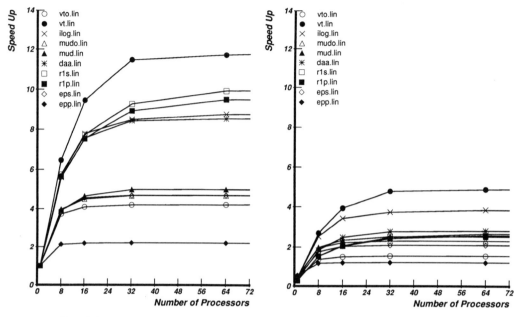

Figure 8-4: Production and action parallelism (nominal speed-up).

Figure 8-5: Production and action parallelism (true speed-up).

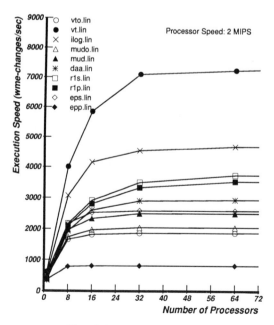

Figure 8-6: Production and action parallelism (execution speed).

8.4. Node Parallelism

Figures 8-7, 8-8, and 8-9 present the data when node parallelism is used to speed-up the execution of production systems. Some of the computed statistics are: (1) The average saturation nominal speed-up is 5.8. This is only a factor of 1.14 better than the corresponding speed-up when production parallelism is used. (2) The average true saturation speed-up is 2.9, which is a factor of 1.50 better than the corresponding speed-up when only production parallelism is used. The improvement in the true speed-up is larger than the improvement in the nominal speed-up because the overheads when exploiting node parallelism are less than the overheads when exploiting production parallelism. The average overhead when using node parallelism is 1.98 as compared to 2.65 when using production parallelism. (3) The average saturation execution speed using node parallelism is 3500 wme-changes/sec as compared to 2350 wme-changes/sec when using production parallelism. (4) The processors needed to obtain the saturation speed-up is still around 8-16 processors.

Studying the nominal speed-up graphs for production and node parallelism shows that systems which achieved relatively high speed-ups with production parallelism (vt.lin, ilog.lin, daa.lin, r1s.lin, r1p.lin) do not benefit much from node parallelism. Systems which did poorly using production parallelism, however, show a more marked improvement. This suggests that systems that were doing well for production parallelism did not suffer from multiple node activations corresponding to the same production when a change to working memory was made, while many of the systems that performed poorly did suffer from such problems.

8.4.1. Effects of Action Parallelism on Node Parallelism

Figures 8-10, 8-11, and 8-12 show the speed-ups for the case when both node parallelism and action parallelism are used. The average statistics are as follows: (1) The saturation nominal speed-up is 10.7 as compared to 5.8 for only node parallelism (a factor of 1.84). (2) The saturation true speed-up is 5.4 as compared to 2.9 for only node parallelism. (3) The average saturation execution speed for the production systems is 6600 wme-changes/sec as compared to 3500 wme-changes/sec for only node parallelism. (4) For most systems it appears that 16 processors are sufficient, though for vt.lin, r1s.lin, and r1p.lin it seems appropriate to use 32 processors.

It is interesting to note that although the sizes of the affect-sets with action parallelism for r1s.lin and r1p.lin are 128.9 and 145.8 respectively, the saturation nominal speed-up is only around 14-fold. This indicates that still a factor of almost 10 is getting lost due to variations in the processing cost of the affected productions. One source of such variation is long chains of dependent node activations, especially since R1-Soar has several productions with large numbers of condition elements. This problem is dealt with in Section 8.6 where the binary Rete networks are considered. The other source of variation is multiple activations of the same node in the network (this may happen due to the cross-product effect as discussed in Section 4.2.3, or due to the multiple changes causing activations of the same node in the Rete network). Since

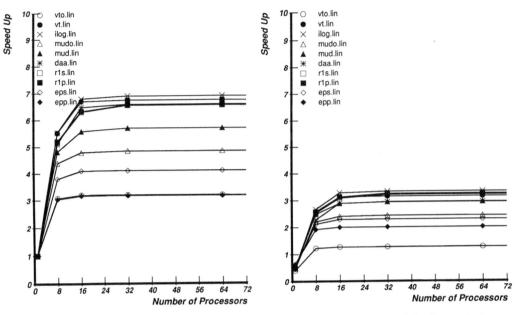

Figure 8-7: Node parallelism (nominal speed-up).

Figure 8-8: Node parallelism (true speed-up).

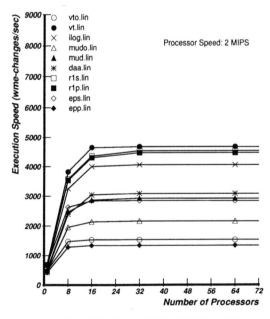

Figure 8-9: Node parallelism (execution speed).

multiple activations of the same node cannot be processed in parallel using node parallelism, they all have to be processed sequentially. The use of intra-node parallelism, which is discussed next, addresses some of these problems.

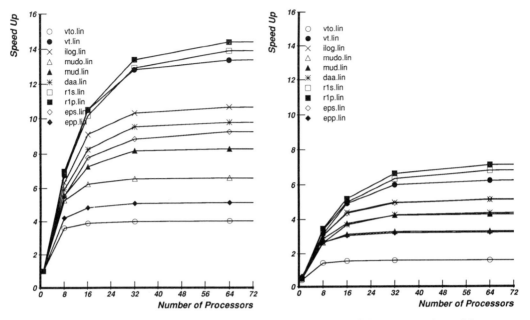

Figure 8-10: Node and action parallelism (nominal speed-up).

Figure 8-11: Node and action parallelism (true speed-up).

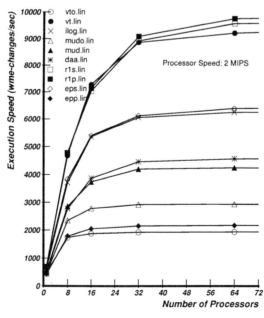

Figure 8-12: Node and action parallelism (execution speed).

120

8.5. Intra-Node Parallelism

Figures 8-13, 8-14, and 8-15 show the speed-up data when intra-node parallelism is used. The average statistics when using intra-node parallelism are: (1) The average saturation nominal speed-up is 7.6 as compared to 5.8 when using node parallelism and 5.1 when using production parallelism. (2) The average saturation true speed-up is 3.9 as compared to 2.9 for node parallelism and 1.9 for production parallelism. (3) The average saturation execution speed is 4460 wme-changes/sec as compared to 3500 when using node parallelism and 2350 when using production parallelism.

It is interesting to observe that the curve for epp.lin has made a sudden upward jump, so that now the saturation nominal speed-up for epp.lin is 7.8 as compared to 3.2 when node parallelism is used and 1.8 when production parallelism is used. This sudden increase can be explained as follows. In the epp.lin system the occurrence of cross-products is very common. While it was not possible to process the cross-products in parallel using production parallelism or node parallelism, it is possible to do so using intra-node parallelism, and hence the large increase in the speed-up. On the other hand the curve for vto.lin shows no extra speed-up at all over what could be achieved using production parallelism. The reason for the low speed-up is that a specific node in the system is affected by all the changes to the working memory, and this node activation takes a really long time to process. Since there is only a single node activation that is involved in the bottleneck, the use of parallelism does not help, unless multiple processors are allocated to process that single node activation. There is some work going on in this direction, though it is not the discussed in this thesis [23].

A general point that emerges from the discussion of the various sources of parallelism is that different production systems pose different bottlenecks to the use of parallelism. While for some programs production parallelism is sufficient (sufficient in the sense that most of the speed-up that is to be gained from using parallelism is obtained by using production parallelism alone), others need to use node parallelism or intra-node parallelism to obtain the full benefits from parallelism. Since this move to finer granularity does not impose any extra overheads, the fine granularity scheme of intra-node parallelism seems to be the scheme of choice.

8.5.1. Effects of Action Parallelism on Intra-Node Parallelism

Figures 8-16, 8-17, and 8-18 present the speed-up data for the case when both intra-node parallelism and action parallelism are used. The average statistics for this case are as follows: (1) The average saturation nominal speed-up is 19.3 as compared to 7.6 when only intra-node parallelism is used. (2) The average saturation true speed-up is 10.2. (3) The average saturation execution speed is 11,260 wme-changes/sec. This corresponds to less than 100μs for match per working-memory change.

It is interesting to note that the highest speed-ups (with the exception of eps.lin) are obtained

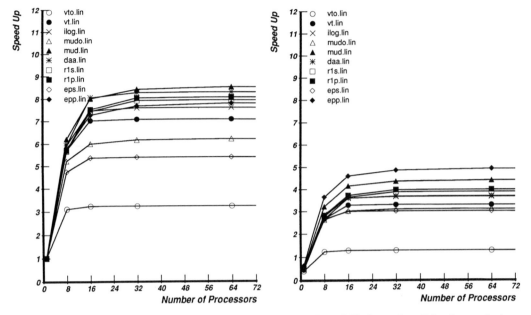

Figure 8-13: Intra-node parallelism (nominal speed-up).

Figure 8-14: Intra-node parallelism (true speed-up).

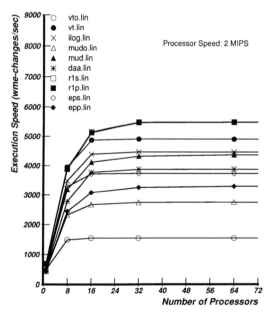

Figure 8-15: Intra-node parallelism (execution speed).

by Soar programs. This is mainly because of the large number of working-memory changes (average of 12.25 changes) that are processed in parallel for these systems. Systems like ilog.lin, daa.lin, vt.lin which did relatively well when action parallel was not used, fall behind due to the small number of working-memory changes (average of 2.44 changes) processed every cycle. Finally, barring a few systems like r1s.lin, r1p.lin, and epp.lin which could use 64 processors, most systems seem to be able to use only about 32 processors effectively.

A summary of the speed-ups obtained using the various sources of parallelism is given in Figures 8-19, 8-20, and 8-21. The curves represent the average nominal speed-up, the average true speed-up, and the average execution speed, with the averages computed over the various production-system traces. As expected, the use of intra-node and action parallelism results in the most speed-up, followed by node and action parallelism, followed by intra-node parallelism alone, with the rest clustered below.

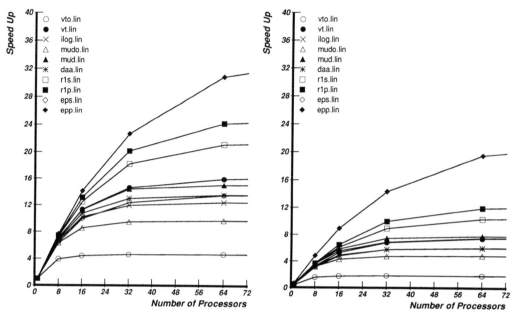

Figure 8-16: Intra-Node and action parallelism (nominal speed-up).

Figure 8-17: Intra-Node and action parallelism (true speed-up).

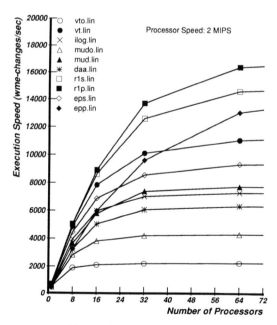

Figure 8-18: Intra-Node and action parallelism (execution speed).

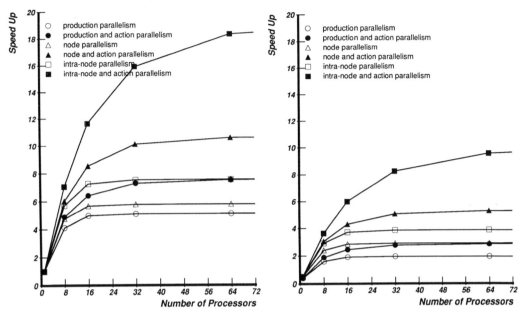

Figure 8-19: Average nominal speed-up.

Figure 8-20: Average true speed-up.

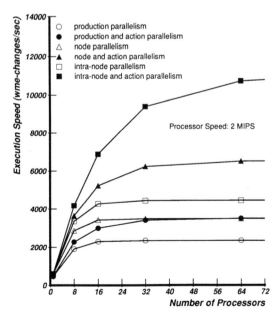

Figure 8-21: Average execution speed.

8.6. Linear vs. Binary Rete Networks

As discussed in Section 5.2.6 there are several advantages of using binary networks instead of linear networks for productions. The main advantage, however, is that it reduces the maximum length that a chain of dependent node activations may have. This section presents simulation results corresponding to production-system runs in which binary networks were used. As done when using linear networks, results are first presented for the binary-network runs on uniprocessors. These data are then used to calibrate the performance of the runs on multiprocessors.

8.6.1. Uniprocessor Implementations with Binary Networks

Tables 8-7 and 8-8 present information about the cost of uniprocessor runs when binary networks are used and when the overheads associated with parallel implementations are eliminated. Lines 1-5 give the number of node activations of each node type and the average cost (in milliseconds) per activation on a 1 MIPS processor. Line 6 gives the cost per wme-change (in milliseconds). Line-7 gives the execution speed in wme-changes per second when binary networks are used and line-8 gives the same information when linear networks are used (line-8 is a copy of line-7 in Tables 8-1 and 8-2). Line-9 gives the ratio of the uniprocessor speeds when binary and linear networks are used.

An important observation that can be made form the data presented in Tables 8-7 and 8-8 is that for all systems other than epp.bin, the binary network version is slower than the linear network version. The average speed decreases by a factor of 1.36. This is because there are many more and-node activations in the binary network version, which in turn is caused by a larger number of and-nodes with no filtering tests (see Section 5.2.6). In fact, in the results reported in this section for the binary network case, there were some productions in each of the programs that were retained in their linear network form to avoid the blow-up of state caused by the binary network form. If this was not done the state grew so much that the lisp system would crash. Thus to perform better than the parallel linear-network implementations, the parallel binary-network implementations have to recover the performance they lose due to the extra node activations.

Table 8-7: Uniprocessor Execution With No Overheads: Part-A

Feature	vto.bin	vt.bin	ilog.bin	mudo.bin	mud.bin
1. root-per-ch, avg cost	1.0, .010	1.0, .010	1.0, .010	1.0, .010	1.0, .010
2. ctst-per-ch, avg cost	22.92, .014	22.92, .013	24.48, .013	41.96, .011	41.96, .011
3. and-per-ch, avg cost	27.82, .093	25.88, .057	28.90, .059	31.71, .077	30.38, .062
4. not-per-ch, avg cost	5.01, .049	4.65, .049	5.84, .051	5.79, .059	5.79, .059
5. term-per-ch, avg cost	1.79, .028	1.03, .028	2.06, .028	3.69, .028	3.69, .028
6. cost per wme-ch (ms)	1.964	1.645	2.033	2.664	2.438
7. bin-speed (wme-ch/sec)	509.2	607.8	491.9	375.4	410.2
8. lin-speed (wme-ch/sec)	603.9	742.9	607.5	443.5	495.3
9. bin-speed/lin-speed	0.84	0.82	0.81	0.85	0.83

126

Table 8-8: Uniprocessor Execution With No Overheads: Part-B

Feature	daa.bin	rls.bin	rlp.bin	eps.bin	epp.bin
1. root-per-ch, avg cost	1.0, .010	1.0, .010	1.0, .010	1.0, .010	1.0, .010
2. ctst-per-ch, avg cost	7.14, .026	5.05, .021	5.07, .021	3.97, .019	3.99, .018
3. and-per-ch, avg cost	36.30, .066	33.37, .078	37.44, .080	28.98, .086	30.05, .087
4. not-per-ch, avg cost	3.97, .062	2.60, .067	2.87, .068	1.04, .069	1.24, .070
5. term-per-ch, avg cost	1.65, .028	0.55, .028	0.55, .028	0.74, .028	0.78, .028
6. cost per wme-ch (ms)	2.248	2.458	2.855	2.415	2.540
7. bin-speed (wme-ch/sec)	444.8	406.8	350.3	414.2	393.8
8. lin-speed (wme-ch/sec)	523.3	704.2	685.9	618.8	335.0
9. bin-speed/lin-speed	0.85	0.58	0.51	0.67	1.18

Tables 8-9 and 8-10 present the overheads in binary networks due to the parallel implementation when node parallelism or intra-node parallelism is used. The average overhead due to the parallel implementation is a factor of 1.84, as compared to 1.98 when linear networks are used. Similarly, Tables 8-11 and 8-12 present the overheads due to the parallel implementation when production parallelism is used. The average overhead in this case is 2.52, as compared to 2.64 when linear networks are used.

Table 8-9: Uniprocessor Execution With Overheads: Part-A
Node Parallelism and Intra-Node Parallelism

Feature	vto.bin	vt.bin	ilog.bin	mudo.bin	mud.bin
1. cost per wme-ch (ms)	4.604	3.333	3.896	5.145	4.551
2. speed (wme-ch/sec)	217.2	300.1	256.7	194.4	219.7
3. (sync+sched+shar) ovrhd	2.344	2.026	1.916	1.931	1.867

Table 8-10: Uniprocessor Execution With Overheads: Part-B
Node Parallelism and Intra-Node Parallelism

Feature	daa.bin	rls.bin	rlp.bin	eps.bin	epp.bin
1. cost per wme-ch (ms)	4.520	4.425	5.032	4.012	4.190
2. speed (wme-ch/sec)	221.2	225.9	198.8	249.3	238.7
3. (sync+sched+shar) ovrhd	2.011	1.800	1.762	1.661	1.650

Table 8-11: Uniprocessor Execution With Overheads: Part-A
Production Parallelism

Feature	vto.bin	vt.bin	ilog.bin	mudo.bin	mud.bin
1. cost per wme-ch (ms)	5.206	3.915	4.724	5.321	4.727
2. speed (wme-ch/sec)	198.8	255.4	211.7	187.9	211.5
3. (sync+sched+shar) ovrhd	2.649	2.381	2.322	1.997	1.938

Table 8-12: Uniprocessor Execution With Overheads: Part-B
Production Parallelism

Feature	daa.bin	rls.bin	rlp.bin	eps.bin	epp.bin
1. cost per wme-ch (ms)	7.316	7.627	8.282	5.233	5.393
2. speed (wme-ch/sec)	136.7	131.1	120.7	191.1	185.4
3. (sync+sched+shar) ovrhd	3.254	3.103	2.900	2.166	2.124

8.6.2. Results of Parallelism with Binary Networks

Results for the speed-up from parallelism for binary networks are presented in Figures 8-22 through 8-25 for production parallelism, in Figures 8-26 through 8-29 for node parallelism, and in Figures 8-30 through 8-33 for intra-node parallelism. Results about average speed-up are presented in Figures 8-34 and 8-35. These graphs are to be interpreted in exactly the same way as the graphs presented earlier for linear networks.

It is interesting to compare the average saturation speed-ups for the linear network case and the binary network case. The results are shown in Table 8-13 — the data on the left is for the binary-network case and the data on the right is for the linear-network case. As can be seen from the Table, most of the time, the average saturation nominal speed-up obtained using binary networks is higher than that obtained using linear networks. However, most of the time, the average saturation execution speed (given in wme-changes/sec) obtained using binary networks is lower than that obtained using linear networks. The answer to this apparent contradiction lies in the fact that programs when using a binary network execute at less speed than when using a linear network on a uniprocessor, as discussed in Section 8.6.1. Looking separately at OPS5 systems and Soar systems, while the linear-network scheme seems to be more suitable for OPS5 systems, the binary-network scheme seems to be more suitable for Soar systems. This is because in OPS5 systems, where the average number of condition elements per production is small, long-chains of dependent node activations do not arise, so binary networks do not help. In Soar systems, where the average number of condition elements per production is much higher than in OPS5, the long-chains are a bottleneck in the exploitation of parallelism, and for that reason using the binary-network scheme helps significantly.

Table 8-13: Comparison of Linear and Binary Network Rete

Sources of Parallelism	Average Saturation Nominal Speed-Up (bin,lin)	Average Saturation Execution Speed (bin,lin)
1. Production Parallelism	5.3, 5.1	1870, 2350
2. Production and Action Parallelism	8.3, 7.6	2850, 3550
3. Node Parallelism	5.6, 5.8	2680, 3490
4. Node and Action Parallelism	11.6, 10.7	5400, 6600
5. Intra-Node Parallelism	8.0, 7.6	3480, 4460
6. Intra-Node and Action Parallelism	25.8, 19.3	12020, 11260

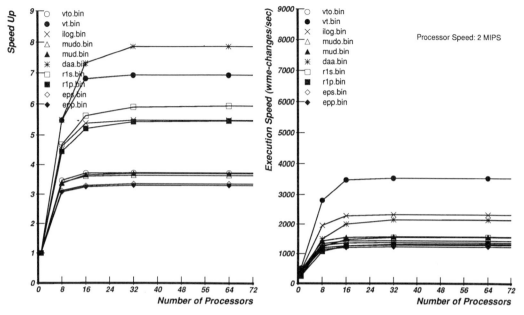

Figure 8-22: Production parallelism (nominal speed-up).   **Figure 8-23:** Production parallelism (execution speed).

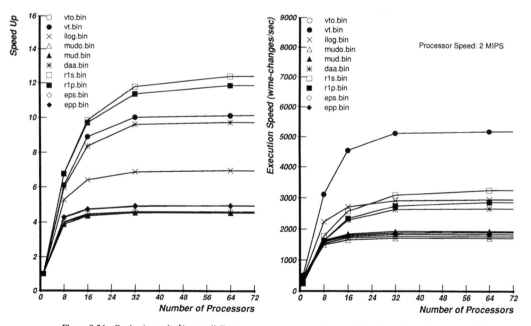

Figure 8-24: Production and action parallelism
(nominal speed-up).

Figure 8-25: Production and action parallelism
(execution speed).

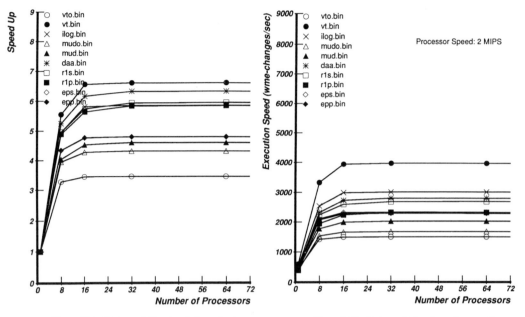

Figure 8-26: Node parallelism (nominal speed-up).

Figure 8-27: Node parallelism (execution speed).

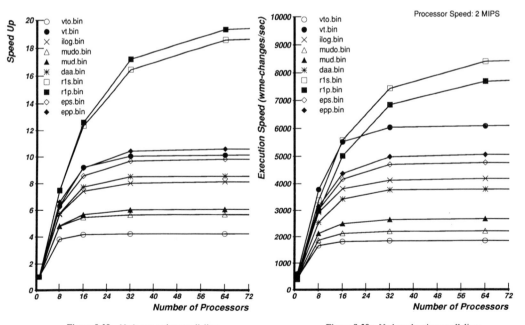

Figure 8-28: Node and action parallelism
(nominal speed-up).

Figure 8-29: Node and action parallelism
(execution speed).

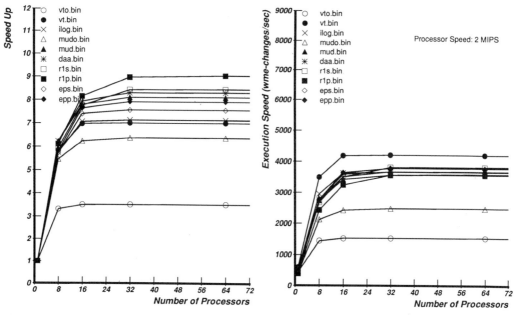

Figure 8-30: Intra-node parallelism (nominal speed-up).

Figure 8-31: Intra-node parallelism (execution speed).

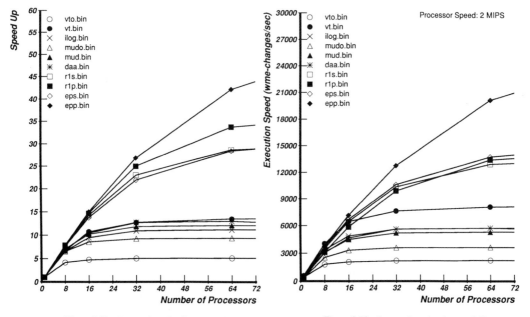

Figure 8-32: Intra-node and action parallelism
(nominal speed-up).

Figure 8-33: Intra-node and action parallelism
(execution speed).

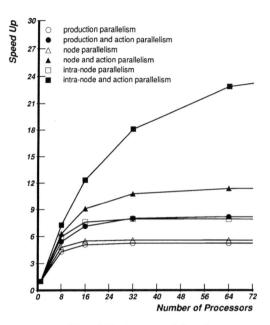

Figure 8-34: Average nominal speed-up.

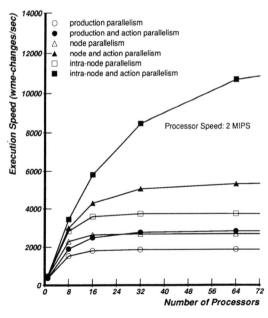

Figure 8-35: Average execution speed.

8.7. Hardware Task Scheduler vs. Software Task Queues

This section presents simulation results for the case when several software task queues are used instead of a hardware task scheduler. The software task queues are modeled in the simulator as suggested in Section 6.2. The actual code from which the cost model used in the simulator is derived is given in Appendix B.2.

It is interesting to consider the overheads in the parallel implementation using software task queues with respect to the uniprocessor implementation with no such overheads. Calculations show that the average overhead when exploiting intra-node parallelism is a factor of 3.23, the average overhead when exploiting node parallelism is a factor of 2.96, and the average overhead when exploiting production parallelism is a factor of 3.70.[71] The corresponding numbers when a hardware task scheduler is being used are 1.98, 1.98, and 2.64 respectively. The overheads are significantly larger because of the much larger costs of enqueueing and dequeueing activations from the software task queues. In the proposed implementation, enqueueing a node activation requires the software task queue be locked for the duration corresponding to about 13 register-register instructions[72] as compared to less than 1 such instruction for the hardware task queue. Similarly, dequeueing a node activation requires the task queue to be locked for a duration corresponding to about 44 register-register instructions[73] as compared to less than 1 such instruction with the hardware task scheduler. Also note that the dequeueing cost is similar in magnitude to the actual cost of processing a node activation. Although the task queues have to be locked for these relatively long durations, reasonable performance can be obtained because many task queues are used.

Once the decision to use software task queues has been made, the next question that arises is "Given some number of processors, how many task queues should be used?". Figure 8-36 plots the performance obtained when the number of processors is fixed at 32 and the number of task queues is varied between 4 and 64. The curves show that when the number of task queues is small (4-16), the execution speed is quite sensitive to this number and increases rapidly with an increase in the number of task queues. When the number of task queues is large (32-64), the execution speed is not sensitive to this number and it decreases slowly with an increase in the number of task queues. In between these two regions, when there are 16-32 schedulers, the

---

[71]The overheads were determined by dividing the cost of the parallel version running on a single processor with a single software task queue, by the cost of the uniprocessor version with no overheads due to parallelism (as described in Tables 8-1 and 8-2).

[72]It is actually composed of 2 synchronization instructions, 3 memory-register instructions, 1 memory-memory-register instruction, and 1 branch instruction. Using the relative cost of instructions given in Table 7-1, the above instructions are equivalent to 12.5 register-register instructions.

[73]It is actually composed of 4 synchronization instructions, 9 register-register instructions, 9 memory-register instructions, 1 memory-memory-register instruction, and 8 branch instructions. Using the relative costs of instructions given in Table 7-1, the above instructions are equivalent to 44 register-register instructions.

execution speed reaches a maximum and then slowly drops. These observations can be explained as follows. When the number of task queues is small, the enqueueing and dequeueing of activations from the task queues is a bottleneck, and thus the low execution speed. Also as a result, provided that there is enough intrinsic parallelism in the programs (unlike ilog.lin, mud.lin, and daa.lin), the performance is almost proportional to the number of task queues that are present, which explains the large slope when the number of task queues is increased. As the number of task queues is increased further, the performance peaks at some point determined by the intrinsic parallelism available in the program and the costs associated with using the task queues. Beyond this point, the effect of a still larger number of task queues is that the processor has to look up several task queues before it finds a node activation to process (as there are an excessive number of task queues, many of them are empty). Since the cost of looking up an extra task queue to see if it is empty is quite small, the slope in this region of the curves is small. All the results presented later in this section, assume that the number of task queues present is half of the number of processors. This number was found to be quite reasonable empirically, in that, beyond this number of task queues the performance does not increase or decrease significantly.

Figures 8-37 to 8-48 show the nominal speed-up and the execution speed obtained using software task queues and different sources of parallelism. The sources of parallelism range from production parallelism to intra-node and action parallelism. Data about the nominal speed-up and the execution speed averaged over the eight traces are presented in Figures 8-49 and 8-50. As can be observed from these graphs, the average saturation execution speed when using production and action parallelism is 2080 wme-changes/sec as compared to 3550 wme-changes/sec when using a hardware task scheduler. When using node and action parallelism, the saturation speed with software task queues is 3330 wme-changes/sec as compared to 6600 wme-changes/sec when using a hardware task scheduler. When using intra-node and action parallelism, the saturation execution speed is 4700 wme-changes/sec as compared to 11260 wme-changes/sec when using a hardware task scheduler. Thus on an average, a factor of 1.7 to 2.4 is lost in performance when software task queues are used.

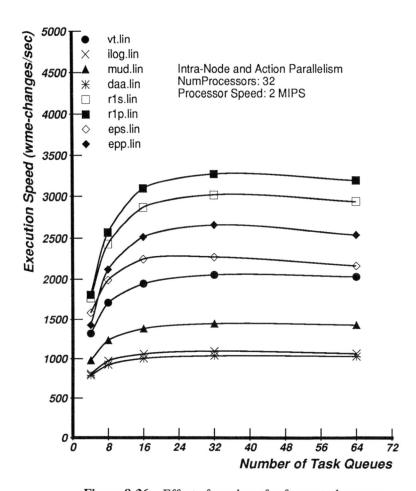

Figure 8-36: Effect of number of software task queues.

135

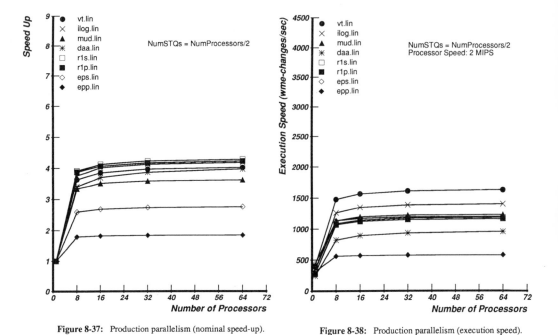

Figure 8-37: Production parallelism (nominal speed-up).

Figure 8-38: Production parallelism (execution speed).

Figure 8-39: Production and action parallelism
(nominal speed-up).

Figure 8-40: Production and action parallelism
(execution speed).

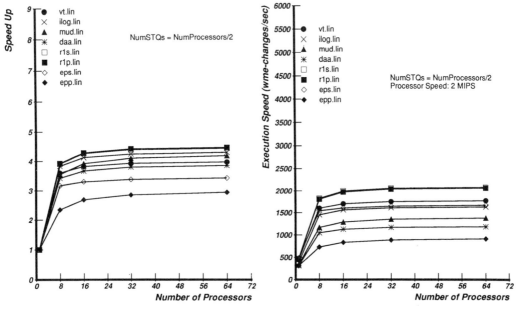

Figure 8-41: Node parallelism (nominal speed-up).

Figure 8-42: Node parallelism (execution speed).

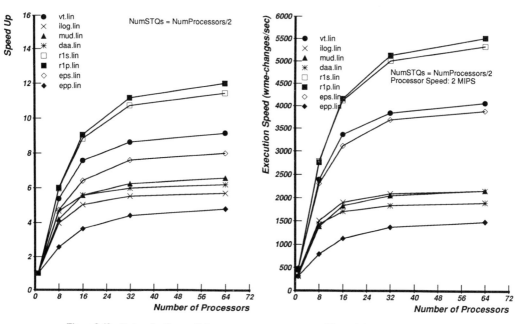

Figure 8-43: Node and action parallelism
(nominal speed-up).

Figure 8-44: Node and action parallelism
(execution speed).

137

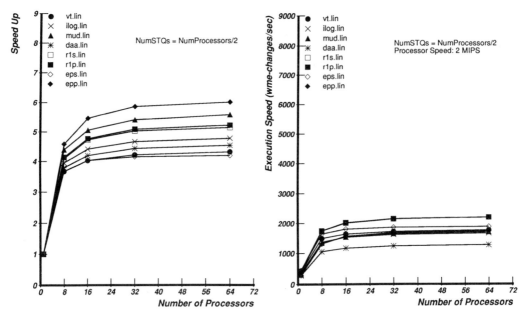

Figure 8-45: Intra-node parallelism (nominal speed-up).

Figure 8-46: Intra-node parallelism (execution speed).

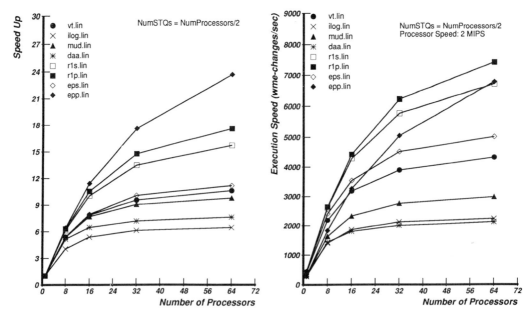

Figure 8-47: Intra-node and action parallelism
(nominal speed-up).

Figure 8-48: Intra-node and action parallelism
(execution speed).

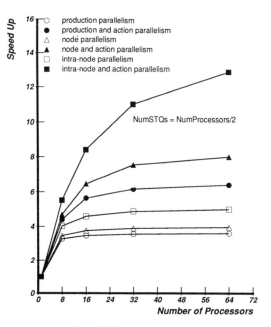

Figure 8-49: Average nominal speed-up.

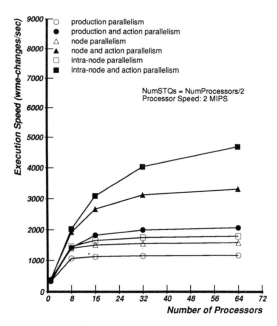

Figure 8-50: Average execution speed.

8.8. Effects of Memory Contention

The simulation results that have been presented so far do not take effects of memory contention into account. This was done in order to keep machine specific data away from the analysis of parallelism. To be more specific, as technology changes and computer buses can handle higher bandwidth, as memories get faster, as new cache coherence strategies evolve, the performance lost due to memory contention will change. Not including memory contention in the simulations provides a measure of parallelism in the programs which is independent of such changes in technology and algorithms — somewhat like an upper-bound result.[74] While it is important to know the intrinsic limits of speed-up from parallelism for programs, it is, of course, also interesting to know the actual speed-up that would be obtained on a real machine, which does have some losses due to memory contention. This section presents simulation results that include the memory contention overhead.

The memory contention overhead is included in the simulation results as per the model described in Section 7.1.1.4. Since one would not design multiprocessors with 8, 16, 32, 64, 128 processors in exactly the same way (for example, using buses with the same bandwidth to connect the processors to memory), different models are used to calculate the contention for multiprocessors with different number of processors. The multiprocessors are divided into three groups: those having 8 or 16 processors, those having 32 or 64 processors, and those having 128 processors (the simulations were run with only these discrete values for number of processors). For the case when there are 8 or 16 processors, it is assumed that the number of memory modules is equal to the number of processors (8 or 16), the bus has a latency of 1µs, the bus is time-multiplexed, and that it can transfer 4 bytes of data every 100ns. For the case when there are 32 or 64 processors, it is assumed that the number of memory modules is 32, the bus has a latency of 1µs, the bus is time-multiplexed, and that it can transfer 8 bytes of data every 100ns. For the case when there are 128 processors, it is assumed that the number of memory modules is 32, the bus has a latency of 1µs, the bus is time-multiplexed, and that it can transfer 8 bytes of data every 50ns. It is further assumed for all the cases that each processor has a speed of 2 MIPS and that the instruction mix consists of 50% register-register instructions and 50% memory-register instructions. Thus each processor when active generates 3 million memory references per second, 2 million references for the instructions and 1 million references for the data. The cache-hit-ratio is uniformly assumed to be 0.85, that is, 85% of the memory accesses are satisfied by the cache and do not go to the bus.[75] Figure 8-51 shows the processor ef-

---

[74]Note some portions of the architecture, like the instruction set of the machine, had to be specified in more detail, because it would not have been possible to do the simulations otherwise.

[75]The cache-hit ratio of 85% is based on the following rough calculations. Since each processor executes at 2 MIPS, there are 2 million references per sec (MRS) generated for instructions and 1 MRS generated for data (assuming that only 50% of the instructions require memory references). Assuming 95% hit-ratio for code and 65% hit-ratio for data, the composite hit-ratio turns out to be 85%.

ficiency for the above cases as a function of the number of processors that are active.[76]

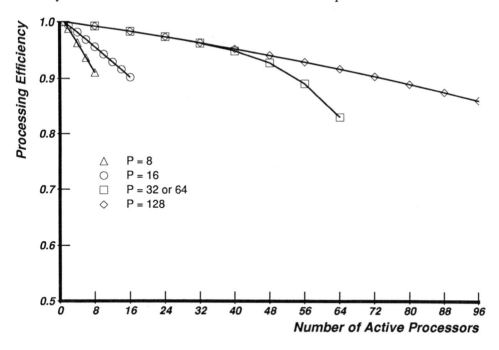

Figure 8-51: Processor efficiency as a function
of number of active processors.

Figures 8-52 and 8-53 present the nominal speed-up and the execution speed for production systems as predicted by the simulator when intra-node and action parallelism are used. The results are presented only for the intra-node and action parallelism case because the combination of these two sources results in the most speed-up, and also because these sources are most affected by the memory contention overhead. The graphs present data for the individual programs (curves with solid lines) and also the average statistics (curves with dotted lines).

It is interesting to compare the average statistics curves in Figures 8-52 and 8-53 with the corresponding curves in Figures 8-19 and 8-21 (when memory contention overheads are not included). The average nominal speed-up (concurrency or average number of active processors) with 128 processors with memory contention is 20.5 and without memory contention is 19.3 (an increase of about 6%). The average execution speed with 128 processors with memory contention is 10950 wme-changes/sec and without memory contention is 11261 wme-changes/sec (a decrease of about 3%). The increase in the concurrency and decrease in the execution speed

---

[76]The variable P in Figure 8-51 refers to the total number of processors (both active and inactive) in the multiprocessor system.

may be understood as follows. Since memory contention causes everything to slow down, the execution speed will obviously be lower. However, since all processors in the multiprocessor are not busy all of the time, the multiprocessor is able to compensate for these slower processors by using some processors that would not be used if memory contention was not present, thus overcoming some of the losses. Thus, although the cost of processing the production systems goes up by 9% due to memory contention, the decrease in the speed of the parallel implementation is only 3%. The remaining 6% is recovered by an increase in the concurrency.

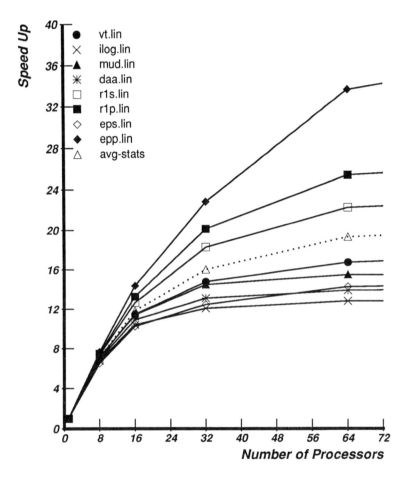

Figure 8-52: Intra-node and action parallelism
(nominal speed-up).

143

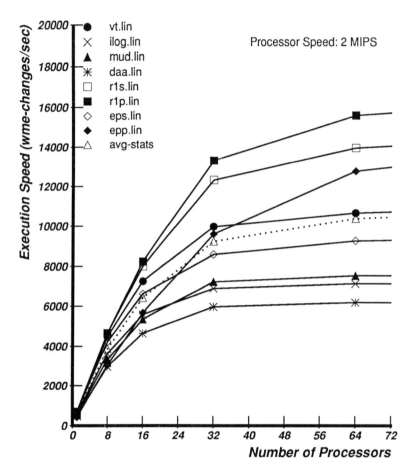

Figure 8-53: Intra-node and action parallelism
(execution speed).

8.9. Summary

In summary, the following observations can be made about the simulation results presented in this chapter:

- When using a hardware task scheduler:
    - A parallel implementation has some intrinsic overheads as compared to a uniprocessor implementation. The overheads occur because of lack of sharing of memory nodes, synchronization costs and scheduling costs. Such overheads when using node or intra-node parallelism result in cost increase by a factor of 1.98, and when using production parallelism result in a cost increase by a factor of 2.64. The overheads are larger when using production parallelism because it is not possible to share two-input nodes between different productions.

    - The average execution speed of production systems on a uniprocessor (without considering the overheads of a parallel implementation) that executes two million register-register instructions per second is about 1180 wme-changes/sec.

    - The average saturation nominal speed-up (concurrency) obtained using production and action parallelism is 7.6, that using node and action parallelism is 10.7, and that using intra-node and action parallelism is 19.3. Using intra-node and action parallelism, the saturation execution speed is about 11,250 wme-changes/sec assuming a multiprocessor with 2 MIPS processors. The speed-up from parallelism is significantly lower when action parallelism is not used. For example, when intra-node parallelism is used, the saturation nominal speed-up is only 7.6 as compared to 19.3 when action parallelism is also used.

    - As a result of the larger number of changes made to working memory per cycle, the Soar systems show much larger benefits from action parallelism than OPS5 systems. For example, when using intra-node parallelism, the speed-up for OPS5 systems increases by a factor of 1.84 as a result of action parallelism, while the speed-up for Soar systems increases by a factor of 3.30.

    - The simulations show that only 32-64 processors are needed to reach the saturation speed-up for most production systems. Thus a multiprocessor system with significantly more processors is not expected to provide any additional speed benefits.

- When using binary Rete networks:
    - The average cost of executing a production system on a uniprocessor (with no overheads due to parallelism) goes up by a factor of 1.39 as compared to when using linear networks. This increase in cost is due to an increased number of node activations per change to working memory. The increased cost sometimes results in situations where the actual execution speed of a production system is less than that of its linear network counterpart, although the nominal speed-up achieved due to parallelism is more.

    - The average overhead due to parallelism when exploiting node or intra-node parallelism is a factor of 1.84 and that when exploiting production parallelism is a factor of 2.52.

- The average saturation nominal speed-up (concurrency) obtained using production and action parallelism is 8.8, that using node and action parallelism is 11.6, and that using intra-node and action parallelism is 25.8. Using intra-node and action parallelism, the saturation execution speed is about 12,000 wme-changes/sec assuming a multiprocessor with 2 MIPS processors.

- The benefits from using binary networks are much more significant for Soar systems than for OPS5 systems. In fact, the average saturation nominal speed-up for the OPS5 systems goes down by 16% (from 14.5 to 12.3) as a result of using binary networks, while the corresponding speed-up for the Soar systems goes up by 62% (from 24.1 to 39.2). The reason for the large increase is that there are several productions in the Soar systems which have very large number of condition elements (resulting in longer chains).

- The above differences between the results for OPS5 systems and Soar systems suggests that there is no single strategy (binary or linear Rete networks) that is uniformly good for all production systems, and that the strategy to use should be determined individually for each production system.

- When using software task queues:
  - The average overhead due to parallelism for intra-node parallelism is a factor of 3.23, for node parallelism is a factor of 2.96, and for production parallelism is a factor of 3.70. These factors are much larger than when a hardware task scheduler is used because of the large cost associated with enqueueing and dequeueing node activations from the task queues.

  - The saturation execution speed is 2080 wme-changes/sec when using production and action parallelism (as compared to 3550 when using a hardware task scheduler), 3330 wme-changes/sec when using node and action parallelism (as compared to 6600), and 4700 wme-changes/sec when using intra-node and action parallelism (as compared to 11,260). Thus the performance loss when using software task queues is a factor between 1.7 and 2.4.

  - Simulations show that the performance of a scheme using software task queues is best when the number of queues is approximately equal to the number of processors.

- When memory contention overheads are included:
  - The memory contention overheads were studied in the simulations by assuming different processor memory interconnect bandwidths for multiprocessors with different number of processors. For multiprocessors with 8 or 16 processors the bandwidth was assumed to be 40 MBytes/sec, for 32-64 processors the bandwidth was assumed to be 80 MBytes/sec, and for 128 processors the bandwidth was assumed to be 160 MBytes/sec.

  - For the case of a multiprocessor with 128 processors it is observed that when memory contention is taken into account, the cumulative cost of executing all node activations goes up by 9%, the nominal speed-up achieved due to parallelism goes up by 6%, and the actual execution speed drops by about 3% (as compared to when memory contention overheads are ignored). It is interesting to note that some of the increase in execution costs due to memory contention is absorbed by the unused processors of the multiprocessor.

9   Related Work

Research on exploiting parallelism to speed up the execution of production systems is not very new, but the efforts have gained significant momentum recently. This gain in momentum has been caused by several factors: (1) There are slowly emerging larger and larger production systems, and their limited execution speed is becoming more noticeable. (2) With the increase in popularity of expert systems, there has been a movement to use expert systems in new domains, some of which require very high performance (for example, real-time control applications). (3) There is a general feeling that the necessary speed-up is not going to come from improvements in hardware technology alone. (4) Finally, the production systems, at least on the surface, appear to be highly amenable to the use of large amounts of parallelism, and this has encouraged researchers to explore parallelism. This chapter briefly describes some of the early and more recent efforts to speed-up the execution of production systems through parallelism.

9.1. Implementing Production Systems on C.mmp

For his thesis [55], Donald McCracken implemented a production-system version of the Hearsay-II speech understanding system [16] on the C.mmp multiprocessor [54].[77] He showed that high degrees of parallelism could be obtained using a shared memory multiprocessor — one of his simulations showed that it was possible to keep 50 processors busy 60% of the time during the match phase. Most of the results presented in his thesis, however, are not applicable to the current research. This is because:

- The characteristics of the Hearsay-II system are distinct enough from current OPS5 and SOAR programs that the results cannot be carried over.

- The speed-up obtained from parallel implementations of production systems is dependent on the underlying computation model. For example, it depends on the quality of the underlying match algorithm. If the underlying match algorithm is naive, it is possible to obtain very large amount of speed-up from parallelism. Since the basic match algorithm used by Don McCracken in his thesis is significantly different from the OPS5-Rete algorithm, it is not possible to interpret his results in the current context.

---

[77]The C.mmp multiprocessor consisted of 16 PDP-11 processors connected to shared memory via a crossbar switch.

- McCracken's thesis addresses issues related to the parallel implementation of Hearsay-II on the C.mmp architecture. Because of the differences in the hardware structure of the PSM considered in this thesis and C.mmp, many issues that were evaluated for C.mmp have no relevance for the PSM. For example, since processors in C.mmp did not have caches, the performance of the parallel implementation was considerably affected by how the code was distributed among the multiple memory modules. In the PSM, since processors have local memory and cache, the distribution of code is not an issue.

9.2. Implementing Production Systems on Illiac-IV

Charles Forgy, in one of his papers [18], has studied the problem of implementing production systems on the Illiac-IV computer system [7]. Since the Illiac-IV is a SIMD (single instruction stream, multiple data streams) computer, the main concern was to develop a match algorithm where all processors would simultaneously execute the same instructions on different data to achieve higher performance.

In the algorithm described in the paper, a production system is initially divided into sixty four partitions, corresponding to the number of processors in Illiac-IV. The paper does not detail the partitioning technique, but suggests that it should be such that similar productions are in different partitions. This is to ensure that the work is uniformly distributed amongst the processors. The Rete network for each partition is constructed and the associated code is placed in corresponding processors. The network interpreter then executes the code in a manner similar to the uniprocessor interpreters, but with one exception. All node evaluations of one type are executed before the node evaluations of another type are begun. For example, the interpreter will finish executing all constant-test nodes before attempting to execute any memory nodes. This ensures that for most of the time all processors are executing nodes of the same type, and since nodes of the same type require the same instructions (they may use different data), the SIMD nature of Illiac-IV is usefully exploited. Although the paper describes the algorithms for executing production systems on Illiac-IV in detail, no estimates are given for the expected speed-up from such an implementation.

9.3. The DADO Machine and the TREAT Match Algorithm

DADO [87, 88] is a highly parallel tree-structured architecture designed to execute production systems at Columbia University by Salvatore J. Stolfo and his colleagues. The proposed machine architecture consists of a very large number (on the order of tens of thousands in the envisioned full-scale version) of processing elements, interconnected to form a complete binary tree. Each processing element consists of its own processor, a small amount of random access memory, and a specialized I/O switch that is constructed using a custom VLSI chip. Figure 9-1 depicts the DADO prototype as described in [87]. The Intel 8751 processors used in the prototype DADO are rated at 0.5 MIPS.

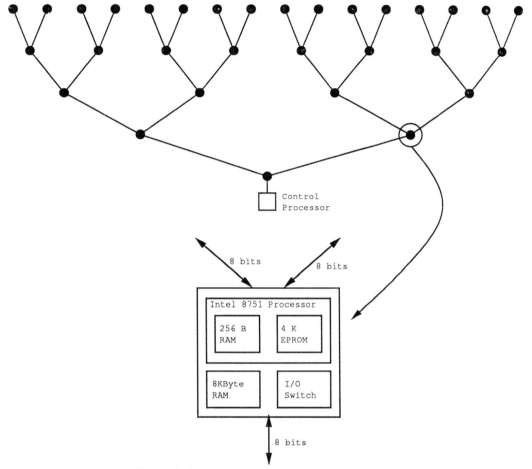

Figure 9-1: The prototype DADO architecture.

Several different algorithms for implementing production systems on DADO have been proposed [31, 61, 89]. Of the many proposed algorithms, the two algorithms offering the highest performance for OPS5-like productions systems on DADO are (1) the parallel Rete algorithm and (2) the Treat algorithm.

In the implementation of the Rete algorithm on DADO [31], the complete production system is divided into 16-32 partitions, the actual number of partitions depending on the amount of production parallelism (see Section 4.2.1) present in the program. Once the production system has been partitioned, separate Rete networks are generated for each of the partitions. Each par-

149

tition is then mapped onto a processing element at the *PM-level*[78] and its associated subtree of processing elements (also called the *WM-Subtree*). Using the processor at the PM-level as a control processor, the processing elements in the WM-subtree are used to associatively match condition elements and working-memory elements, to associatively locate tokens to be deleted, and to perform other similar operations. The processors above the PM-level are used for performing conflict-resolution. The performance of the parallel Rete algorithm on the prototype DADO is predicted to be around 175 wme-changes/sec (for more details, assumptions, and limitations of the analysis see [31]).

The implementation of the Treat algorithm on DADO [61] is similar to the implementation of the parallel Rete algorithm described above, but varies in one fundamental way. While the Rete algorithm stores state corresponding to both α-memory and β-memory nodes in the Rete network, the Treat algorithm stores state corresponding only to the α-memory nodes.[79] It is argued that storing the state corresponding to the β-memory nodes is not very useful for DADO (especially for production systems where a large fraction of the working memory changes on every recognize-act cycle), because it is possible to compute the *relevant* portion of the β-memory state[80] very efficiently on DADO. This is because:

- It is possible to dynamically change the order in which tokens matching individual condition elements are combined, so as to reduce the amount of β-memory state that is computed. Such reordering is not possible in the Rete algorithm, where the combinations of condition elements for which state is stored is frozen at compile time (see Section 5.2.6).[81]

- In case the number of working-memory elements matching some condition element of a production is zero, the Treat algorithm does not compute the β-memory state at all. This is because an instantiation of such a production cannot enter the conflict-set. The Rete algorithm in such a case would anyway go ahead and compute β-memory state in the hope that it would be useful at some later time.

- Finally, the associative match capabilities of the DADO WM-subtree help speed up

---

[78]The PM-level (the production-memory level) is determined by the number of partitions that are made. For example, if the number of partitions is 16 the PM-level would be 4, and if the number of partitions is 32 the PM-level would be 5.

[79]Recall from Section 2.4.2 that the Treat algorithm falls on the low-end of the spectrum of state-saving match algorithms.

[80]The relevant portion of the β-memory state corresponds to those tokens that include a reference to the working-memory change being processed. This is because only tokens involving the new working-memory element can cause a change to the existing conflict-set.

[81]Note that since each change to working memory results in several changes to the conflict-set, there are at least a few productions for which the Treat algorithm has to compute the complete relevant β-memory state. For example, it has to compute tokens matching the first two condition elements of the production, the tokens matching the first three condition elements of the productions, and so on for the entire production. Since much of this computation is done serially on DADO, the variation in the processing times for different productions is expected to be quite large, and consequently the speed-up from parallelism is expected to be less.

computation of the β-memory state that is necessary. For example, using the WM-subtree it is possible to associatively match a given token against all tokens in the opposite memory node. Similarly, all tokens containing a pointer to a given working-memory element can be deleted associatively.

The performance of the Treat algorithm on the prototype DADO is predicted to be around 215 wme-changes/sec. The performance of the Rete algorithm is predicted to be around 175 wme-changes/sec.

More recently, Miranker has been looking at the uniprocessor performance of the Treat algorithm [62, 63]. Data gathered for five different OPS5 programs shows that the total number of comparisons required to do variable bindings under Treat is significantly less than the number of comparisons required by Rete (often, by a factor of two). On this basis, Miranker claims that Treat is a better (*faster*) algorithm for doing match in production systems. We find the following problems with Miranker's analysis as it stands:

- Miranker computes the number of comparisons done by Rete for an implementation that uses linear-list based memory nodes — recent implementations of Rete use hash-table based memory nodes [34]. This optimization reduces the number of comparisons required by Rete by a factor of 10 for many of the programs. It is not easily possible to use the same optimization for Treat because it is not known in advance which condition element will be combined next (result of dynamic ordering), which in turn implies that we do not know which variables to hash on. It is possible that the factor gained by Rete due to hash-table based memory nodes may invalidate Miranker's current conclusions.

- Another place where Treat does fewer comparisons than Rete is when processing removes from working memory. Many of the ideas used in Treat to reduce the number of comparisons (although not all) can also be incorporated into Rete implementations, thus reducing the comparisons made by Rete further.

- we do not think that it is a good idea to base the goodness of one match algorithm over the other simply on the basis of the number of comparisons that they make — there are more complex issues involved. For example, one reason why the number of comparisons is smaller in Treat is that the order in which state associated with condition elements is combined is decided at run time. However, it takes computation resources to decide the order in which the state is to be combined, and such costs should also be taken into account in the final evaluation of the algorithm. As another example, due to the dynamic order in which the state associated with condition elements is combined in Treat, it is not possible to compile the variable-binding tests in Treat into efficient assembly code, as is done in current Rete compilers which combine state in a fixed order. (In Rete, the exact set of tests to be performed at each node and the exact locations from which the values to be compared are to be extracted are known at compile time.) Because of the efficiency gained from such optimizations, it is possible for Rete to overcome some disadvantages that it may have from performing a larger number of comparisons.

Finally, to conclude, we think that there are a number of good ideas in the Treat algorithm — in the way it manages the state associated with condition elements and how such state is combined to determine the conflict set. However, in our opinion, it is too early to claim that one algorithm is better than the other at this point. In fact, we think that an algorithm which combines the good points of both Treat and Rete would turn out to be better than either of them.

9.4. The NON-VON Machine

NON-VON [82, 83] is a massively parallel tree-structured architecture designed for AI applications at Columbia University by David Elliot Shaw and his colleagues. The proposed machine architecture consists of a very large number (anywhere from 16K in the prototype version to one million in the envisioned full-scale supercomputer) of *small processing elements* (SPEs) interconnected to form a complete binary network. Each small processing element consists of 8-bit wide data paths, a small amount of random-access memory (32-256 bytes), a modest amount of processing logic, and an I/O switch that permits the machine to be dynamically reconfigured to support various forms of inter-processor communication. The leaf nodes of the SPE-tree are also interconnected to form a two-dimensional orthogonal mesh. In addition to the small processing elements, the NON-VON architecture provides for a small number of *large processing elements* (LPEs). Specifically, each small processing element above a certain fixed level in the binary network is connected to its own large processing element. The large processing elements are to be built out of off-the-shelf 32-bit microprocessors (for example, the Motorola 68020), with a significant amount of local random-access memory. A large processing element normally stores the programs that are to be executed by the SPE-subtree below it, and it can broadcast instructions at a very high speed with the assistance of a high-speed interface called the *active memory controller*. With the assistance of the large processing elements the NON-VON architecture is capable of functioning in multiple-SIMD (single instruction stream, multiple data stream) mode. Figure 9-2 shows a picture of the proposed NON-VON architecture.

The proposed implementation of production systems on the NON-VON machine [38] is similar to the implementation of the Rete algorithm suggested for the DADO machine in the previous section. However, many changes were made to accommodate the proposed data structures into the small amount of memory available within each SPE. For example, it was often necessary to distribute a single memory-node token across multiple SPEs. This fine distribution of state amongst the processing elements permits a greater degree of associative parallelism than what was possible in the DADO implementation. The performance predicted for the execution of OPS5 on NON-VON [38] is about 2000 wme-changes/sec. The performance numbers correspond to the case when both the large processing elements and the small processing elements in NON-VON function at a speed of about 3 MIPS. (Note that the significantly better performance of NON-VON over DADO can be partly attributed to the facts that (1) NON-VON processing elements are 6 times faster than the prototype DADO processing elements, and (2) NON-VON LPEs have 4 times wider datapaths than the prototype DADO processing elements.)

At this point, it might be appropriate to contrast architectures using a small number (32-64) of

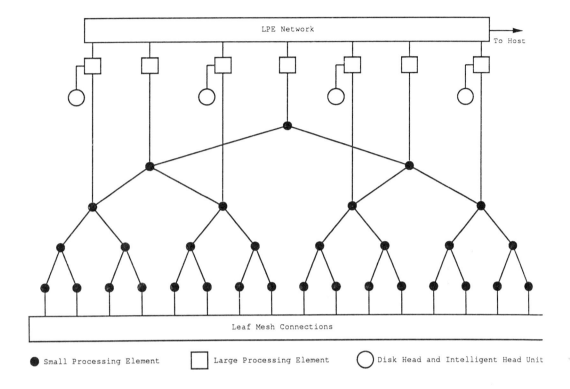

Figure 9-2: The NON-VON architecture.

high-performance processors (for example, the scheme proposed in this thesis) against architectures using a very large number (10,000-1000,000) of *weak* processors (for example, DADO and NON-VON). Studies for uniprocessor implementations show that using a single 3 MIPS processor, it is possible to achieve a performance of about 1800 wme-changes/sec, which is only 10% slower than the performance achieved by the NON-VON machine using thirty-two LPEs of 3 MIPS each and several thousand SPEs. The performance for the DADO machine is even smaller. There are two main reasons for the low performance of these highly parallel machines: (1) The amount of intrinsic parallelism available in OPS5-like production systems is quite small, as shown in the previous chapter. As a result, researchers have used the large number of processors available in the massively-parallel machines as associative memory. However, this does not buy them too much, because hashing on a single powerful processor works just as well. (2) While a scheme using a small number of processors can use expensive and very high performance processors, schemes using a very large number of processors cannot afford fast processors for each of the processing nodes. The performance lost in the highly parallel machines due to the weak individual processing nodes is difficult to recover by simply using a large number of such nodes (since the parallelism is limited). Note, however, the massively parallel machines may do better for highly *non-temporal* production systems (production systems where a large fraction of the working-memory changes on every cycle), or for production systems where the number of rules affected per change to working memory is very large.[82]

9.5. Oflazer's Work on Partitioning and Parallel Processing of Production Systems

Kemal Oflazer in his thesis [70] explores a number of issues related to the parallel processing of production systems. (1) He explores the task of partitioning production systems so that the work is uniformly distributed amongst the processors. (2) He proposes a new parallel algorithm for performing match for production systems. (3) He proposes a parallel architecture to execute the proposed algorithm. The new algorithm is especially interesting in that it stores much more state than the Rete algorithm in an attempt to cut down the variance in the processing required by different productions.

9.5.1. The Partitioning Problem

The partitioning problem for production systems addresses the task of assigning productions to processors in a parallel computer in a way such that the load on processors is uniformly distributed. While the problem of partitioning the production systems amongst multiple processors may be bypassed in shared-memory architectures, like the one proposed in this thesis, it is central in all architectures that do not permit such sharing (for example, partitioning is essential for the algorithms proposed for the DADO and NON-VON machines). The advantages of schemes not relying on the shared-memory architectures are that scheduling, synchronization, and memory-contention overheads are not present. The first part of Oflazer's thesis presents a formulation of the partitioning problem as a minimization problem, which may be described as follows. The execution of a production-system run may be characterized by the sequence $T=<e_1,e_2, \ldots ,e_t>$, where t is the number of changes made to the working memory during the run and where e_i is the set of productions affected by the ith change to working memory.[83] Let $\Pi=(\Pi_1, \ldots ,\Pi_k)$ be some partitioning of the production system onto k processors. With such a partitioning, the cost of executing the production system on a parallel processor is $Cost_{T,\Pi}=\sum_{i=1}^{t} \max_{1 \leq j \leq k}(\sum_{p \in e_i \cap \Pi_j} c_i(p))$, where c_i is a cost function that gives the processing required by productions for the ith change to working memory. Using this terminology, the

---

[82]Note that the techniques developed in this thesis will also result in larger speed-ups for programs on which the massively parallel machines are expected to do well. The only problem arises when the possible speed-ups are of the order of several hundreds. This is because it is difficult to construct shared memory multiprocessors with hundreds or thousands of processors. It is suggested that in such a case it would be best to use a mixture of the partitioning approach (for example, as used in implementations of Rete on DADO and NON-VON) and the fine-grained approach (as proposed in this thesis), and implement it on top of a hierarchical multiprocessor.

[83]Recall that a production is said to be *affected* by a change to working memory, if the working-memory element matches at least one of its condition elements, that is, if the state corresponding to that production has to be updated.

partitioning problem is simply stated as the problem of discovering a partitioning Π such that $Cost_{T,\Pi}$ is minimized. The complexity of finding the exact solution to this minimization problem is shown by Oflazer to be NP-complete [26].

In addition to analysis of some simple partitioning methods like random, round-robin, and context-based, Oflazer's thesis presents a more complex heuristic method for partitioning that relies on data obtained from actual production-system runs. The inputs to the new partitioning method consist of the affect-sets for each of the changes to working memory and the cost associated with each affected production in these affect-sets. The algorithm is very fast and gives results that are 1.15 to 1.25 times better than the results of the simpler partitioning strategies.

9.5.2. The Parallel Algorithm

The second part of Oflazer's thesis concerns itself with a highly parallel algorithm for the state-update phase of match in production systems. The algorithm is based on the contention that both Treat and Rete algorithms are too conservative in the amount of state they store. For example, Treat only stores tokens matching the individual condition elements of productions, and Rete only stores tokens that match the individual condition elements and some fixed combinations of the condition elements. Oflazer's parallel algorithm proposes that the tokens matching not some but all combinations of condition elements of a production should be stored. The main motivation for doing so is to reduce the variance in the processing requirements of the various affected productions in any given match cycle. For example, consider the Treat algorithm. Since it does not store state corresponding to any of the combinations of condition elements, a lot of state has to be computed when a change is made to the working memory. Much of the state computation that is done after the change is made to the working memory could have been done beforehand, thus reducing the interval between the time the working-memory change is made and the time the conflict-set is ready. A similar argument is used against the Rete algorithm.[84]

Oflazer also proposes a new representation for storing state corresponding to the partial matches for a production. He introduces the notion of a *null* working-memory element that matches all condition elements, satisfies all inter-condition tests for productions, and is always present in the working memory. The state of a production is represented by a set of *instance elements* (IEs), where each instance element has the form $\langle (t_1,w_1)(t_2,w_2) \dots (t_c,w_c) \rangle$, where c is the number of condition elements in the production, t_i is the tag associated with the ith slot, and w_i is the working-memory element associated with the ith slot. The working-memory element w_i must satisfy the ith condition element of the production, and the c-tuple $\langle w_1,w_2, \dots ,w_c \rangle$ must

---

[84]Oflazer's thesis, however, does not demonstrate clearly if the variation in the processing requirements of productions is actually reduced by the proposed scheme. Storing state for all combinations of condition elements can result in some productions requiring very large amount of processing, a situation which may not have occurred in the Treat or Rete algorithms (see Section 9.5.4).

consistently satisfy the complete production, that is, the working-memory elements together should satisfy all the inter-condition element tests (note that some of the slots may point to the *null* working-memory element). The tags are used to help detect and delete some of the redundant state generated for a production.

When a change is made to the working memory, the new state for a production is obtained as a result of the interaction between the old state and the new change. An advantage of the proposed representation for state is that the interaction of the new change to each instance element of the old state may be computed independently and in parallel. There is, however, one problem. As a result of the state-update processing, it is possible to generate redundant instance elements (multiple copies of the same instance element or instance elements whose information content is a subset of the information content of other instance elements). It is necessary to eliminate these redundant instance elements, because otherwise they can cause the match to give incorrect results and they also use up scarce processing resources. The elimination of redundant instance elements is problematic because it is essentially a sequential process — it requires that each potentially redundant instance element be compared to all other instance elements for that production. Oflazer presents the detailed algorithms and a hardware architecture to help detect and eliminate redundant instance elements.

9.5.3. The Parallel Architecture

The architecture proposed for the algorithm described above is a parallel reconfigurable tree-structured machine, with fast processors located at the leaf nodes and specialized switches with simple processing capabilities located at the interior nodes of the tree. Figure 9-3 shows a high-level picture of the proposed architecture.

In mapping the proposed algorithm onto the suggested architecture, each production is assigned to some subset of the leaf processors, and as a result each processor is responsible for some subset of the productions in the program. The processors assigned to a production are responsible for processing the instance elements associated with that production and for keeping the state of that production updated.[85] The internal switch nodes of the tree are used to send information to/from the controller located at the root. They are also used to isolate small sections of the tree during the redundant-instance-element-removal phase of the algorithm.

The thesis presents some performance figures based on simulations done for the XSEL [57] and R1 [56] production systems. The simulations assume that (1) processors take 100ns to execute an instruction from the on-chip memory and 200ns to execute an instruction from the external memory, (2) each stage of switch nodes takes 200ns to compute and transfer infor-

---

[85]The number of processors assigned to a production depends on how large its associated state becomes during actual runs. A modified version of the partitioning algorithm given earlier in the thesis is used to partition the productions amongst the processors.

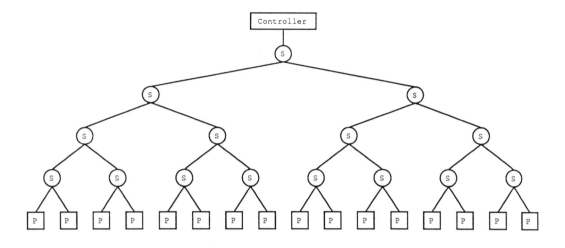

P: Instance Element Processors

S: Switches

Figure 9-3: Structure of the parallel processing system.

mation to the next stage, and (3) the number of processors allocated to a production is the next power of two that is larger than the average number of instance elements for that production. Under these assumptions the time to perform match for a single change to working memory for XSEL is around 150μs (6666 wme-changes/sec), and for R1 it is around 210μs (4750 wme-changes/sec). In all these runs an average of about 300 processors were used to update the instance elements. However, if required on any given match cycle, more processors were assumed to be available.

9.5.4. Discussion

The most interesting aspect of Oflazer's research is the proposed parallel state-update algorithm. It provides yet another distinct data point (at the high-end of the spectrum) in the space of state-saving algorithms for match. The proposed architecture (using 256-1024 processors) also forms a distinct data point as far as the number of processors is concerned. It falls in between the multiprocessor architecture proposed in this thesis with 32-64 processors, and the DADO and NON-VON architectures with 10000 or more processors.

A possible problem with Oflazer's parallel algorithm is that potentially the state associated with a production may become extremely large. Such a production would then require an extremely large number of processors to update its state, or it will become a bottleneck. For example, consider the following production which locates blocks that are at height 6 from a table and prints the result.

157

```
(p blocks-at-height-6
    (on    ^block <a>    ^block table)
    (on    ^block <b>    ^block <a>)
    (on    ^block <c>    ^block <b>)
    (on    ^block <d>    ^block <c>)
    (on    ^block <e>    ^block <d>)
    (on    ^block <f>    ^block <e>)
-->
    (call print "block" <f> "is at height 6"))
```

Now suppose there are 100 blocks in the blocks world, and with each block there is the property "on ^block <x> ^block <y>", where this property is represented as a working-memory element. Thus there would be 100 working-memory elements matching CE-2 (condition element 2), and similarly 100 working-memory elements matching each of condition elements CE-3 through CE-6. Since Oflazer's algorithm stores state corresponding to all possible combinations of condition elements, consider the number of tokens that would be matching CE-2, CE-4, and CE-6 together. Since there are no common variables between these condition elements, the total number of tokens matching these condition elements together would be $100 \times 100 \times 100 = 1,000,000$. If a single new block is added to the system, the number of matching tokens would go to $101 \times 101 \times 101 = 1,030,031$, that is, about 30,000 new tokens would have to be processed.

Oflazer suggests a solution to the above problem by splitting such productions into two or several pieces, so that the combinations of condition elements for which the state is stored is controlled. For example, the above production may be split into the following two productions.

```
(p blocks-at-height-6-part-1
    (on    ^block <a>    ^block table)
    (on    ^block <b>    ^block <a>)
    (on    ^block <c>    ^block <b>)
-->
    (send-message blocks-at-height-6-part-2   ^vars <c>))

(p blocks-at-height-6-part-2
    (message ^vars <c>)
    (on    ^block <d>    ^block <c>)
    (on    ^block <e>    ^block <d>)
    (on    ^block <f>    ^block <e>)
-->
    (call print "block" <f> "is at height 6"))
```

While splitting the production into two parts reduces the number of tokens that are generated, it reintroduces some of the sequentiality in state processing, which is exactly what the algorithm was trying to avoid. The goodness of the proposed solution depends on the number of productions that have to be split, and the performance penalty they cause. Oflazer notes that for the XSEL system 42 productions had to be split and for the R1 system 22 productions had to be split. However, no clear numbers about the performance lost due to such splitting are available at this time.

Another drawback of Oflazer's algorithm is that it cannot exploit action parallelism, that is, it cannot easily process multiple changes to working memory in parallel. This is because (1) often the multiple changes to working memory affect the same set of productions, which requires that the instance elements for such productions respond to the effect of several changes to their slots, and (2) the algorithm requires that multiple changes to the slots of an instance element be processed sequentially. Since action parallelism is exploited very usefully by the implementation proposed in this thesis, not being able to exploit it is a significant disadvantage.

Finally, it is interesting to compare the performance of the proposed algorithm to that of the Rete algorithm. Oflazer's algorithm using about three hundred 5-10 MIPS 16-bit processors achieves 4500-7000 wme-changes/sec. The Rete algorithm on a 5 MIPS 32-bit uniprocessor can achieve a speed of 3000 wme-changes/sec. The reasons for the small amount of speed-up after using so many more processors appear to be: (1) The intrinsic parallelism in production systems is limited, so large amounts of speed-up cannot be expected. (2) The strategy of keeping large amounts of state for productions is not working, that is, while keeping large state is increasing the number of processors that is required, it is not at the same time helping in significantly reducing the variation in the processing times of productions. (3) There is significant overhead in the proposed parallel implementation, for example, the time taken to remove redundant instance elements, that nullifies much of the potential speed-up.

9.6. Honeywell's Data-Flow Model

Researchers at Honeywell CSC have also been exploring the use of parallelism for executing production-system programs [74]. They have proposed a tagged token data-flow computation model[86] for capturing the inherent parallelism present in OPS5 production systems. The proposed model is based on the Rete algorithm, and the key idea is to translate the Rete network into a data-flow graph that explicitly shows the data dependencies. Similarly, operations performed in the Rete algorithm are encapsulated into appropriate activities (or tasks) in the data-flow model, which can then be executed on the available physical processing resources. For example, consider the case when a token arriving at an and-node of the Rete network finds n

---

[86]A tagged token data-flow model is different from the conventional data-flow models. While there can be only one token present on an output arc in the conventional data-flow model, there can be multiple tokens present on the output arcs of the tagged token data-flow model.

tokens in the opposite memory node. In such a case, n activities would be generated in the proposed data-flow model — an activity each for testing the incoming token for consistent variable bindings with one of the n opposite memory tokens.

The paper [74] presents details about the kinds of nodes that are required in the data-flow graph and the functionality associated with those nodes. However, details about the hardware structure on which the proposed model is to be mapped, and how the necessary synchronization and scheduling is to be performed are not given in the paper. Since the size of the individual activities in the proposed data-flow model is very small (about 10 machine instructions or less), extremely efficient scheduling and synchronization methods will have to be developed if the approach is to be successful.

9.7. Other Work on Speeding-up Production Systems

In addition to the efforts mentioned above, which specifically address the issue of speeding up OPS production systems through parallelism, there are several other efforts [8, 50, 72, 75, 80, 92] going on to speed up production systems. Two of these, noted below, have been carried out within the PSM project and complement the work done in this thesis.

Jim Quinlan has done a comparative analysis of computer architectures for production-system machines [72]. He uses run-time measurements on production systems to evaluate the performance of five computer architectures (the VAX-11/780, the Berkeley RISC II computer, a custom designed microcoded machine for production systems, a custom RISC processor for production systems, and the Pyramid computer). His main conclusions are: (1) The custom designed microcoded machine is the best CPU architecture for production systems. Although it takes more machine cycles than the custom designed RISC processor, it has lower processor-memory bandwidth requirements. (2) The difference in the performance of the six architectures is not very large. As a result the motivation for building a custom processor is small.

Ted Lehr presents a custom pipelined RISC architecture for production-system execution [50]. The proposed architecture has a static branch prediction strategy, a large register file, and separate instruction and data fetch units. Since the proposed architecture is very simple, he also discusses the viability of implementing it in GaAs.

10 Summary and Conclusions

In this thesis we have explored the use of parallelism to speed up the execution of production-system programs. We have discussed the sources of parallelism available in OPS5 and Soar production systems, the design of a suitable parallel match-algorithm, the design of a suitable parallel architecture, and the implementation of the parallel match-algorithm on the parallel architecture. This chapter reiterates the main results of the thesis and discusses directions for future research.

10.1. Primary Results of Thesis

The study of parallelism in OPS5 and Soar production systems in this thesis leads us to make the following conclusions:

1. The Rete-class of algorithms is highly suitable for parallel implementation.

2. The amount of speed-up available from parallelism is quite limited, about 10-fold, in contrast to initial expectations of 100-fold to 1000-fold.

3. To obtain the limited speed-up that is available, it is necessary to exploit parallelism at a very fine granularity.

4. To exploit the suggested sources of parallelism, a multiprocessor architecture with 32-64 high-performance processors and special hardware support for scheduling the fine-grained tasks is desirable.

The above conclusions are expanded in the following subsections.

10.1.1. Suitability of the Rete-Class of Algorithms

The thesis empirically shows that the Rete-class of algorithms is highly suitable for parallel implementation of production systems. While Rete-class algorithms use significantly fewer processors than other proposed algorithms [38, 61, 70] (and in that sense are less concurrent[87]), simulations show that they perform better than these other algorithms.

---

[87]Statements about the amount of parallelism available in a class of programs can often be misleading. This is because it is always possible to construct parallel algorithms that can keep a very large numbers of processors busy without providing any significant speed-up over the known sequential algorithms. Thus simply talking about the average number of processors that are kept busy by a parallel algorithm is not very useful, at least not in isolation of the absolute speed-up over the best known sequential algorithms.

Some of the reasons for choosing and parallelizing the Rete class of algorithms are the following (see Section 2.4 for details). In designing a parallel algorithm, the first choice is between state-saving algorithms and non-state saving algorithms. State-saving algorithms are the obvious choice since only a very small fraction (less than 1%) of the global working-memory changes on each recognize-act cycle. Within the class of state-saving algorithms itself, however, many different algorithms can be designed, each storing different amounts of state. The Rete-class of algorithms store an intermediate amount of state (between the low extreme of the Treat algorithm [61] and the high extreme of Oflazer's parallel algorithm [70]). The state stored for a production in Rete corresponds to (1) matchings between individual condition elements and working-memory elements, and (2) matchings between some fixed combinations of condition elements occurring in the left-hand side of the production and tuples of working-memory elements. In algorithms like Treat, where the state stored is small, the disadvantage is that much of the information about partial matches with the unchanged part of the working memory has to be recomputed. In algorithms like Oflazer's parallel algorithm, where the state stored is large, the disadvantage is that a large amount of processing resources are wasted in computing partial matches that never reach the conflict-set.

We believe that the Rete class of algorithms avoids the disadvantages of both Treat and Oflazer's parallel algorithm. However, note that we do not wish to argue that the Rete class is the best class of parallel algorithms, but only that the Rete-class algorithms fall in an interesting part of the spectrum of state-saving algorithms. The suitability of Rete as a parallel algorithm is also based on its other features, for example, the discrimination net used for the selection-phase computation and the data-flow like nature of the overall computation graph. Finally, the claim for suitability of the Rete-class of algorithms for parallel implementation is based on the results of simulations, which show the execution speeds obtained by parallel Rete to be favorable compared to other proposed algorithms.

10.1.2. Parallelism in Production Systems

One of the main results of this thesis is that the speed-up obtainable from parallelism is quite limited, of the order of a few tens rather than of the order of few hundreds or thousands.[88] The initial expectations about the speed-up from parallelism for production-system programs were very high, especially for large programs. The general idea was that if match for each production is performed in parallel, then speed-up proportional to the number of productions in the program would be achieved [87]. This idea was quickly abandoned, as results from actual measurements on production systems were obtained (see Chapter 3 and [30, 31]). The reasons for the limited speed-up were found to be: (1) The number of productions that are affected as a result of a change to working memory is very small (about 26), and since affected productions take most of

---

[88]Note that the speed-up numbers in the following discussion are with respect to the sequential Rete algorithm, which is so far the fastest sequential algorithm for implementing production systems.

the processing time, assigning a processor to each production can result in only 26-fold speed-up. (2) The speed-up is actually much less than 26-fold, because there is a large variance in the processing requirements of the affected productions. In fact, using production parallelism in a straightforward manner was found to result in less than 5.1-fold nominal speed-up.[89] (3) Overheads due to loss of sharing in the Rete network and overheads due to the parallel implementation cause the real speed-up to be only 1.9-fold (a factor of 2.64 is lost). An attempt to increase the size of the affect-sets by processing all changes resulting from a production firing in parallel (use of action parallelism) results in a nominal speed-up of 7.6-fold, instead of the 5.1-fold achieved otherwise. The increase in speed-up is much smaller than the number of working-memory changes processed in parallel, because the affect-sets of the multiple changes overlap significantly.

Since the number of productions that are affected on each cycle is not controlled by the implementor of the production-system interpreter (it is governed mainly by the author of the program and the nature of the task), one solution to the problem of limited speed-up is to somehow decrease the variance in the processing required by the affected productions. This requires that the processing associated with an affected production be distributed amongst multiple processors by exploiting parallelism at a finer granularity. To achieve this end, the thesis proposes the use of node parallelism, that is, processing activations of distinct nodes in the Rete network in parallel. Using node parallelism and action parallelism results in a nominal speed-up of about 10.7-fold, as compared to 7.6-fold achieved for production and action parallelism. The overheads in this case are a factor of 1.98, so that the real speed-up is 5.4-fold. Studying the results in detail, two bottlenecks were found to be limiting the speed-up. These were (1) the cross-product effect and (2) the long-chain effect.

The cross-product effect refers to the case when an incoming token finds several matching tokens in the opposite memory node, and as a result of which a large number of tokens are sent to the successor of that node. Since multiple activations of any given node are processed sequentially when using node parallelism, the cross-product effect resulted in large processing times for some of the productions, thus reducing the speed-up obtained.

The long-chain effect refers to the occurrence of long chains of dependent node activations. Since these activations, as their name suggests, cannot be processed concurrently, they result in some productions taking much longer to finish than others, thus resulting in small speed-ups. The long-chain effect is especially bad for Soar systems, where the number of condition elements per production is larger than in OPS5 systems and as a result of which the networks for productions often contain long chains.

---

[89]*Nominal* speed-up or concurrency refers to the average number of processors that are busy in a parallel implementation. In contrast, the *real* speed-up refers to the speed-up with respect to the highest performance sequential algorithm.

As a solution to the problem of the cross-product effect, the thesis proposes the use of intra-node parallelism, where in addition to processing activations of different nodes in the Rete network in parallel, it is possible to process the relevant activations of the same node in parallel. Using intra-node and action parallelism it is possible to achieve 19.3-fold nominal speed-up, as compared to node and action parallelism where only 10.6-fold speed-up is achieved. The corresponding average execution speed on a multiprocessor with 2 MIPS processors is 11,250 wme-changes/sec. The nominal speed-up for individual systems actually varies between 12-fold for some OPS5 systems and 35-fold for some Soar systems, and the execution speed varies between 7000 wme-changes/sec and 17,000 wme-changes/sec.

As a solution to the problem of the long-chain effect, the thesis proposes using binary networks for productions rather than linear networks as used in the original Rete algorithm.[90] This way the maximum length of a chain can be reduced to the logarithm of the number of condition elements in a production. The average nominal speed-up obtained using binary networks and intra-node and action parallelism is 25.8-fold. The corresponding average execution speed achieved is 12,000 wme-changes/sec. Although the average nominal speed-up is significantly larger than the 19.3-fold achieved with linear networks, the execution speed is not much higher than the 11,250 wme-changes/sec achieved with linear networks. This is because, for many of the systems, using binary networks results in a larger number of node activations per change to working memory. Thus, even though the speed-up with respect to the uniprocessor implementation using binary networks is higher, the uniprocessor implementation using binary networks is slower than that using linear networks, so that not much is gained on the whole.

The speed-up for the individual systems when using binary networks varies between 11-fold and 56-fold. The benefits of using the binary networks are small (or sometimes even negative) for OPS5 systems since the average number of condition elements per production is small. The benefits for Soar systems are much larger since the average number of condition elements in Soar productions is much higher. Thus the decision whether or not to use binary networks should be made depending on the characteristics of the individual production systems. In fact, there is no reason not to have a mixture in the same program, that is, have some productions with linear networks, some productions with binary networks, and some productions with a mixture of linear and binary network forms. The overall aim is to minimize the state that is computed, while at the same time avoiding long chains. This job of selecting the network form for productions may be done by a programmer who understands the underlying implementation, or by a program which uses static and run-time information, or by some combination of the two.

---

[90]This corresponds to varying the fixed combinations of condition elements for which partial matches are stored by the Rete algorithm.

10.1.3. Software Implementation Issues

The thesis addresses a number of issues related to the correctness and the efficiency of the parallel Rete algorithm. Some of the issues discussed are: (1) the use of hashing for constant-test nodes at the top-level of the Rete network, (2) the lumping of multiple constant-test node activations when scheduling them on a processor, (3) the lumping of memory-nodes with the associated two-input nodes, (4) the use of hash tables to store tokens in memory nodes, (5) the set of concurrently processable activations of a node, (6) the processing of conjugate pairs of tokens, (7) the locks necessary for manipulating the contents of memory nodes, and (8) the use of binary networks versus linear networks. Although the details are not relevant here, the above features have considerable impact on the overheads that are imposed by the parallel implementation, and are consequently very important if a parallel implementation is to be successful.

10.1.4. Hardware Architecture

To implement the parallel Rete class of algorithms, as described in the previous paragraphs, the thesis proposes the use of a shared-memory multiprocessor architecture. The basic characteristics of the proposed architecture are: (1) Shared-memory multiprocessor with 32-64 processors. (2) The individual processors should be high performance computers, each with a cache and a small amount of private memory. (3) The processors should be connected to the shared memory via one or more shared buses. (4) The multiprocessor should support a hardware task scheduler to help enqueue node activations on the task queue and to assign pending tasks to idle processors.

The main reason for suggesting the shared-memory multiprocessor is a consequence of the fine granularity at which the parallelism is exploited by the parallel Rete algorithm. The parallel Rete algorithm requires that the data structures be shared amongst multiple concurrent processes, which makes it appropriate to use a shared-memory architecture. When used in conjunction with a centralized task queue, a shared-memory multiprocessor also makes it possible to bypass the load distribution problem. The reason for using only 32-64 processors is that simulations show that no additional speed-up is gained by using a larger number of processors. Since only a small number of processors are used, it is possible to use expensive high performance processors. Each processor should have a cache and some private memory to enable high speed of operation (to avoid the large latency to the shared memory), and also to reduce contention for the shared memory-modules and the shared bus.

The thesis recommends a bus-based architecture instead of an architecture based on a crossbar or other processor-memory interconnects because it is easier to construct intelligent cache-coherence schemes for shared buses and because simulations show that a single bus would be able to support the load generated by 32-64 processors (provided reasonable cache-hit ratios are obtained).[91] To avoid the problem of load distribution, the thesis suggests the use of a central-ized task queue containing all pending node activations. The task queue required for this job is quite complex since not all node activations in the task queue can be processed concurrently, in fact, the set of concurrently processable node activations changes dynamically (see Section 5.2.4 for details). Furthermore, since the average processing required by a node activation is only 50-100 instructions, it is necessary to have a mechanism whereby the node activations can be enqueued and dequeued extremely fast, so that the task queue does not become a bottleneck. The thesis proposes two mechanisms for solving the scheduling problem: the use of a hardware scheduler and the use of multiple software task queues. The proposed hardware task scheduler makes use of content-addressable memory to maintain a list of concurrently processable node activations, and is expected to perform at the bus-speed of the multiprocessor. The software task queues are studied as an alternative to building the custom hardware task scheduler. Simulations show that the performance when using multiple software task queues is about half of the performance when using the hardware task scheduler.

10.2. Some General Conclusions

Amongst Treat, Rete, and Oflazer's algorithm three very distinct points in the space of pos-sible state-saving match algorithms are covered. Alongside in the implementations of the above algorithms, three distinct points in the architecture space have also been covered — small-scale parallel architectures like a 32-node multiprocessor, medium-scale parallel architectures like Oflazer's 512 processor parallel machine, and highly parallel architectures like DADO and NON-VON with tens of thousands of processors. In terms of performance, Treat on DADO is expected to execute at a rate of about 215 wme-changes/sec, assuming sixteen thousand 0.5 MIPS node processors [61]; Rete on NON-VON is expected to execute at about 2000 wme-changes/sec, assuming thirty-two 3 MIPS large processing elements and sixteen thousand 3 MIPS small processing elements [38]; Oflazer's algorithm is expected to execute at about 4750-7000 wme-changes/sec, assuming five-hundred-and-twelve 5-10 MIPS custom processors [70]; Rete on a single 2 MIPS processor is expected to execute at about 1200 wme-changes/sec; and Rete on the production-system machine proposed in this thesis is expected to execute at 11000 wme-changes/sec, assuming thirty-two node multiprocessor using 2 MIPS processors.[92]

---

[91]Many of the the design recommendations made in the thesis are highly technology dependent. Future advances in the processor technology and the interconnection-network technology may make it necessary to reevaluate the recommendations.

[92]No attempt has been made to normalize the speeds of the processors used in the architectures discussed above. For example, the speed of production-system execution on the DADO machine is given when processors have 8-bit wide datapaths and execute at 0.5 MIPS (as described in the original paper), and not when the processors have 32-bit datapaths and execute at 2 MIPS. This is because the overall effect on the feasibility of the different architectures is very different when individual processors are speeded up. For example, in Oflazer's machine, 5 MIPS processors are fine because they work out of their local memory. Using 5 MIPS processors for the PSM may, however, cause problems since the shared bus would become a bottleneck. The reader may, however, wish to do some such normalization (based on architectural feasibility) to gain more comparability.

The first general conclusion that can be derived from the relative comparison of various algorithms and architectures discussed above is that the speed-up over the best existing sequential algorithm by any of the parallel implementations is small, and this is irrespective of the type of algorithm or architecture being used. Thus the answer to the question "Is it the sequentiality of the Rete algorithm that is blocking the speed-up from the use of parallelism?" is most probably no, because other algorithms at both ends of the state-saving spectrum have not shown any better results. Thus it appears that it is not the Rete algorithm, or the Treat algorithm, or Oflazer's algorithm that is preventing the use of parallelism, but it is the inherent nature of the computation involved in implementing production systems that prevents significant speed-up from parallelism.

Another conclusion that we can draw is that while massively parallel architectures like DADO and NON-VON may be *effective* for the task of executing production systems, that is, they can execute production systems at reasonably high speeds, the approach of using a small number of tightly-coupled high-performance processors with the migration of critical functionality to special purpose hardware seems to be *preferred*.

Since the results in this thesis are based on the analysis of existing programs, an interesting question to ask is: "Are existing production-system programs not able to exploit parallelism because they were not written with parallel implementations in mind, or alternatively, will future production-system programs when written with parallel implementations in mind be able to exploit more parallelism?" The answer is undoubtedly yes, but probably to a limited extent only. We believe that while additional factors of two, four, or eight are very probable, it is doubtful that additional factors of fifty, a hundred, or more will be obtained in the future. There are reasons to believe that the two main factors limiting the speed-up (the small number of affected productions per cycle and the small number of changes to working memory per cycle) will not change significantly in the near future, and maybe not even in the long run (see Section 4.7 for more details).[93] On the positive side, however, the techniques that have been developed in this thesis will still be applicable to the new class of systems, the only difference being that the speed-up will be larger.

10.3. Directions for Future Research

Although many issues regarding the use of parallelism in implementing production systems have been addressed in this thesis, many more remain to be addressed. This section discusses some such issues.

In the area of design of algorithms and architectures it is extremely useful to have a generally

---

[93]There may be exceptions to the above claims for special classes of programs, for example, production-system programs working on low-level vision. But for a large majority of tasks in Artificial Intelligence they are expected to be true.

accepted set of benchmark programs that can be used by all researchers. At this point there are no such established benchmarks for production-system programs and as a result one often ends up comparing apples to oranges. The PSM group at Carnegie-Mellon University is beginning an effort to assemble such a set of programs.[94] When selecting such a set of programs it is necessary to ensure that there is sufficient variability in them, so that the proposed algorithms and architectures can be tested along various dimensions. For example, there should be programs that are knowledge-search intensive, those that are problem-space search intensive, those with small and those with large working memory, those with small and those with large production memory, and so on. The final success of such an effort, of course, would be established only if the selected set of benchmark programs is adopted by the rest of the research community and used to evaluate many architectures.

A criticism that has often been cited for the current work being done in parallel implementations of production systems is that, existing programs were written with sequential implementations in mind, and that they do not reflect the true parallelism which is to be found in programs written with parallel implementations in mind [41, 89]. As stated a few paragraphs earlier, while we believe that small factors of two or four may be achieved in such a way, factors of fifty or hundred will not be achieved. However, factors of two or four are not small enough to be ignored, and much work needs to be done in developing production-system formalisms that permit more explicit expression of parallelism (for example, the Herbal language being developed at Columbia University), or those that implicitly allow much more parallelism to be used (for example, the Soar formalism as compared to the OPS5 formalism).

An obvious direction for further work is to implement the ideas proposed in this thesis on an actual multiprocessor. Such an implementation will bring many interesting issues to light, and a running parallel implementation will certainly encourage production-system programmers to adapt their styles to make better use of the parallelism. Such an implementation is currently underway by the PSM group. The thesis does not explore the issue of using multiple software task schedulers in a very comprehensive way, and additional work is needed to help clarify the trade-offs involved. Another interesting task would be to build a program that uses static and run-time information to decide on the network forms (linear, binary, or some mixture) for the productions [86]. The criteria of goodness for such a program is that it should minimize the total amount of state computed on every cycle, while avoiding the occurrence of long chains of dependent node activations.

Another interesting direction for future work is to analyze the relative merits of different AI programming languages. To be more specific, with the start of the Japanese Fifth Generation Computing Project [24], the language Prolog has gained very wide usage [13, 81]. Prolog has

---

[94]The collection of programs that we have been using in our experiments represents a start, but it is still inadequate in various ways. For example, most of the programs are too large to be recoded in other related languages, and many programs are of a proprietary nature and cannot be shipped outside of CMU.

also been put forward as a language for building expert systems, and it has been claimed that massive amounts of parallelism can be used in its implementations [12, 27, 51, 64, 91]. It would be interesting to implement a common set of tasks using Prolog, OPS5, Soar, Multilisp, Actors, and other such languages [1, 15, 25, 36, 60, 67, 96], and see the amount of parallelism that each of the formalisms permits, and the absolute performance that can be achieved by each of them.

References

[1]   Gul Agha and Carl Hewitt.
        Concurrent Programming Using Actors: Exploiting Large-Scale Parallelism.
        A.I. Memo 865, Massachusetts Institute of Technology, October, 1985.

[2]   J.R. Anderson.
        The Architecture of Cognition.
        Harvard University Press, 1983.

[3]   Mario R. Barbacci.
        An Introduction to ISPS.
        In Daniel P. Siewiorek, C. Gordon Bell, and Allen Newell (editor), *Computer Science*:
            Computer Structures: Principles and Examples, chapter 4. McGraw-Hill, 1982.

[4]   Avron Barr and Edward A. Feigenbaum.
        The Handbook of Artificial Intelligence, Volume 1.
        William Kaufmann, Inc., 1981.

[5]   Forest Baskett and Alan Jay Smith.
        Interference in Multiprocessor Computer Systems with Interleaved Memory.
        Communications of the ACM 19(6), June, 1976.

[6]   D. P. Bhandarkar.
        Analysis of Memory Interference in Multiprocessors.
        IEEE Transactions on Computers C-24(9), September, 1975.

[7]   W. J. Bouknight, Stewart A. Denenberg, David E. McIntyre, J.M. Randall, Amed
        H. Sameh, and Daniel L. Slotnick.
        The Illiac IV System.
        Proceedings of the IEEE , April, 1972.

[8]   Ruven Brooks and Rosalyn Lum.
        Yes, An SIMD Machine Can Be Used For AI.
        In *International Joint Conference on Artificial Intelligence*. 1985.

[9]   George Broomell and J. Robert Heath.
        Classification Categories and Historical Development of Circuit Switching Topologies.
        Computing Surveys 15(2):95-133, June, 1983.

[10]   Lee Brownston, Robert Farrell, Elaine Kant, and Nancy Martin.
        Programming Expert Systems in OPS5: An Introduction to Rule-Based Programming.
        Addison-Wesley, 1985.

[11]   B.G. Buchanan and E.A. Feigenbaum.
         DENDRAL and Meta-DENDRAL: Their Applications Dimensions.
         Artificial Intelligence 11(1,2), 1978.

[12]   Yaohan Chu and Kozo Itano.
         Organization of a Parallel Prolog Machine.
         In *International Workshop on High-Level Computer Architecture*. 1984.

[13]   W.F. Clocksin and C.S. Mellish.
         Programming in Prolog.
         Springer-Verlag, 1981.

[14]   R.O. Duda, J.G. Gaschnig, and P.E. Hart.
         Model Design in the PROSPECTOR Consultant System for Mineral Exploration.
         In D. Michie (editor), *Expert Systems in the Micro-Electronic Age*. Edinburgh University
             Press, Edinburgh, 1979.

[15]   J. Fain, F. Hayes-Roth, S.J. Rosenschein, H. Sowizral, and D. Waterman.
         The ROSIE Language Reference Manual.
         Technical Report N-1647-ARPA, Rand Corporation, 1981.

[16]   Richard D. Fennell and Victor R. Lesser.
         Parallelism in Artificial Intelligence Problem Solving: A Case Study of Hearsay II.
         IEEE Transactions on Computers C-26(2), February, 1977.

[17]   Charles L. Forgy.
         On the Efficient Implementations of Production Systems.
         PhD thesis, Carnegie-Mellon University, Pittsburgh, 1979.

[18]   Charles L. Forgy.
         Note on Production Systems and ILLIAC-IV.
         Technical Report CMU-CS-80-130, Carnegie-Mellon University, Pittsburgh, 1980.

[19]   Charles L. Forgy.
         OPS5 User's Manual.
         Technical Report CMU-CS-81-135, Carnegie-Mellon University, Pittsburgh, 1981.

[20]   Charles L. Forgy.
         Rete: A Fast Algorithm for the Many Pattern/Many Object Pattern Match Problem.
         Artificial Intelligence 19, September, 1982.

[21]   Charles L. Forgy.
         The OPS83 Report.
         Technical Report CMU-CS-84-133, Carnegie-Mellon University, Pittsburgh, May, 1984.

[22]   Charles Forgy, Anoop Gupta, Allen Newell, and Robert Wedig.
         Initial Assessment of Architectures for Production Systems.
         In *National Conference for Artificial Intelligence*. AAAI-1984.

[23]   Charles Forgy and Anoop Gupta.
         Preliminary Architecture of the CMU Production System Machine.
         In *Hawaii International Conference on System Sciences*. January, 1986.

[24] Kazuhiro Fuchi.
Revisiting Original Philosophy of Fifth Generation Computer Systems Project.
In *International Conference on Fifth Generation Computer Systems*. ICOT, 1984.

[25] Richard P. Gabriel and John McCarthy.
Queue-based Multi-processing Lisp.
In *ACM Symposium on Lisp and Functional Programming*. ACM, 1984.

[26] Michael R. Garey and David S. Johnson.
Computers and Intractability: A Guide to the Theory of NP-Completeness.
W. H. Freeman and Company, 1979.

[27] Atsuhiro Goto, Hidehiko Tanaka, and Tohru Moto-oka.
Highly Parallel Inference Engine -- Goal Rewriting Model and Machine Architecture.
New Generation Computing 2:37-58, 1984.

[28] A. Gottileb, R. Grishman, C.P. Kruskal, K.P. McAuliffe, L. Rudolph, and M. Snir.
The NYU Ultracomputer -- Designing a MIMD Shared-memory Parallel Machine.
In *The 9th Annual Symposium on Computer Architecture*. IEEE and ACM, 1982.

[29] J.H. Griesmer, S.J. Hong, M. Karnaugh, J.K. Kastner, M.I. Schor, R.L. Ennis, D.A. Klein, K.R. Milliken, H.M. VanWoerkom.
YES/MVS: A Continuous Real Time Expert System.
In *National Conference on Artificial Intelligence*. AAAI-1984.

[30] Anoop Gupta and Charles L. Forgy.
Measurements on Production Systems.
Technical Report CMU-CS-83-167, Carnegie-Mellon University, Pittsburgh, 1983.

[31] Anoop Gupta.
Implementing OPS5 Production Systems on DADO.
In *International Conference on Parallel Processing*. IEEE, 1984.

[32] Anoop Gupta.
Parallelism in Production Systems: The Sources and the Expected Speed-up.
Technical Report CMU-CS-84-169, Carnegie-Mellon University, Pittsburgh, 1984.
Also in Proceedings of *Fifth International Workshop on Expert Systems and Applications*, Avignon, France, May 1985.

[33] Anoop Gupta, Charles Forgy, Allen Newell, and Robert Wedig.
Parallel Algorithms and Architectures for Production Systems.
In *13th International Symposium on Computer Architecture*. June, 1986.

[34] Anoop Gupta, Charles Forgy, Dirk Kalp, Allen Newell, and Milind Tambe.
Results of Parallel Implementation of OPS5 on the Encore Multiprocessor.
Technical Report, Carnegie-Mellon University, Pittsburgh, 1987.
In preparation.

[35] P. Haley, J. Kowalski, J. McDermott, and R. McWhorter.
PTRANS: A Rule-Based Management Assistant.
Technical Report, Carnegie-Mellon University, Pittsburgh, 1983.

[36] Robert H. Halstead, Jr.
      Multilisp: A Language for Concurrent Symbolic Computation.
      ACM Transactions on Programming Language and Systems 7(4):501-538, October,
          1985.

[37] J.L. Hennessy, N. Jouppi, S. Przybylski, C. Rowen, and T. Gross.
      The MIPS Machine.
      In *Computer Conference.* February, 1982.

[38] Bruce K. Hillyer and David E. Shaw.
      Execution of OPS5 Production Systems on a Massively Parallel Machine.
      Technical Report, Columbia University, September, 1984.

[39] Keki B. Irani and Ibrahim H. Onyuksel.
      A Closed-Form Solution for the Performance Analysis of Multiple-Bus Multiprocessor
          Systems.
      IEEE Transactions on Computers C-33(11), November, 1984.

[40] Gary Kahn and John McDermott.
      The MUD System.
      In *First Conference on Artificial Intelligence Applications.* IEEE Computer Society and
          AAAI, December, 1984.

[41] Dennis F. Kibler and John Conery.
      Parallelism in AI Programs.
      In *International Joint Conference on Artificial Intelligence.* 1985.

[42] Jin Kim, John McDermott, and Daniel Siewiorek.
      TALIB: A Knowledge-Based System for IC Layout Design.
      In *National Conference on Artificial Intelligence.* AAAI-1983.

[43] Ted Kowalski and Don Thomas.
      The VLSI Design Automation Assistant: Prototype System.
      In *20th Design Automation Conference.* ACM and IEEE, June, 1983.

[44] Ted Kowalski.
      The VLSI Design Automation Assistant: A Knowledge-Based Expert System.
      PhD thesis, Carnegie-Mellon University, April, 1984.

[45] John E. Laird.
      Universal Subgoaling.
      PhD thesis, Carnegie-Mellon University, Pittsburgh, December, 1983.

[46] John E. Laird and Allen Newell.
      A Universal Weak Method: Summary of Results.
      In *International Joint Conference on Artificial Intelligence.* 1983.

[47] John E. Laird and Allen Newell.
      A Universal Weak Method.
      Technical Report CMU-CS-83-141, Carnegie-Mellon University, Pittsburgh, June, 1983.

[48] John E. Laird, Paul S. Rosenbloom, and Allen Newell.
      Towards Chunking as a General Learning Mechanism.
      In *National Conference on Artificial Intelligence.* AAAI-1984.

[49]   John E. Laird.
Soar User's Manual
4th edition, Xerox PARC, 1986.

[50]   Theodore F. Lehr.
The Implementation of a Production System Machine.
Master's thesis, Department of Electrical and Computer Engineering, Carnegie-Mellon
      University, 1985.

[51]   G.J. Lipovski and M.V. Hermenegildo.
B-LOG: A Branch and Bound Methodology for the Parallel Execution of Logic
      Programs.
In *International Conference on Parallel Processing*. IEEE, 1985.

[52]   Sandra Marcus, John McDermott, Robert Roche, Tim Thompson, Tianran Wang, and
George Wood.
Design Document for VT.
1984.
Carnegie-Mellon University.

[53]   M. A. Marsan.
Bounds on Bus and Memory Interference in a Class of Multiple-Bus Multiprocessor Sys-
      tems.
In *Third International Conference on Distributed Computer Systems*. October, 1982.

[54]   Henry H. Mashburn.
The C.mmp/Hydra Project: An Architectural Overview.
In Daniel P. Siewiorek, C. Gordon Bell, and Allen Newell (editor), *Computer Struc-
      tures: Principles and Examples*. McGraw-Hill, 1982.

[55]   Donald McCracken.
A Production System Version of the Hearsay-II Speech Understanding System.
PhD thesis, Carnegie-Mellon University, Pittsburgh, 1978.

[56]   John McDermott.
R1: A Rule-based Configurer of Computer Systems.
Technical Report CMU-CS-80-119, Carnegie-Mellon University, Pittsburgh, April,
      1980.

[57]   John McDermott.
XSEL: A Computer Salesperson's Assistant.
In J.E. Hayes, D. Michie, and Y.H. Pao (editor), *Machine Intelligence*. Horwood, 1982.

[58]   John McDermott.
R1: A Rule-Based Configurer of Computer Systems.
Artificial Intelligence 19(1):39-88, 1982.

[59]   John McDermott.
Extracting Knowledge from Expert Systems.
In *International Joint Conference on Artificial Intelligence*. 1983.

[60]   W. Van Melle, A.C. Scott, J.S. Bennett, and M. Peairs.
The Emycin Manual.
Technical Report STAN-CS-81-885, Stanford University, October, 1981.

[61] Daniel P. Miranker.
      Performance Estimates for the DADO Machine: A Comparison of Treat and Rete.
      In *Fifth Generation Computer Systems*. ICOT, Tokyo, 1984.

[62] Daniel P. Miranker.
      Treat: A Better Match Algorithm for AI Production Systems.
      In *National Conference on Artificial Intelligence*. AAAI-1987.

[63] Daniel P. Miranker.
      Treat: A New and Efficient Match Algorithm for AI Production Systems.
      PhD thesis, Columbia University, New York, 1987.

[64] Tohru Moto-oka, Hidehiko Tanaka, Hitoshi Aida, Keiji Hirata, and Tsutomu Maruyama.
      The Architecture of a Parallel Inference Engine -- PIE --.
      In *International Conference on Fifth Generation Computer Systems*. ICOT, 1984.

[65] Allen Newell and Herbert A. Simon.
      Human Problem Solving.
      Prentice-Hall, 1972.

[66] Allen Newell.
      HARPY, Production Systems and Human Cognition.
      Technical Report CMU-CS-78-140, Carnegie-Mellon University, Pittsburgh, September,
      1978.

[67] H.P. Nii and N. Aiello.
      AGE(Attempt to Generalize): A Knowledge-Based Program for Building Knowledge-
      Based Programs.
      In *International Joint Conference on Artificial Intelligence*. 1979.

[68] Nils J. Nilsson.
      Computer Science Series: Problem-Solving Methods in Artificial Intelligence.
      McGraw-Hill, New York, 1971.

[69] Kemal Oflazer.
      Parallel Execution of Production Systems.
      In *International Conference on Parallel Processing*. IEEE, August, 1984.

[70] Kemal Oflazer.
      Partitioning in Parallel Processing of Production Systems.
      PhD thesis, Carnegie-Mellon University, (in preparation), 1986.

[71] D.A. Patterson and C.H. Sequin.
      A VLSI RISC.
      Computer 9, 1982.

[72] James E. Quinlan.
      A Comparative Analysis of Computer Architectures for Production System Machines.
      Master's thesis, Department of Electrical and Computer Engineering, Carnegie-Mellon
      University, 1985.

[73] G. Radin.
      The 801 Minicomputer.
      IBM Journal of Research and Development 27, May, 1983.

[74]   Raja Ramnarayan.
         A Tagged Token Data Flow Computation Model for OPS5 Production Systems.
         1984.
         Working Draft, Honeywell CSC, Bloomington, MN.

[75]   Bruce Reed, Jr.
         The ASPRO Parallel Inference Engine (P.I.E.): A Real Time Production Rule System.
         1985.
         Goodyear Aerospace.

[76]   Paul S. Rosenbloom.
         The Chunking of Goal Hierarchies: A Model of Stimulus-Response Compatibility.
         PhD thesis, Carnegie-Mellon University, Pittsburgh, August, 1983.

[77]   Paul S. Rosenbloom, John E. Laird, John McDermott, Allen Newell, and Edmund Or-
         ciuch.
         R1-Soar: An Experiment in Knowledge-Intensive Programming in a Problem-Solving
             Architecture.
         In *IEEE Workshop on Principles of Knowledge Based Systems*. 1984.

[78]   Paul S. Rosenbloom, John E. Laird, Allen Newell, Andrew Golding, and Amy Unruh.
         Current Research on Learning in Soar.
         In *International Workshop on Machine Learning*. 1985.

[79]   Larry Rudolph and Zary Segall.
         Dynamic Decentralized Cache Schemes for MIMD Parallel Processors.
         In *International Symposium on Computer Architecture*. 1984.

[80]   Mike Rychener, Joe Kownacki, and Zary Segall.
         Parallel Production Systems: OPS3.
         Cm*: An Experiment in Multiprocessing.
         Digital Press, 1986.

[81]   Ehud Y. Shapiro.
         A Subset of Concurrent Prolog and Its Interpreter.
         Technical Report, ICOT -- Institute for New Generation Computer Technology,
             February, 1983.

[82]   David Elliot Shaw.
         The NON-VON Supercomputer.
         Technical Report, Columbia University, New York, August, 1982.

[83]   David Elliot Shaw.
         On the Range of Applicability of an Artificial Intelligence Machine.
         Technical Report, Columbia University, January, 1985.

[84]   E. H. Shortliffe.
         Computer-Based Medical Consultations: MYCIN.
         North-Holland, 1976.

[85]   Herbert A. Simon.
         The Architecture of Complexity.
         The Sciences of the Artificial.
         MIT Press, 1981, Chapter 7.

[86] David E. Smith and Michael R. Genesereth.
      Ordering Conjunctive Queries.
      Artificial Intelligence 26(2):171-215, 1985.

[87] Salvatore J. Stolfo and David E. Shaw.
      DADO: A Tree-Structured Machine Architecture for Production Systems.
      In *National Conference on Artificial Intelligence*. AAAI-1982.

[88] Salvatore J. Stolfo, Daniel Miranker, and David E. Shaw.
      Architecture and Applications of DADO: A Large-Scale Parallel Computer for Artificial
          Intelligence.
      In *International Joint Conference on Artificial Intelligence*. 1983.

[89] Salvatore J. Stolfo.
      Five Parallel Algorithms for Production System Execution on the DADO Machine.
      In *National Conference on Artificial Intelligence*. AAAI-1984.

[90] S.N. Talukdar, E. Cardozo, L. Leao, R. Banares, and R. Joobbani.
      A System for Distributed Problem Solving.
      In *Workshop on Coupling Symbolic and Numerical Computing in Expert Systems*.
          August, 1985.

[91] Stephen Taylor, Christopher Maio, Salvatore J. Stolfo, and David E. Shaw.
      *PROLOG on the DADO Machine: A Parallel System for High-Speed Logic
          Programming*.
      Technical Report, Columbia University, New York, January, 1983.

[92] M.F.M. Tenorio and D.I. Moldovan.
      Mapping Production Systems into Multiprocessors.
      In *International Conference on Parallel Processing*. IEEE, 1985.

[93] Jeffrey D. Ullman.
      Principles of Database Systems.
      Computer Science Press, 1982.

[94] Shinji Umeyama and Koichiro Tamura.
      A Parallel Execution Model of Logic Programs.
      In *The 10th Annual International Symposium on Computer Architecture*. IEEE and
          ACM, June, 1983.

[95] D.A. Waterman and Frederick Hayes-Roth.
      Pattern-Directed Inference Systems.
      Academic Press, 1978.

[96] S.M. Weiss and C.A. Kulikowski.
      EXPERT: A System for Developing Consultation Models.
      In *International Joint Conference on Artificial Intelligence*. 1979.

Appendix A   ISP of Processor Used in Parallel Implementation

```
! This is an ISPS description [3] of the architecture of the individual
! processors used in the PSM.  The cost models used in the simulator are
! based on this description.  The instruction-set is designed so that
! the instructions may be partitioned into a small number of classes, with
! the cost of executing all instructions within a class being the same.
! For example, almost all instructions make either 0 or 1 memory reference.
! There are only a very small number of instructions that need more memory
! references and they are treated specially when computing the cost models
! for the simulator.


**PC.State**

R[0:31]<0:31>,              ! General Purpose Registers
IR<0:31>,                   ! Instruction Register
PSW<0:31>,                  ! Prog Status Word and Cond Code Register
PREFIX<0:31>,               ! Prefix Register

PC      := R[31],           ! Program Counter
SP      := R[30],           ! System Stack Pointer
Link    := R[29],           ! System Link Register
Zero    := R[28];           ! Zero Register

Z<>     := PSW<0>,          ! zero
V<>     := PSW<1>,          ! overflow
N<>     := PSW<2>,          ! negative
C<>     := PSW<3>,          ! carry bit

**Instruction.Register.Fields**
opcode<0:5>     := IR<26:31>,   ! opcode
type<0:1>       := IR<24:25>,   ! type of operands, eg., byte, word,..
rd<0:4>         := IR<19:23>,   ! destination register for instruction
mode<0:1>       := IR<17:18>,   ! used in instruction interpretation
rs<0:4>         := IR<12:16>,   ! source register for instruction
rx<0:4>         := IR<12:16>,   ! index register/ base register

r1<0:4> := IR<19:23>,           ! first reg specified by instruction
r2<0:4> := IR<12:16>,           ! second reg specified by instruction
r3<0:4> := IR<7:11>,            ! third reg specified by instruction

xd<0:4>                 := IR<19:23>,   ! 5 bit  signed/unsigned constant
```

```
xs<0:4>                := IR<12:16>,   ! 5 bit  signed/unsigned constant
disp/const<0:6>        := IR<0:6>,     ! 7 bit displacement or constant
ldisp/lconst<0:11>     := IR<0:11>,    ! 12 bit displacement or constant
lldisp/llconst<0:16>   := IR<0:16>,    ! 17 bit displacement or constant
llldisp/lllconst<0:23> := IR<0:23>,    ! 24 bit displacement or constant
```

! Note: The difference between constants and displacements is that, the
! displacements are shifted by the type (byte/word/long/..) of the instr.,
! while constants are not affected by the type of the instruction. All
! constants may be signed or unsigned as relevant in the context of the
! instruction. For example, if the constant is used to specify a bit
! within a word, it will be unsigned.

```
|------------------------------------------------------------------------|
|                                         |  r3 |      disp/const        |
|                                         |-----|------------------------|
|                                         |  5  |           7            |
|                                         |                              |
|                               |r2/rs/rx|        ldisp/lconst           |
|                               |--------|------------------------------|
|                               |   5    |             12               |
|                               |                                       |
| opcode | type |r1/rd/xd|mode/xs|          lldisp/llconst               |
|--------|------|--------|-------|--------------------------------------|
|   6       2   |   5       2                    17                      |
|               |                      llldisp/lllconst                 |
|               |-----------------------------------------------------  |
|                                     24                                 |
|                                                                        |
|                          INSTRUCTION REGISTER                          |
|------------------------------------------------------------------------|
31                                                                      0
```

Instructions-Set

Arithmetic & Logical Instructions

! The arithmetic and logical instructions exist in both two-operand and
! three-operand formats. For each instruction the variants which deal
! with the three primitive data types (byte, word, longword) also exist.
! Thus to determine the type of the instruction:
```
  DECODE type<0:1> =>
    begin
      00: type = byte;
      01: type = word;
      10: type = longword;
      11: type is part of opcode. (instructions that do not need type bits)
    end
```

! Instructions in the two-operand form.
! instr   Args   Mode   Interpretation

```
! -----      ----            ----          ----------------
   add2     llconst,rd       00            rd <-- rd + llconst
            rs,rd            01            rd <-- rd + rs
            (rx)ldisp,rd     10            rd <-- rd + M[rx + ldisp]
            (rx)r3,rd        11            rd <-- rd + M[rx + r3]
! Note, when mode = 11, the contents of r3 are shifted according to the
! type of the instruction, just like any other displacement.  Other instr.
! with the same format are:
   addc2                    ! add with carry
   sub2                     ! subtract
   subc2                    ! subtract with carry
   and2                     ! logical and
   or2                      ! logical or
   xor2                     ! logical xor


! Instructions in the three-operand form.
! instr    Args             Mode          Interpretation
! -----    ----             ----          ----------------
   add3     rs,r3,rd         00            rd <-- rs + r3
            rs,lconst,rd     01            rd <-- rs + lconst
            rs,(r3)disp,rd   10            rd <-- rs + M[r3 + disp]
            xs,(r3)disp,rd   11            rd <-- xs + M[r3 + disp]
! Other instructions with the same format are:
   addc3                    ! add with carry
   sub3                     ! subtract
   subc3                    ! subtract with carry
   and3                     ! logical and
   or3                      ! logical or
   xor3                     ! logical xor


** Shift Instructions **

! instr    Args             Mode          Interpretation
! -----    ----             ----          ----------------
   shl      rs,r3,rd         00            rd <-- r3 shifted-by rs
            xs,r3,rd         01            rd <-- r3 shifted-by xs
            xs,(r3)disp,rd   10            rd <-- M[r3 + disp] shifted-by xs
! Other related instructions with the same format are:
   shr                      ! shift right
   shra                     ! shift right arithmetic


** Bit-Field Extract/Insert Instructions **

! The following two instructions do not make use of the type bits.  The
! modes 10 and 11 are also not used.  The reason is that pos and siz fields
! take up the bits that would be needed to specify a useful memory address.
pos<0:4>         := IR<7:11>,
siz<0:4>         := IR<0:4>,

! instr    Args             Mode          Interpretation
```

```
! -----     ----          ----         ---------------
   bfx     rs,pos,siz,rd   00          rd<0,siz-1> <-- rs<pos,pos+siz-1>
           xs,pos,siz,rd   01          rd<0,siz-1> <-- xs<pos,pos+siz-1>
   bfi     rs,pos,siz,rd   00          rd<pos,pos+siz-1> <-- rs<0,siz-1>
           xs,pos,siz,rd   01          rd<pos,pos+siz-1> <-- xs<0,siz-1>
```

** Load/Store Instructions **

```
! Note:  The instructions ld (load) and st (store) are special, in that
! these two instructions also have a quad-word type (type = 11).  The
! quad-word type is necessary to accommodate the hardware task scheduler.

! instr    Args            Mode         Interpretation
! -----    ----            ----         ---------------
   ld      llconst,rd      00          rd <-- llconst
           rs,rd           01          rd <-- rs
           (rx)ldisp,rd    10          rd <-- M[rx + ldisp]
           (rx)r3,rd       11          rd <-- M[rx + r3]

   st      xd,(rx)ldisp    00          M[rx + ldisp] <-- xd
           xd,(rx)r3       01          M[rx + r3]    <-- xd
           r1,(rx)ldisp    10          M[rx + ldisp] <-- r1
           r1,(rx)r3       11          M[rx + r3]    <-- r1

   lda     (rx)ldisp,rd    10          rd <-- rx + ldisp (shifted by type)
           (rx)r3,rd       11          rd <-- rx + r3 (shifted by type)

   ldpi    const:IR<0:25>  --          PREFIX<0:25> <-- IR<0:25>

! lda:  is the load-address instruction.
! ldpi: is the load-prefix instruction.  The bits IR<0:5> of the following
! instruction are combined with with PREFIX<0:25> to form a 32 bit
! displacement or constant, the number being PREFIX<0:25>:IR<0:5>.
```

** Push/Pop Instructions **

```
! instr    Args            Mode         Interpretation
! -----    ----            ----         ---------------
   push    llconst,rd      00          (rd)++; M[rd] <-- llconst
           rs,rd           01          (rd)++; M[rd] <-- rs
           (rx)ldisp,rd    10          (rd)++; M[rd] <-- M[rx + ldisp]
           (rx)r3,rd       11          (rd)++; M[rd] <-- M[rx + r3]

   pusha   (rx)ldisp,rd    10          (rd)++; M[rd] <-- rx + ldisp;
           (rx)r3,rd       11          (rd)++; M[rd] <-- rx + r3;

   pop     rs,rd           --          rd <-- M[rs]; (rs)--;
```

** Subroutine Linkage Instructions **

```
! instr     Args           Mode    Interpretation
! -----     ----           ----    ---------------
  brlink    r1,lldisp      00      Link <-- PC; PC <-- r1 + lldisp;
            r1,r2          01      Link <-- PC; PC <-- r1 + r2;

  brlinki   (r1)lldisp     00      Link <-- PC; PC <-- M[r1 + lldisp];
            (r1)r2         01      Link <-- PC; PC <-- M[r1 + r2];

  jsb       r1,lldisp      00      (SP)++; M[SP] <-- PC; PC <-- r1 + lldisp;
            r1,r2          01      (SP)++; M[SP] <-- PC; PC <-- r1 + r2;

  bsb       llldisp        --      (SP)++; M[SP] <-- PC; PC <-- PC + llldisp;

  rsb       --             --      PC <-- M[SP]; (SP)--;
```

! NOTE: The brlinki (branch-link-indirect) instruction is especially useful
! when code for the various nodes in the Rete network is shared. For
! example, it can be used to branch to one of several MakeToken routines
! depending on the size of the token.

** Comparison and Control Flow Instructions **

! There are four types of instructions in this category: compare (cmp),
! branch (br), compare-and-branch (cb), and jump (jmp). The compare
! instructions set the Z, V, N, C, bits in the PSW. The branch instruction
! can then jump of some combination of these bits in the PSW.

```
! instr     Args           Mode    Interpretation
! -----     ----           ----    ---------------
  cmp       r1, llconst    00      compare(r1, llconst)
            r1, r2         01      compare(r1, r2)
            r1, (rx)ldisp  10      compare(r1, M[rx + ldisp])
            r1, (rx)r3     11      compare(r1, M[rx + r3])


  br        llldisp        --      PC <-- PC + llldisp
  br_xx     llldisp        --      if xx(N,Z,V,C) then PC <-- PC + llldisp
! where xx = z, nz, ovf, neg, eq, neq, lt, gt, le, ge


  cb_xx     r1,r2,ldisp    00      if xx(r1, r2)      then PC <-- PC + ldisp
            r1,(r2),ldisp  01      if xx(r1, M[r2])   then PC <-- PC + ldisp
            xd,r2,ldisp    10      if xx(xd, r2)      then PC <-- PC + ldisp
            xd,(r2),ldisp  11      if xx(xd, M[r2])   then PC <-- PC + ldisp
! where xx = eq, neq, lt, gt, le, ge


  jmp       llldisp        --      PC <-- llldisp
  jmpi      (r1)lldisp     00      PC <-- M[r1 + lldisp]
            (r1)r2         01      PC <-- M[r1 + r2]
  jmpx      r1,lldisp      00      PC <-- r1 + lldisp
            r1,r2          01      PC <-- r1 + r2
```

183

** Synchronization Instructions **

```
! tsi: test-and-set-interlocked
! tci: test-and-clear-interlocked
pos<0:4>        := xs
```

! instr	Args	Mode	Interpretation
! -----	----	----	---------------
tsi	(r1)ldisp,pos	00	cmp(M[r1+ldisp]<pos>,0);
			M[r1+ldisp]<pos> <-- 1;
	(r1)r2,pos	01	cmp(M[r1 + r2]<pos>,0);
			M[r1 + r2]<pos> <-- 1;
tci	(r1)ldisp,pos	00	cmp(M[r1+ldisp]<pos>,1);
			M[r1+ldisp]<pos> <-- 0;
	(r1)r2,pos	01	cmp(M[r1 + r2]<pos>,1);
			M[r1 + r2]<pos> <-- 0;

! instr	Args	Mode	Interpretation
! -----	----	----	---------------
incr_i	(rx)ldisp,rd	00	rd = (M[rx + ldisp] += 1); Also set flags
	(rx)r3,rd	01	rd = (M[rx + r3] += 1); Also set flags
decr_i	(rx)ldisp,rd	00	rd = (M[rx + ldisp] -= 1); Also set flags
	(rx)r3,rd	01	rd = (M[rx + r3] -= 1); Also set flags

```
! The increment_interlocked and decrement_interlocked instructions are
! useful to maintain shared counters in multiprocessors.  It is possible to
! do the incr/decr operations at the memory-board itself, so that these
! instructions should not be any more expensive than a read from memory.
```

** Miscellaneous Instructions **

! instr	Args	Mode	Interpretation
! -----	----	----	---------------
put_psw	.....		
get_psw	.....		
.	.....		
.	.....		
.	.....		

Appendix B   Code and Data Structures for Parallel Implementation

B.1. Code for Interpreter with Hardware Task Scheduler

```
/*
 * Cost Model for OPS5 Production Systems.  To be used in the parallel
 * implementation using the Hardware Task Scheduler.
 */

/* Data Structure Declarations */

typedef struct TokenTag
        {
          struct TokenTag      *tNext;
          int                  nid;
          int                  refCount;/* required for left-not tokens */
          struct TokenTag      *tLeft;  /* Beta-Token: Left  Component */
          struct TokenTag      *tRight; /* Beta-Token: Right Component */
          struct WmeTag        *wptr[32];
        } Token;

typedef struct TokPtrTag
        {
          Token          *ltok;
          Token          *rtok;
        } TokPtr;

/*
 *           +------+-----+--------------------------------------------+
 * word1:    | Flag | Dir |                   Node-ID                  |
 *           +------+-----+--------------------------------------------+
 *           31     30    29                                           0
 *
 *
 *           +--------------------------------------------------------+
 * word2:    |            tokPtr: pointer to Token or TokPtr          |
 *           +--------------------------------------------------------+
 *           31                                                       0
 *
 * Structure of data sent to the HTS:  The data consists of two words.
 * The first word is received and sent from register R'-nid.  This consists
 * of three pieces of information.  R'-nid<31> := Flag, i.e. Insert/Delete,
 * R'-nid<30> := Dir, i.e. Left/Right, and R'-nid<29:0> := Node-ID. The
 * second word is received and sent from register R'-tokPtr.  This word
```

185

```
 * contains a pointer to Token or TokPtr.
 */




#define MaxWmeFields    128     /* max fields in working-memory element */
#define WmeHTSize       4096    /* size of Wme hash table               */

typedef struct WmeTag
        {
           struct WmeTag        *wNext;
           int                  wTimeTag;
           int                  wVal[MaxWmeFields];
        } Wme;

typedef struct
        {
           int   lock;     /* lock for modifying wList               */
           Wme   *wList;   /* list of wmes associated with this entry */
        } WmeHTEntry;

extern-shared   WmeHTEntry      *WmeHT[WmeHTSize];

/*
 * Register R-wmeHT contains a pointer to the shared structure WmeHT.
 *
 * Both symbolic and numeric-integer data are encoded within the wVal
 * fields of the Wme.  Integer data is encoded as (val * 2), while
 * symbolic data is enoded as (sym-val * 2 + 1).  Standard integer
 * comparisons work properly between numeric values.
 */




#define TokenHTSize     4096     /* size of Token hash table       */

typedef struct
        {
           short        lock;     /* lock to modify refCount safely */
           short        refCount; /* -1: writeLock, 0: free, +k: k readers */
           Token        *tList;   /* ptr to token list */
        } TokHTEntry;

extern-shared TokHTEntry  LTokHT[TokenHTSize]; /* hash table for left toks */
extern-shared TokHTEntry  RTokHT[TokenHTSize]; /* hash table for right toks */
/*
 * Pointers to the two token hash tables are available in registers
 * R-ltokHT and R-rtokHT.
 */




#define MaxNodes        10000
```

```c
#define NodeTableSize    MaxNodes

typedef struct nodeTag
        {
          struct nodeTag    *next;
          unsigned          dir.succNid;
        } Node;

typdef struct
        {
          unsigned addr-lef-act;       /* code address for left activation  */
          unsigned addr-rht-act;       /* code address for right activation */
          unsigned addr-mak-tok;       /* code address for makTok-lces-rces */
          unsigned addr-lef-hash;      /* code address for left hash fn     */
          unsigned addr-rht-hash;      /* code address for right hash fn    */
          unsigned addr-do-tests;       /* code for tests assoc with node   */
          short   lock;        /* for safe modification of other fields */
          short   refCount;    /* used by implementation with STQs        */
          Token   *leftExtraRem;  /* extra removes due to conjugate pairs  */
          Token   *rightExtraRem; /* extra removes due to conjugate pairs  */
          Node    *succList;      /* set of successors of the node         */
        } NodeTableEntry;

extern-shared  NodeTableEntry   NodeTable[NodeTableSize];
/*
 * Pointer to the NodeTable is available in the register R-nodTab.
 * Note: Most of the fields in the node-table data structure are wasted for
 * the txxx nodes.  If space is at a premium, an extra test just before the
 * end of PopG routine can be used to check for txxx-nodes.  Subsequently
 * the code can branch using the appropriate table.
 */



/* Some data structures for conflict-resolution */

typedef struct ConResComTag
        {
          struct ConResComTag    *next;
          TokPtr                 *ltok;
          TokPtr                 *rtok;
          int                    flag;
        } ConResCom;

extern-shared    ConResCom   *ConflResCommList;      /* Confl-Res Command List */
extern-shared    int          ConflResCommListLock; /* the associated lock      */



/*
 *                ** Register Definitions **
 * Note: The register allocation is done by hand for all the code.
 * The system defined registers are:
 * R[31] == PC, R[30] == SP, R[29] == Link, and R[28] == Zero
 */
```

```
#define        R'-nid       R[27]   /* temp-reg to sto flg-dir-nid in HTS */
#define        R'-tokPtr    R[26]   /* temp-reg to store token ptr in HTS */

#define        R-nid        R[25]   /* node-id for activation         */
#define        R-tokPtr     R[24]   /* token ptr for activation       */

#define        R-flg        R[23]   /* Flag (ins/del) for cur-actvn */
#define        R-dir        R[22]   /* Direction of activation        */

#define        R-ltokPtr    R[21]   /* left  token of struct-TokPtr */
#define        R-rtokPtr    R[20]   /* right token of struct-TokPtr */
#define        R-state      R[20]   /* Position in opp-token-mem      */
! R-state is the same physical register as R-rtokPtr, since they are never
! used at the same time.

#define        R-ltok       R[19]   /* ptr to left  tok being matched */
#define        R-rtok       R[18]   /* ptr to right tok being matched */
#define        R-wmePtr     R[18]   /* Ptr to wme for alpha-actvns */
! R-wmePtr is the same physical register as R-rtok.  This is possible because
! these registers are never used at the same time.

#define        R-hIndex     R[17]   /* Hash value for token */
#define        R-nodTab     R[16]   /* Address of NodeTable */

#define        R-wmeHT      R[15]   /* Address of WmeHT      */
#define        R-ltokHT     R[14]   /* Address of LTokenHT   */
#define        R-rtokHT     R[13]   /* Address of RTokenHT   */


#define        R-HTS        R[12]   /* Contains the address of the
                                     * hardware task scheduler.*/

#define        R-globTab    R[11]   /* Many global variables can be
                                     * accessed as offsets of this
                                     * register value -- something like
                                     * a pointer to the name-table. */


#define        R-node       R[10]   /* Ptr to relevant NodeTableEntry */



/*
 * The following pages give the code for the parallel implementation.  The
 * code is given for each of the primitive operations, which are then
 * combined to form code for more complex operations.  All code is expected
 * to be expanded in-line, so that the individual sequences of code are like
 * macros and not procedures.
 */


! ** PopG **
!------------
```

```
! When the processor is looking for new tasks, it executes the following
! piece of code.  Note that when no tasks are available, the value of tokPtr
! fetched is NULL, and the processor does not cause any traffic on the bus.

PopG:   ldq     (R-HTS),R-nid---R-tokPtr
        cb_eq   NULL,R-tokPtr,PopG      ! loop out of cache when idle.
        bfx     R-nid,#31,#1,R-flg      ! extract flag field from R-nid
        bfx     R-nid,#30,#1,R-dir      ! extract dir field from R-nid
        bfx     R-nid,#0,#30,R-nid      ! extract node-id field from R-nid
        shl     #3,R-nid,r0             ! r0 contains offset into NodeTable
        add2    R-nid,r0               ! done as siz of nodTabRow is 10 lwords
        add2    R-nid,r0               ! done as siz of nodTabRow is 10 lwords
        ldal    (R-nodTab)r0,R-node     ! get base of relevant node-table entry
        jmpi    (R-node)R-dir          ! jump to code specific to this
                                       ! activation type.

! The activation types are: dir=left/right, lev=alpha/beta, type=and/not/prod
! Both insert and delete operations are handled by the same code.  Txxx nodes
! jump to all custom code.




! ** PushG **
!-------------

! The code executed to schedule a new task on the HTS.  The registers R'-nid
! and R'-tokPtr already contain the relevant data.

        stq     R'-nid---R'-tokPtr,(R-HTS)




! ** ReleaseNodeLock **
!------------------------

! This code is executed when a globally scheduled node activation finishes.

        bfi     R-flg,#31,#1,R-nid      ! Insert val of flag field in bit 31
        bfi     R-dir,#30,#1,R-nid      ! Insert val of dir field in bit 30
        stl     NULL,(R-HTS)1          ! Set value of tokPtr field to NULL
        stl     R-nid,(R-HTS)          ! inform HTS about end of processing
        br      PopG                   ! PopG is a global label

! It is assumed that PendingTasksCount is being maintained by the HTS.  The
! flg-dir-nid info is sent to the HTS again to speed up processing there. The
! value of (R-HTS)1 is set to NULL, so that when PopG is looping to find a
! task, it will find the value NULL until the HTS modifies it.




! ** Root-Node **
!------------------

! The root-node receives a list of wme-changes to be processed in each
! cycle.  The structure of each entry in the list is as follows:
```

189

```
!      struct tokTag  {
!            int                 flag;
!            Token              *tokPtr;
!            struct tokTag      *tNext; } Tok;

        ldl      (R-globTab)wme-toks,r0  ! get list of changes to process
        ldpi     prefix_dir.&bus-nid
        ldl      restof_dir.&busnid,R'-nid
L_beg:  cb_eq    #0,r0,L_end
        or2      (r0),R'-nid
        ldl      (r0)tokPtr,R'-tokPtr
        PUSHG
        ldl      (r0)tNext,r0
        bfi      #0,#31,#1,R'-nid            ! clear the flag field
        br       L_beg
L_end   RELEASE-NODE-LOCK


! ** Bus Node **
!---------------

! Note:  Some of the successors may be processed as subtasks (processed on
! the same processor), while others may be processed as independent tasks
! (scheduled through HTS).

        ----------------------------------------------------------------
        ldpi     prefix_dir.succ-nid          ! Several repetitions of this code
        ldl      restof_dir.succ-nid,R'-nid   ! depending on # of beta-lev succs
        bfi      R-flg,#31,#1,R'-nid          ! and # of non-teqa/non-teqn succs.
        PUSHG
        ----------------------------------------------------------------
        ldpi     prefix_L_exit
        push     restof_L_exit,SP
        ----------------------------------------------------------------
        ldpi     prefix_nodeAddress           ! 0 or more, if some non-teqa/
        push     restof_nodeAddress,SP        ! non-teqn done as subtasks.
        ----------------------------------------------------------------
        ldl      (R-tokPtr)wme,R-wmePtr
        and3     b'11100',(R-wmePtr)2,r0      ! (R-wmePtr)2 is type of wme.
        add2     LocTabOffset,r0
        jmpi     (PC)r0
L_exit: RELEASE-NODE-LOCK
LocTab: address-of-succ-node1
        address-of-succ-node2
        .

        .

        address-of-succ-node8


! ** Constant-Test Nodes or Txxx Nodes **
!-----------------------------------------
```

```
! The code below corresponds to a teqa node.  The code is custom for each
! txxx node in the rete network.  Depending on the number, type, and the way
! in which successors of the node are to be scheduled, there are several
! cases: (1) When the txxx-node has some teqa/teqn successors for
! which hashing can be used beneficially.  (2) When there are no teqa/teqn
! successors .... to make hashing useful, but there are some txxx nodes which
! are to be processed as subtasks.  (3)  Same as case-2, but when there are
! no txxx nodes to be processed as subtasks.


! Case-I: When hashing is used.

        ldl     (R-tokPtr)wme,R-wmePtr  ! executed, iff sched (through HTS)
        ldpi    prefix_type.val         ! recall: num = 2*val, sym = 2*val+1
        ldl     restof_type.val,r0
        ldl     (R-wmePtr)field,r1
        cb_neq  r0,r1,L_fail/L_exit     ! if (thru HTS) L_exit else L_fail
        ----------------------------------------------------------------
        ldpi    prefix_dir.succ-nid           ! Several repetitions of this code
        ldl     restof_dir.succ-nid,R'-nid    ! depending on # of beta-lev succs
        bfi     R-flg,#31,#1,R'-nid           ! and # of non-teqa/non-teqn succs.
        PUSHG
        ----------------------------------------------------------------
        ldpi    prefix_L_exit           ! Done iff node is scheduled
        push    restof_L_exit,SP        ! through HTS.
        ----------------------------------------------------------------
        ldpi    prefix_nodeAddress      ! 0 or more, if some non-teqa/
        push    restof_nodeAddress,SP   ! non-teqn done as subtasks.
        ----------------------------------------------------------------
        and3    b'11100',(R-wmePtr)fld,r0  ! extract from field to hash on
        add2    LocTabOffset,r0
        jmpi    (PC)r0
L_fail: rsb                             ! Pop one of the subtasks
L_exit: RELEASE-NODE-LOCK               ! used only if sched through HTS.
LocTab: address-of-succ-node1
        address-of-succ-node2
        .
        .
        address-of-succ-node8


! Case-II: When hashing is NOT used, but some txxx-nodes as subtasks.

        ldl     (R-tokPtr)wme,R-wmePtr  ! executed, iff sched (through HTS)
        ldpi    prefix_type.val         ! recall: num = 2*val, sym = 2*val+1
        ldl     restof_type.val,r0
        ldl     (R-wmePtr)field,r1
        cb_neq  r0,r1,L_fail/L_exit     ! if (thru HTS) L_exit else L_fail
        ----------------------------------------------------------------
        ldpi    prefix_dir.succ-nid           ! Several repetitions of this code
        ldl     restof_dir.succ-nid,R'-nid    ! depending on # of beta-lev succs
        bfi     R-flg,#31,#1,R'-nid           ! and # of non-teqa/non-teqn succs.
        PUSHG
```

```
            ----------------------------------------------------------------
            ldpi    prefix_L_exit              ! Done iff the node is scheduled
            push    restof_L_exit,SP           ! through the HTS.
            ----------------------------------------------------------------
            ldpi    prefix_nodeAddress         ! one or more of txxx nodes
            push    restof_nodeAddress,SP      ! done as subtasks.
            ----------------------------------------------------------------
L_fail:     rsb                                ! Pop one of the subtasks
L_exit:     RELEASE-NODE-LOCK                  ! used only if sched through HTS.



! Case-III: When hashing is NOT used, and no txxx-nodes as subtasks.

            ldl     (R-tokPtr)wme,R-wmePtr  ! executed, iff sched (through HTS)
            ldpi    prefix_type.val         ! recall: num = 2*val, sym = 2*val+1
            ldl     restof_type.val,r0
            ldl     (R-wmePtr)field,r1
            cb_neq  r0,r1,L_exit
            ----------------------------------------------------------------
            ldpi    prefix_dir.succ-nid           ! Several repetitions of this code
            ldl     restof_dir.succ-nid,R'-nid    ! depending on # of beta-lev succs.
            bfi     R-flg,#31,#1,R'-nid           ! and # of non-teqa/non-teqn succs.
            PUSHG
            ----------------------------------------------------------------
L_exit:     RELEASE-NODE-LOCK/rsb          ! if (thru HTS) REL-N... else rsb




! ** Left Beta And Node **
!------------------------

! The code for a right activation can be obtained by minor substitutions.

            ldl     (R-tokPtr), R-ltokPtr
            ldl     (R-tokPtr)1,R-rtokPtr
            HASH-TOKEN-LEFT
            cb_eq   Delete,R-flg,L_del
            ldal    (R-node)LefExRem,r0    ! check extra-removes field for node
            cb_eq   NULL,(r0),L10
            CHECK-EXTRA-REMOVES           ! result in r5. 0=>OK, 1=>ExtraRemoves
            cb_eq   #1,r5,L_exit
L10:        MAKE-TOKEN
            INSERT-LTOKEN
            br      L11
L_del:      DELETE-LTOKEN
            cb_neq  NULL,R-ltok,L11
            INSERT-EXTRA-REMOVE
            br      L_exit
L11:        ldal    (R-rtokHT)R-hIndex,r5  ! see if hash bucket is empty
            cmp     NULL,(r5)tList
            br_eq   L_exit
```

```
        LOCK-RTOKEN-HT
        ldl     (r5)tList,R-state
L_loop: NEXT-MATCHING-RTOKEN              ! L12 is used within NextMatchingTok
        SCHEDULE-SUCCESSORS
        br      L_loop
L12:    RELEASE-RTOKEN-HT
L_exit: FREE-TOKPTR
        RELEASE-NODE-LOCK
```

! Note: In the previous version, the code between LOCK-TOKEN-HT and
! RELEASE-TOKEN-HT was skipped if the number of tokens in the opp-mem
! was zero. In this version, that section of the code is skipped if
! the hash bucket is NULL. This has the following advantages: (1) The
! overhead of maintaining the counts of tokens in the memory nodes is no
! longer present. (2) Even if the opp-mem has several tokens, if there are
! no matching tokens, there is a large probability that the hash-bucket where
! we look is empty, so that the above code is skipped, while if the decision
! was based on counts the code would not have been skipped. (3) It saves
! 4 bytes of space per node table entry. The disadvantage of the scheme is
! that if the hash table gets pretty full, that is, most buckets have some
! tokens in them, then even if there are no tokens in the opposite memory,
! we will execute the above sequence of code.

! ** Left Alpha And Node **
!-------------------------


```
        HASH-TOKEN-LEFT
        cb_eq   Delete,R-flg,L_del
L10:    MAKE-TOKEN
        INSERT-LTOKEN
        br      L11
L_del:  DELETE-LTOKEN
L11:    ldal    (R-rtokHT)R-hIndex,r5   ! see if hash bucket is empty
        cmp     NULL,(r5)tList
        br_eq   L_exit
        LOCK-RTOKEN-HT
        ldl     (r5)tList,R-state
L_loop: NEXT-MATCHING-RTOKEN              ! L12 is used within NextMatchingToken
        SCHEDULE-SUCCESSORS
        br      L_loop
L12:    RELEASE-RTOKEN-HT
L_exit: RELEASE-NODE-LOCK
```


! ** Left Beta Not Node **
!-------------------------


```
        ldl     (R-tokPtr), R-ltokPtr
```

193

```
            ldl     (R-tokPtr)1,R-rtokPtr
            HASH-TOKEN-LEFT
            cb_eq   Delete,R-flg,L_del
            ldal    (R-node)LefExRem,r0        ! check extra-removes field for node
            cb_eq   NULL,(r0),L10
            CHECK-EXTRA-REMOVES               ! result is returned in r5
            cb_eq   #1,r5,L_exit
L10:        MAKE-TOKEN
            INSERT-LTOKEN
            stl     #0,(R-ltok)refC           ! Initialize refCount to 0
            ldal    (R-rtokHT)R-hIndex,r0
            cmp     NULL,(r0)tList
            br_eq   L12                        ! skip DetRefCount if hash-bucket=NULL
            LOCK-RTOKEN-HT
            DETERMINE-REFCOUNT
            RELEASE-RTOKEN-HT
            br      L11
L_del:      DELETE-LTOKEN
            cb_neq  NULL,R-ltok,L11
            INSERT-EXTRA-REMOVE
            br      L_exit
L11:        cmp     Zero,(R-ltok)refC          ! check value found by DetRefCount
            br_neq  L_exit
L12:        SCHEDULE-SUCCESSORS
L_exit:     FREE-TOKPTR
            RELEASE-NODE-LOCK




! ** Left Alpha Not Node **
!------------------------

            HASH-TOKEN-LEFT
            cb_eq   Delete,R-flg,L_del
L10:        MAKE-TOKEN
            INSERT-LTOKEN
            stl     #0,(R-ltok)refC           ! Initialize refCount to 0
            ldal    (R-rtokHT)R-hIndex,r0
            cmp     NULL,(r0)tList
            br_eq   L12                        ! skip DetRefCount if hash-bucket=NULL
            LOCK-RTOKEN-HT
            DETERMINE-REFCOUNT
            RELEASE-RTOKEN-HT
            br      L11
L_del:      DELETE-LTOKEN
L11:        cmp     Zero,(R-ltok)refC          ! check value found by DetRefCount
            br_neq  L_exit
L12:        SCHEDULE-SUCCESSORS
L_exit:     RELEASE-NODE-LOCK
```

```
! ** Right Beta Not Node **
!------------------------

        ldl     (R-tokPtr), R-ltokPtr
        ldl     (R-tokPtr)1,R-rtokPtr
        HASH-TOKEN-RIGHT
        cb_eq   Delete,R-flg,L_del
        ldal    (R-node)RightExRem,r0    ! check extra-removes field for node
        cb_eq   NULL,(r0),L10
        CHECK-EXTRA-REMOVES             ! result is returned in r5
        cb_eq   #1,r5,L_exit
L10:    MAKE-TOKEN
        INSERT-RTOKEN
        br      L11
L_del:  DELETE-RTOKEN
        cb_neq  NULL,R-rtok,L11
        INSERT-EXTRA-REMOVE
        br      L_exit
L11:    ldal    (R-node)R-hIndex,r5     ! see if hash bucket is empty
        cmp     NULL,(r5)tList
        br_eq   L_exit
        xor2    #1,R-flg               ! R-flg gets value of opp-flag
        LOCK-LTOKEN-HT
        ldl     (r5)tList,R-state      ! Note: LockTokenHT does not use r5
L_loop: NEXT-MATCHING-LTOKEN-NOT       ! L12 used within NextMatch....
        SCHEDULE-SUCCESSORS
        br      L_loop
L12:    xor2    #1,R-flg               ! restore R-flg to not(opp-flag)
        RELEASE-LTOKEN-HT
L_exit: FREE-TOKPTR
        RELEASE-NODE-LOCK




! ** Right Alpha Not Node **
!--------------------------

        HASH-TOKEN-RIGHT
        cb_eq   Delete,R-flg,L_del
L10:    MAKE-TOKEN
        INSERT-RTOKEN
        br      L11
L_del:  DELETE-RTOKEN
L11:    ldal    (R-ltokHT)R-hIndex,r5   ! see if hash bucket us empty
        cmp     NULL,(r5)tList
        br_eq   L_exit
        xor2    #1,R-flg               ! R-flg gets value of opp-flag
        LOCK-LTOKEN-HT
        ldl     (r5)tList,R-state
L_loop: NEXT-MATCHING-LTOKEN-NOT       ! L12 used within NextMatch....
        SCHEDULE-SUCCESSORS
        br      L_loop
L12:    xor2    #1,R-flg               ! restore value of R-flg
```

```
              RELEASE-LTOKEN-HT
L_exit:  RELEASE-NODE-LOCK




! * GetNewToken *
!----------------

! This is used by code for MakeToken.  The token ptr is returned in R-ltok,
! making this useful for insert command from left.  Note, although the
! tokens are allocated from shared memory, each processor keeps its own
! list of free tokens.  Thus no locks are required to get this storage.
! To obtain the code for right activations, simply replace R-ltok by R-rtok.

         ldl     (R-globTab)TokFr,R-ltok ! load value of _TokenFreeList
         cb_neq  NULL,R-ltok,L10
         ALLOCATE-MORE-SPACE
L10:     ldl     (R-ltok),r0              ! value of next field of token
         stl     r0,(R-globTab)TokFr




! ** MakeToken **
!----------------

! Code for a left-alpha-token
         GET-NEW-TOKEN
         stl     R-nid,(R-ltok)nid       ! copy node-id in token
         ldl     (R-tokPtr)wme,r0        ! get pointer to wme
         stl     r0,(R-ltok)wptr         ! copy wme pointer in token

! Code for a left-beta-token
         GET-NEW-TOKEN
         stl     R-nid,(R-ltok)nid       ! copy node-id in token
         stq     R-ltokPtr---R-rtokPtr,(R-ltok)tLeft; ! copy constituent tokens
         brlinki (R-node)addr-mak-tok


! Node specific code for make-token.  There is one such routine for each
! combination of lces and rces that occurs in the rete network.  Thus for
! the case where a linear Rete network is used (with MaxCEs = 32), 32 such
! routines would be present.

         ldl/ldq (R-ltokPtr)wme,r0       ! get wme pointer/s
         stl/stq r0,(R-ltok)wptr         ! store wme pointer/s in token
         .
         .. similar stmts to copy rest of wme ptrs from R-ltokPtr to R-ltok.
         ldl/ldq (R-rtokPtr)wme,r0       ! get wme pointer/s
         stl/stq r0,(R-ltok)wptr         ! store wme pointer/s in token
         .
         .. similar stmts to copy rest of wme ptrs from R-rtokPtr to R-ltok.
         jmpx    Link
```

```
! ** GetNewTokPtr **
!-------------------

! Returns the pointer in R'-tokPtr, which will then be sent to the HTS.

        ldl     (R-globTab)TokFr,R'-tokPtr      ! load value of _TokPtrFreeList
        cb_neq  NULL,R'-tokPtr,L10
        ALLOCATE-MORE-SPACE
L10:    ldl     (R'-tokPtr),r0                  ! value of next field of tokptr
        stl     r0,(R-globTab)TokFr
```

```
! ** FreeTokPtr **
!-----------------

! Note:  The token to be freed is still in R-tokPtr

        ldl     (R-globTab)TokFr,r0       ! r0 <-- TokPtrFreeList
        stl     r0,(R-tokPtr)             ! tokPtr->tNext  <-- TokPtrFreeList
        stl     R-tokPtr,(R-globTab)TokFr ! TokPtrFreeList <-- tokPtr
```

```
! ** HashToken-Left/Right **
!----------------

        ldl     R-nid,r0                  ! the hash value is accumulated in r0
        brlinki (R-node)addr-lef/rht-hash
        bfx     r0,#1,#12,R-hIndex        ! extract bits <1:12> for hash value
        shl     #1,R-hIndex,R-hIndex      ! since size of each entry in tokHT
                                          ! and wmeHT is 2 lwords.  This way
                                          ! R-hIndex gives the correct offset.
```

```
! ** Node-specific Hash Function Code **
!---------------------------------------
```

! Code for beta activations. Here the two components of the token to be
! hashed are available in R-ltokPtr and R-rtokPtr. The final value is
! accumulated in r0.

```
        ldl     (R-ltokPtr)wme,r1         ! move wptr to r1
        xor2    (r1)val-x, r0             ! xor value into r0
        xor2    (r1)val-y,r0              ! multiple value from same wme
        .
        .
        ldl     (R-rtokPtr)wme',r1        ! get wmes from R-rtokPtr
        xor2    (r1)val-z, r0             ! xor value into r0
        .
        ... and so on, depending on the tests associated with the node
```

```
        jmpx    Link                            ! Pop back to generic code

! Code for alpha activations.  Here the pointer to the token is available
! in R-tokPtr.  R-ltokPtr ans R-rtokPtr are not used.  Note that there can
! only be one wme associated with the token.

        ldl     (R-tokPtr)wme,r1                ! move wptr to r1
        xor2    (r1)val-x, r0                   ! xor value into r0
        xor2    (r1)val-y,r0                    ! multiple value from same wme
        .
        .
        .
        ... and so on, depending on the tests associated with the node
        jmpx    Link                            ! Pop back to generic code



! ** InsertToken **
!-------------------

! The following code corresponds to inserting token pointed to by R-ltok
! in left-token hash table.

        add3    #1,R-hIndex,r1                  ! tokList is second longword in bucket
        LOCK-LTOKEN-HT
        ldl     (R-ltokHT)r1,r0                 ! get tokList in r0
        stl     r0,(R-ltok)next                 ! ltok->tNext <-- tokList
        stl     R-ltok,(R-ltokHT)r1             ! tokList <-- ltok
        RELEASE-LTOKEN-HT



! ** DeleteToken **
!-------------------

! The following code corresponds to the deletion of a left token, which
! is formed jointly by R-ltokPtr and R-rtokPtr.

        add3    #1,R-hIndex,r0
        LOCK-LTOKEN-HT
        ldl     (R-ltokHT)r0,r1
        ldl     NULL,r2
L_loop: cb_eq   NULL,r1,L20
        cmp     R-nid,(r1)nid                   ! compare node-ids
        br_neq  L_fail
        v--------------------------------------------------------------------v
        ! The enclosed code corresponds to deletion of a left beta token

        ldl     (R-ltok)tLeft,r3                ! load ptr to left-part of tok in r3
        cmp     r3,(r1)tLeft                    ! see if the two have same left-part
        br_neq  L_fail
        ldl     (R-ltok)tRight,r3               ! load ptr to left-part of tok in r3
        cmp     r3,(r1)tRight                   ! see if the two have same left-part
        br_neq  L_fail
        ^--------------------------------------------------------------------^
```

```
v-------------------------------------------------------------------v
        ! The enclosed code corresponds to deletion of a left alpha token

        ldl     (R-ltok)wptr,r3             ! load ptr to the only wme in r3
        cmp     r3,(r1)wptr                 ! compare with the other token
        br_neq  L_Fail
        ^-------------------------------------------------------------------^
        br      L_succ
L_fail: ldl     r1,r2
        ldl     (r1)next,r1
        br      L_loop
L_succ: ldl     (r1)next,r3
        cb_eq   NULL,r2,L10                 ! token to be del is at head of tList
        stl     r3,(r2)next
        br      L20
L10:    stl     r3,(R-ltokHT)r0
L20:    RELEASE-LTOKEN-HT
        ldl     r1,R-ltok                   ! deleted token is returned in R-ltok
        cbeq    NULL,r1,L30                 ! if tok==NULL, then return.
        ldl     (R-globTab)DelTokList,r0    ! token cannot be freed now
        stl     r0,(r1)next
        stl     r1,(R-globTab)DelTokList
L30:
```

```
! ** LockTokenHT **
!------------------

! The following code implements lock-left-token-HT.  Note that cb_neq instr
! can be used because "lock" is the first field of hash table entry.

        ldal    (R-ltokHT)R-hIndex,r6
L1:     cb_neqw #0,(r6),L1                  ! if lock is busy loop out of cache
        tsi_w   (r6),#0                     ! try and obtain the lock
        br_nz   L1
        cmp     Zero,(r6)refC               ! 0: free, -1: writer, +k: k readers
        br_neq/lt L100                      ! neq:write-lock, lt:read-lock
        add3_w  #-1/#1,(r6)refC,r7          ! decr/incr refC dep-on write/read
        stw     r7,(r6)refC
        tci_w   (r6),#0
        br      L200
L100:   tci_w   (r6),#0
        br      L1                          ! try again
L200:
```

```
! ** ReleaseTokenHT **
!---------------------

! Note: r6 already has the correct address for the lock in it.
```

```
L1:      cb_neqw  #0,(r6),L1
         br_neq   L1
         tsi_w    (r6),#0
         br_nz    L1
         add3_w   #1/#-1,(r6)refC,r7      ! incr/decr refC dep-on write/read
         stw      r7,(r6)refC
         tci_w    (r6),#0
```

! Note: The time inside the lock for LockTokenHT and ReleaseTokenHT (without
! any contention) is around 12 instructions. Thus, if the average node takes
! 100 instructions, then for tokens arriving on the same hash-table bucket
! no more than a factor of 8 in speed-up can be achieved. If specialized
! hardware is being designed the above code will benefit from cmp_incr_i,
! and cmp_decr_i (compare-and-if-equal-incr/decr-interlocked) instructions.

! ** NextMatchingToken **
!------------------------

! Code below corresponds to a left activation. The register R-state stores
! a pointer to the next token that should be tried for match.

```
L_loop: cb_eq    NULL,R-state,L12       ! L12 occurs within calling code
        cmp      R-nid,(R-state)nid     ! check if node-ids are same
        br_neq   L_fail
        ldl      R-state,R-ltok         ! This is needed so that the code to do
                                        ! tests is not direction dependent
        brlinki  (R-node)addr-do-tests  ! result returned in r5
        cb_eq    #1,r5,L_succ           ! all tests must have succeeded
L_fail: ldl      (R-state)next,R-state
        br       L_loop
L_succ: ldl      (R-state)next,R-state  ! update R-state, so that next time
                                        ! we return to L_loop we check new
                                        ! value in R-state, and not old one.
```


! ** NextMatchingTokenNOT **
!---------------------------

! Code below corresponds to a right-not-activation. The register R-state
! stores a pointer to the next token that should be tried for match. The code
! makes extensive use of the fact that the tests are known at compile time.

```
L_loop: cb_eq    NULL,R-state,L12       ! L12 occurs within calling code
        cmp      R-nid,(R-state)nid     ! check if node-ids are same
        br_neq   L_fail
        ldl      R-state,R-ltok
        brlinki  (R-node)addr-do-tests  ! result returned in r5
        cb_eq    #0,r5,L_fail
        incr_iw/decr_iw (R-state)refC,r0 ! All tests must have succeeded
```

```
                                        ! incr:Insert-flag, decr:Del-flag
                                        ! Updated value returned in r0
          cb_eq    #1/#0,r0,L_succ      ! #1:Insert-flag, #0: Del-flag
                                        ! #1: 0=>1, #0:1=>0 transition.
L_fail: ldl      (R-state)next,R-state
        br       L_loop
L_succ: ldl      (R-state)next,R-state
```

```
! ** DetermineRefCount **
!-----------------------
```

! This code is executed on the left-activation of a not-node.

```
          add3     #1,R-hIndex,r0        ! offset to get access to tList
          ldal     (R-rtokHT)r0,r0       ! get tList of opp-mem in r0
          ldl      #0,r1                 ! the # of match-toks is accum in r1
L_loop: cb_eq    NULL,r0,L_exit
          cmp      R-nid,(r0)nid         ! check if node-ids are same
          br_neq   L_fail
          brlinki  (R-node)addr-do-tests ! result returned in r5
          cb_eq    #0,r5,L_fail
          add2     #1,r1                 ! all tests must have succeeded
                                         ! incr num of matching opp-tokens
L_fail: ldl      (r0)next,r0
        br       L_loop
L_exit: stl      r1,(R-ltok)refC         ! store count in refC field of ltok
                                         ! Note this update does not have to
                                         ! be done in an interlocked manner.
```

```
! ** Do Tests **
!--------------
```

! This piece of code is node specific and performs the tests associated with
! a given node. The result of the tests is returned in r5. The code below
! corresponds to the case when the number of tests associated with the node
! is greater than zero.

```
      -----------------------------------------------------------------
      ldl      (R-ltok)wptr,r0           ! get wme from left-tok in r0
      ldl      (R-rtok)wptr',r1          ! get wme from opp-tok  in r1
      ldl      (r0)field,r2              ! get value to be compared
      cmp      r2,(r1)field'             ! compare values
      br_xx    L_fail                    ! xx depends on the test type
      .
      .. the last three instructions for each test between the same wmes
      .
      .. the above sequence for tests between different wmes
      -----------------------------------------------------------------
      ldl      #1,r5                     ! all tests must have succeeded
      jmpx     Link                      ! Pop back to generic code
```

```
L_fail: ldl     #0,r5
        jmpx    Link                        ! Pop back to generic code


! Case when the number of tests associated with a node is zero.  The following
! code can be shared by all nodes that have zero tests.

        ldl     #1,r5
        jmpx    Link                        ! Pop back to generic code




! ** ScheduleSuccessors **
!-------------------------

! Generic code to schedule successors of a node.


        ldl     (R-node)succList,r3     ! get pointer to successor list
loop:   ldl     (r3)dir.succNid,R'nid   ! first time thru loop, r3 can't be NULL
        bfi     R-flg,#31,#1,R'-nid
        GET-NEW-TOKPTR                      ! ptr is returned in R'-tokPtr
        stl     R-ltok,(R'-tokPtr)
        stl     R-rtok,(R'-tokPtr)1
        PUSHG
        ldl     (r3)next,r3
        cb_neq  NULL,r3,loop




! ** CheckExtraRemoves **
!-------------------------

! This routine will be executed only in exceptional circumstances, and for
! that reason need not be highly optimized.  The code corresponds to a left-
! beta-insert operation.  The result is returned in r5.

L1:     cmp_w   #0,(R-node)lock
        br_neq  L1
        tsi_w   (R-node)lock,#0
        br_nz   L1
        ldl     (R-node)LefExRem,r1
        ldl     NULL,r2
L_loop: cb_eq   NULL,r1,L_notF
        cmp     R-nid,(r1)nid
        br_neq  L_fail
        cmp     R-ltokPtr,(r1)tLeft
        br_neq  L_fail
        cmp     R-rtokPtr,(r1)tRight
        br_neq  L_fail
        br      L_succ
L_fail: ldl     r1,r2
```

```
        ldl      (r1)next,r1
        br       L_loop
L_succ: ldl      (r1)next,r3
        cb_eq    NULL,r2,L10              ! Token to be del is at head of list
        stl      r3,(r2)next
        br L20
L10:    stl      r3,(R-node)LefExRem
L20:    tci_w    (R-node)lock,#0
        ldl      (R-globTab)DelTokList,r0
        stl      r0,(r1)next
        stl      r1,(R-globTab)DelTokList
        ldl      #1,r5                    ! value being returned in r5
        br       L30
L_notF: ! case if a matching token is not found in the Extra-Removes-List
        ldl      #0,r5
L30:
```

```
! ** InsertExtraRemove **
!-----------------------
```

! This routine will be executed only in exceptional circumstances, and for
! that reason need not be highly optimized.

```
        MAKE-TOKEN                        ! ptr to token is returned in R-ltok
L1:     cmp      #0,(R-node)lock
        br_neq   L1
        tsi_w    (R-node)lock,#0
        br_nz    L1
        ldl      (R-node)LefExRem,r0
        stl      r0,(R-ltok)next
        stl      R-ltok,(R-node)LefExRem
        tci_w    (R-node)lock,#0
```

```
! ** Prod Node **
!----------------
```

! The code for prod-node corresponds to the act of preparing a command
! for some process/es doing conflict-resolution, and inserting this
! command into a command-list.

```
        ldl      (R-tokPtr), R-ltokPtr
        ldl      (R-tokPtr)1,R-rtokPtr
        MAKE-CR-COMMAND                   ! make confl-res command. (ptr in r0)
        INSERT-CR-COMMAND                 ! insert command in cr-list
        FREE-TOKPTR
        RELEASE-NODE-LOCK                 ! inform HTS that proc is finished.
```

```
! ** MakeCRCommand **
!--------------------

        ldl     (R-globTab)comFreeList,r0       ! get command from free-list
        cb_neq  NULL,r0,L10
        ALLOCATE-MORE-SPACE
L10:    ldl     (r0)next,r1
        stl     r1,(R-globTab)comFreeList
        stl     R-ltokPtr,(r0)ltok
        stl     R-rtokPtr,(r0)rtok
        stl     R-flg,(r0)flag



! ** InsertCRCommand **
!---------------------

        ldal    (R-globTab)crListLock,r1
L1:     cb_neq  #0,(r1),L1                      ! spin on cache
        tsi     (r1)
        br_nz   L1
        ldl     (R-globTab)crList,r2
        stl     r2,(r0)next                     ! recall new-comm is ret in r0
        stl     r0,(R-globTab)crList
        tci     (r1)
```

B.2. Code for Interpreter Using Multiple Software Task Schedulers

```
! Extensions to the code and data structures for the use of software task
! schedulers.  Most of the code written for the HTS remains the same even for
! the implementation using software task schedulers.  There are only three
! routines that change significantly.  Note: Only the changes are given here.


! Extensions to Data structures:
!------------------------------

#define MaxSchedulers   32

#define NumSchedulers   XX

typedef struct
        {
            unsigned    flg-dir-nid;    ! flag, dir, nid for activation
            Token       *tokPtr;        ! ptr to token causing activation;
        } TaskStackEntry;

#define TaskStackSize 512

typedef struct
```

```
    {
        int             lock;            ! lock for entering scheduler
        int             sTop;            ! index of top entry in Task Stack
        TaskStackEntry *taskStk;         ! ptr to task stack of size TStkSize
        int             dummy;           ! place filler to make size 2^2 lwords
    } Sched;

extern-shared   Sched   Scheduler[NumSchedulers];
extern-shared   int     PendTaskCount;  ! sum of tasks pending in all scheds

extern  int     SchedID;        ! global var, local to each processor.  It
                                ! refers to the schedID from which the task
                                ! being serviced was obtained, or the schedID
                                ! of the sched being searched for new task.
extern  int     Random;         ! global variable per processor.
extern-shared int NewCycleLock; ! Lock so that only one processor goes off
                                ! to process beginNextCycle.

! Note that the register R-HTS is no longer needed in the STS implementation.
#define R-sched R-HTS           ! points to the base of the Scheduler array.
#define R-stk   R-hIndex        ! points to task stack of given scheduler


! Note: The lock field of the node-table-row now consists of three pieces
! of information. bit<0>:lock-bit, bit<1>:direction-bit, and bit<2>:flag-bit.


! Extensions to the code
!------------------------


! THE FOLLOWING CODE EXTENSIONS ARE FOR THE CASE WHEN INTRA-NODE PARALLELISM
! IS USED.  THE CODE EXTENSIONS WHEN NODE PARALLELISM OR PRODUCTION
! PARALLELISM IS USED ARE GIVEN LATER.


! ** ReleaseNodeLock **
!---------------------


! This routine corresponds to the action that is taken when a processor
! is done with evaluating a node activation.  At this it may want to look
! for a new node activation to evaluate, or it may mark the beginning of
! a new recognize-act cycle.

        decr_iw (R-node)refC,r0         ! decrement the refC assoc with node
        ldal    (R-globTab)PendTaskC,r0
        decr_i  (r0)                    ! decr PendingTaskCount interlocked
        cb_neq  #0,(r0),L1              ! check if end of prod cycle
        ldal    (R-globTab)NewCycLock,r7 ! load address of NewCycleLock
        tsi     (r7)
        br_nz   L1                      ! if the lock is busy it implies that
                                        ! some other processor is scheduling
                                        ! the new cycle, so this proc need not
```

```
                                            ! worry about it.
            cb_neq  #0,(r0),L2             ! Get value of PendingTaskCount again.
                                            ! Even if this proc gets the lock, it
                                            ! is possible that another processor
                                            ! already went in, scheduled the next
                                            ! cycle, and then released the lock.
                                            ! Must check for that case.
            BEGIN-NEXT-CYCLE               ! confl-res and act phases
L2:         tci     (r7)
L1:
PopG:                                       ! PopG is a global label
```

! ** PushG **
!------------

! This piece of code is executed whenever a pending node activation is to be
! globally scheduled.

```
            ldl     (R-globTab)random,r0   ! random-seed from last time
            xor2    #4513,r0               ! xor with some prime number
            bfx     r0,#(31-x),#x,r8       ! #x depends on NumScheds.  We also
                                            ! rotate the rand-seed by #x bits
            shl     #x,r0,r0
            bfi     r8,#0,#x,r0            ! rotation is complete
            stl     r0,(R-globTab)random   ! store back value into random-seed
            shl     #2,r8,r9              ! note r8 has indx of rand-sched
            ldal    (R-sched)r9,r9         ! get base-addr of that scheduler
L1:         cb_neq  #0,(r9),L1             ! check sched-lock; spin in cache
            tsi     (r9)lock,#0           ! try and get lock
            br_nz   L1
            add3    #2,(r9)sTop,r0         ! sTop += 2, as each entry is 2 lwords
            stl     r0,(r9)sTop
            add3    r0,(r9)taskStk,r1      ! get address where to push data
            stq     R'-nid---R'-tokPtr,(r1) ! actually push data.
            tci     (r9)lock
            ldal    (R-globTab)PendTaskC,r0
            incr_i  (r0)                   ! increment_interlocked PendTaskCount
```

! ** PopG **
!------------

! This code determines the processability of a node in addition to performing
! the task of PopG routine as described in the HTS version of code.

```
PopG:                                       ! PopG is a global label
            ldl     (R-globTab)schID,r8    ! get ID of last sched used
L2:         add2    #1,r8
            cb_le   (NumScheds-1),r8,L1
```

```
        sub2    r8,NumScheds             ! increment modulo NumScheds
L1:     shl     #2,r8,r9
        ldal    (R-sched)r9,r9
        cmp     Zero,(r9)sTop            ! check sTop -- Is stack empty?
        br_z    L2                       ! if empty then try next sched
        cb_neq  #0,(r9),L2               ! if sched-lock is busy, try next sched
        tsi     (r9),#0
        br_nz   L2                       ! if cant get lock, try next sched
        ldl     (r9)taskStk,R-stk        ! get base-addr of task stack
        ldl     (r9)sTop,r0              ! get sTop
L_loop: cb_le   #0,r0,L_fail
        ldal    (R-stk)r0,r1             ! get base address of stack entry
        ldq     (r1),R-nid---R-tokPtr
        bfx     R-nid,#31,#1,R-flg
        bfx     R-nid,#30,#1,R-dir
        bfx     R-nid,#0,#30,R-nid
        shl     #3,R-nid,r0
        add2    R-nid,r0
        add2    R-nid,r0                 ! done as siz of nodTabRow is 10 lwords
        ldal    (R-nodTab)r0,R-node      ! R-node gets bas Addr of nod-tab-entry
        cmp     R-nid,#10000             ! check if txxx-node
        br_gt   L_succ                   ! if so success
L3:     tsi_w   (R-node)lock,#0          ! lock node tab entry
        br_nz   L3
        cb_eq   Insert,R-flg,L_Ins
          .
        .. two similar symm. cases, consider only one here
L_Ins:  cb_eq   Left,R-dir,LefIns
          .
        .. two similar symm. cases, consider only one here
LefIns: cmp_w   Zero,(R-node)refC        ! check if refCount is zero
        br_neq  L91
L92:    stw     flg-dir-lock,(R-node)lock ! flg-dir-lock is compile-time const
L94:    add3_w  #1,(R-node)refC,r3
        stw     r3,(R-node)refC          ! update refCount
        tci_w   (R-node)lock,#0          ! release lock on node table entry
        br      L_succ
L91:    cmp_w   flg-dir-lock,(R-node)lock ! check if flg-dir-lock match
        br_eq   L94                      ! if same then incr refC and succeed
L93:    tci_w   (R-node)lock,#0          ! release lock
        sub2    #2,r0                    ! sub size of tskstk entry from offset
        br      L_loop                   ! see if next entry is processable
L_fail: tci     (r9)lock,#0              ! release lock on scheduler
        br      L2                       ! try the next scheduler for pr-task
L_succ: cmp_w   r0,(r9)sTop              ! check if task was picked of the
                                         ! top of task stack or from in between
        br_eq   L95                      ! if from top, no compaction neccessary
        ldl     (r9)sTop,r0              ! get value of sTop. I can destroy r0,
                                         ! as r1 contains info in better form.
        ldal    (R-stk)r0,r0             ! get pointer to top entry
        ldq     (r0),r3-r4               ! load top slot of stack
        stq     r3-r4,(r1)               ! store back into the middle slot
L95:    sub3    #2,(r9)sTop,r0
        stl     r0,(r9)sTop              ! decrement stack-top field
```

```
        tci      (r9)lock,#0              ! release scheduler lock
        stl      r8,(R-globTab)schID      ! store schedID from which task was
                                          ! obtained into the global var schedID.
        jmpi     (R-node)R-dir            ! jump to code specific to this
                                          ! activation type.
```

! THE FOLLOWING CODE CORRESPONDS TO THE CASE WHEN NODE PARALLELISM IS
! USED. THE CODE WHEN PRODUCTION PARALLELISM IS USED IS SIMILAR, AND
! THE COST-MODEL DERIVED FROM THIS CODE CAN BE USED THERE TOO.

```
typdef struct
        {
        unsigned addr-lef-act;          /* code address for left activation  */
        unsigned addr-rht-act;          /* code address for right activation */
        unsigned addr-mak-tok;          /* code address for makTok-lces-rces */
        unsigned addr-lef-hash;         /* code address for left hash fn     */
        unsigned addr-rht-hash;         /* code address for right hash fn    */
        unsigned addr-do-tests;         /* code for tests assoc with node    */
        short    lock;            /* for safe modification of other fields */
        short    refCount;        /* used by STS. (not needed here)        */
        Token    *leftExtraRem;   /* extra removes due to conjugate pairs  */
        Token    *rightExtraRem;  /* extra removes due to conjugate pairs  */
        Node     *succList;       /* set of successors of the node         */
        } NodeTableEntry;
```

! ** ReleaseNodeLock' **
!----------------------

! Only the first line is changed as respect to the previous version. Overall
! cost remains the same.

```
        tci_w    (R-node)lock,#0          ! release lock associated with node
        ldal     (R-globTab)PendTaskC,r0
        decr_i   (r0)                     ! decr PendingTaskCount interlocked
        cb_neq   #0,(r0),L1               ! check if end of prod cycle
        ldal     (R-globTab)NewCycLock,r7 ! load address of NewCycleLock
        tsi      (r7)
        br_nz    L1                       ! if the lock is busy it implies that
                                          ! some other processor is scheduling
                                          ! the new cycle, so this proc need not
                                          ! worry about it.

        cb_neq   #0,(r0),L2               ! Get value of PendingTaskCount again.
                                          ! Even if this proc gets the lock, it
                                          ! is possible that another processor
                                          ! already went in, scheduled the next
                                          ! cycle, and then released the lock.
                                          ! Must check for that case.
        BEGIN-NEXT-CYCLE                  ! confl-res and act phases
L2:     tci      (r7)
L1:
```

! ** PushG' **
!------------

! The version of PushG does not change between node parallelism and intra-node
! parallelism. So the cost also remains the same.

```
        ldl     (R-globTab)random,r0    ! random-seed from last time
        xor2    #4513,r0                ! xor with some prime number
        bfx     r0,#(31-x),#x,r8        ! #x depends on NumScheds.  We also
                                        ! rotate the rand-seed by #x bits
        shl     #x,r0,r0
        bfi     r8,#0,#x,r0             ! rotation is complete
        stl     r0,(R-globTab)random    ! store back value into random-seed
        shl     #2,r8,r9                ! note r8 has indx of rand-sched
        ldal    (R-sched)r9,r9          ! get base-addr of that scheduler
L1:     cb_neq  #0,(r9),L1             ! check sched-lock; spin in cache
        tsi     (r9)lock,#0            ! try and get lock
        br_nz   L1
        add3    #2,(r9)sTop,r0         ! sTop += 2, as each entry is 2 lwords
        stl     r0,(r9)sTop
        add3    r0,(r9)taskStk,r1      ! get address where to push data
        stq     R'-nid---R'-tokPtr,(r1) ! actually push data.
        tci     (r9)lock
        ldal    (R-globTab)PendTaskC,r0
        incr_i  (r0)                    ! increment_interlocked PendTaskCount
```

! ** PopG' **
!------------

! This code determines the processability of a node in addition to performing
! the task of PopG routine as described in the HTS version of code.

! This version of the code changes significantly when node parallelism
! is used. The main place of change corresponds to the portion where the
! processability of the selected node activation is being established.

```
PopG:                                   ! PopG is a global label
        ldl     (R-globTab)schID,r8    ! get ID of last sched used
L2:     add2    #1,r8
        cb_le   (NumScheds-1),r8,L1
        sub2    r8,NumScheds           ! increment modulo NumScheds
L1:     shl     #2,r8,r9
        ldal    (R-sched)r9,r9
        cmp     Zero,(r9)sTop          ! check sTop -- Is stack empty?
        br_z    L2                     ! if empty then try next sched
        cb_neq  #0,(r9),L2             ! if sched-lock is busy, try next sched
```

```
          tsi      (r9),#0
          br_nz    L2                      ! if cant get lock, try next sched
          ldl      (r9)taskStk,R-stk       ! get base-addr of task stack
          ldl      (r9)sTop,r0             ! get sTop
L_loop:   cb_le    #0,r0,L_fail
          ldal     (R-stk)r0,r1            ! get base address of stack entry
          ldq      (r1),R-nid---R-tokPtr
          bfx      R-nid,#31,#1,R-flg
          bfx      R-nid,#30,#1,R-dir
          bfx      R-nid,#0,#30,R-nid
          shl      #3,R-nid,r0
          add2     R-nid,r0
          add2     R-nid,r0               ! done as siz of nodTabRow is 10 lwords
          ldal     (R-nodTab)r0,R-node     ! R-node gets bas Addr of nod-tab-entry
          cmp      R-nid,#10000           ! check if txxx-node
          br_gt    L_succ                 ! if so success
L3:       tsi_w    (R-node)lock,#0        ! lock node tab entry
          br_z     L_succ                 ! if lock_obtained then success
          sub2     #2,r0                  ! sub size of tskstk entry from offset
          br       L_loop                 ! see if next entry is processable
L_fail:   tci      (r9)lock,#0            ! release lock on scheduler
          br       L2                     ! try the next scheduler for pr-task
L_succ:   cmp_w    r0,(r9)sTop            ! check if task was picked of the
                                          ! top of task stack or from in between
          br_eq    L95                    ! if from top, no compaction neccessary
          ldl      (r9)sTop,r0            ! get value of sTop. I can destroy r0,
                                          ! as r1 contains info in better form.
          ldal     (R-stk)r0,r0           ! get pointer to top entry
          ldq      (r0),r3-r4             ! load top slot of stack
          stq      r3-r4,(r1)             ! store back into the middle slot
L95:      sub3     #2,(r9)sTop,r0         ! decrement stack-top field
          stl      r0,(r9)sTop
          tci      (r9)lock,#0            ! release scheduler lock
          stl      r8,(R-globTab)schID    ! store schedID from which task was
                                          ! obtained into the global var schedID.
          jmpi     (R-node)R-dir          ! jump to code specific to this
                                          ! activation type.
```

Appendix C Derivation of Cost Models for the Simulator

C.1. Cost Model for the Parallel Implementation Using HTS

```
/*
 *      This cost model was designed for the case where a single Hardware Task
 *      Scheduler (HTS) is used.
 *
 * Exports:
 *      double TaskProcCost(tptr: *Task);
 *      double TaskFinishCost(tptr: *Task);
 *      double TaskLoopCost(tptr: *Task);
 *      double TaskSchedCost(tptr: *Task);
 *
 */


/*
                                     T_deq
    +====<=============================================================<======+
    |                                                                         |
    |                              T_il                                       |
    V                      +-<----------<-+                                   ^
    |                      |              |                                   |
    |   T_b         T_ls   |    T_enq     |   T_le            T_e             |
    +----------->+---------->+============>+---------->+-------------->+
  Start          |                        |                           End
                 |              T_nl       |
                 +------>---------------------->-----+

 * The cost model described in this Appendix may be understood in terms of
 * diagram given above.  The processing required by a node activation
 * usually consists of the following steps: (1) Do some basic processing
 * associated with the node.  (2) If the node fails to find any matching
 * tokens in the opposite memory, then simply go to the end. (3) If the
 * node has successor node activations, then enqueue each of those on the
 * scheduler, before going onto the end. (4) Once the processing for a node
 * is finished, fetch another pending node activation to process.  In the
 * above diagram:  T_b is Beginning cost; T_e is Ending cost; T_ls is
 * Loop-Start cost; T_le is Loop-End cost; T_il is Inner-Loop cost; T_nl is
```

```
 * No-Loop cost; T_enq is cost of enqueuing an activation in the HTS; T_deq
 * is cost of dequeueing an activation from the HTS.  The procedures exported
 * by this file correspond to the following costs:
 *
 * TaskProcCost(tptr: *Task)    := T_b + (if no_succ then T_nl; else T_ls;);
 * TaskLoopCost(tptr: *Task)    := T_il;
 * TaskFinishCost(tptr: *Task)  := T_e + (if no_succ then 0; else T_le;);
 * TaskSchedCost(tptr: *Task)   := T_enq := T_deq;  for the HTS version.
 */


#include "sim.h"
#include "stats.h"


/*
 * Some constant definitions for cost of tasks
 */

#define RR        1.0      /* cost of reg-reg instruction */
#define MR        1.0      /* cost of mem-reg instruction */
#define M2R       2.0      /* cost of mem-mem-reg instruction  */
#define SYN       3.0      /* cost of interlocked instructions */
#define CBR       1.5      /* compare&branch on register value */
#define CBM       1.5      /* compare&branch on memory   value */
#define BRR       1.5      /* branch on register value        */
#define BRM       1.5      /* branch requiring memory-ref   */

#define C_PushG   (M2R)
#define C_PopG    (6*RR + MR + M2R + CBR + BRM)

#define C_GetNewTokPtr (3*MR + CBR)
#define C_GetNewToken  (3*MR + CBR)
#define C_FreeTokPtr   (3*MR)

#define C_ReleaseNodeLock   (2*RR + 2*MR + BRR)

#define C_LockTokenHT    (4*MR + 2*SYN + CBM + 3*BRR)
#define C_ReleaseTokenHT (2*MR + 2*SYN + CBM + 2*BRR)

#define C_MakeCRCommand      (6*MR + CBR)
#define C_InsertCRCommand    (4*MR + 2*SYN + CBM + BRR)


/*
 * The following variable names are used in the functions below to mean:
 *
 * nid:    node-id.
 * toksz:  number of wme pointers in token.
 * ntests: number of tests associated with a two-input node.
 * nteq:   number of equality tests made at the two-input node.
 * ntok:   number of tokens in a given memory node.
```

212

```
 * ntokOmem: number of tokens in the opposite memory node.
 * nsucc:  number of successor node activations generated by a given activation.
 * primTask: true if a given task is scheduled through the global HTS.
 * dir:  direction of activation (left or right).
 * flag: whether a token is being inserted or deleted.
 * lces: the number of condition elements to the left of the two-input node.
 * rces: the number of condition elements to the right of the two-input node.
 * MemConFlag:    true if memory contention is to be taken into account
 * NumActiveProc: number of active processors.
 *
 */


double C_MakeToken(toksz)
int toksz;
{
/*
 * if (tok_size <= 1) then assume that alpha-token is being made.  "<="
 * because the right side of a not-node may have rces listed as 0.
 */

    double   cost;

    if (toksz <= 1)
        cost = 3 * MR + C_GetNewToken;
    else
        cost = MR + (2 * toksz) * MR + M2R + BRR + BRM + C_GetNewToken;

    return (cost);
}


double C_InsertToken()
{
double cost;
   cost = RR + 3*MR + C_LockTokenHT + C_ReleaseTokenHT;
   return(cost);
}

double C_DeleteToken(toksz, nteq, ntok)
int toksz, nteq, ntok;
{
double cost;

   cost = C_LockTokenHT + C_ReleaseTokenHT;
   if (toksz <= 1)   /* delete alpha-token */
      {
        if (nteq > 0) /* hashing works */
          {
             cost += 3*RR + 9*MR + 3*CBR + 3*BRR;
          }
        else
          {
             cost += (3*RR + 6*MR + 2*CBR + BRR) + (3*MR + CBR + 3*BRR);
```

```
                cost += (ntok/2) * (RR + 4*MR + CBR + 3*BRR);
            }
        }
    else
        {
          if (nteq > 0) /* hashing works */
            {
                cost += 3*RR + 11*MR + 3*CBR + 4*BRR;
            }
          else
            {
                cost += (3*RR + 6*MR + 2*CBR + BRR) + (5*MR + CBR + 4*BRR);
                cost += (ntok/2) * (RR + 5*MR + CBR + 3.5*BRR);
            }
        }

    return(cost);
}


double C_HashToken(toksz,nteq)
int toksz,nteq;
{
double cost;

  if (toksz <= 1)
    cost = 3*RR + MR + nteq*MR + BRR + BRM;
  else
    cost = 3*RR + MR + 2*nteq*MR + BRR + BRM;

  return(cost);
}


double C_DoTests(ntests,pass)
int ntests;
bool pass;
{
double cost;

  if (ntests == 0)
      cost = RR + BRR;
  else
    {
      if (pass) /* the tests succeed */
          cost = ntests * (4*MR + BRR) + RR + BRR;
      else
          cost = (ntests/2) * (4*MR + BRR) + RR + BRR;
    }

  return(cost);
}
```

```
double C_NextMatchTok(nsucc, nteq, ntests, ntokOmem)
int nsucc, nteq, ntests, ntokOmem;
{
double cost, k;
  cost = 0.0;
  if (nteq == 0)
    {
      if (nsucc == 0)
        {
          cost` += ntokOmem * (RR + 2*MR + 2*CBR + 2*BRR + BRM);
          cost += ntokOmem * C_DoTests(ntests,False) + CBR;
        }
      else
        {
          k = ntokOmem/nsucc;
          cost += (k - 1) * (RR + 2*MR + 2*CBR + 2*BRR + BRM);
          cost += (k - 1) * C_DoTests(ntests,False);
          cost += RR + 3*MR + 2*CBR + BRR + BRM + C_DoTests(ntests,True);
        }
    }
  else /* hashing is useful */
    {
      if (nsucc == 0)
        cost += CBR;
      else
        cost += RR + 3*MR + 2*CBR + BRR + BRM + C_DoTests(ntests,True);
    }
  return(cost);
}


double C_NextMatchTokNOT(nsucc, nteq, ntests, ntokOmem)
int nsucc, nteq, ntests, ntokOmem;
{
double cost, k;
  cost = 0.0;
  if (nteq == 0)
    {
      if (nsucc == 0)
        {
        /* It is still possible that successful matches with the tokens of the
         * opposite node happened.  It only implies that there were no 0->1
         * transitions for an insert or 1->0 transitions for a delete.
         */
          k = ntokOmem/2;
          cost += k * (RR + 2*MR + 2*CBR + 2*BRR + BRM);
          cost += k * C_DoTests(ntests,False) + CBR;
          cost += k * (RR + 2*MR + SYN + 3*CBR + 2*BRR + BRM);
          cost += k * C_DoTests(ntests,True);
        }
      else
        {
          k = ntokOmem/nsucc;
          cost += (k - 1) * (RR + 2*MR + 2*CBR + 2*BRR + BRM);
```

```
            cost += (k - 1) * C_DoTests(ntests,False);
            cost += RR + 2*MR + SYN + 3*CBR + BRR + BRM + C_DoTests(ntests,True);
          }
      }
   else /* hashing is useful */
      {
        if (nsucc == 0)
          cost += CBR;  /* the opposite bucket is hopefully empty */
        else
          cost += RR + 2*MR + SYN + 3*CBR + BRR + BRM + C_DoTests(ntests,True);
      }
   return(cost);
}


double C_DetermineRefCount(nsucc, nteq, ntests, ntokOmem)
int nsucc, nteq, ntests, ntokOmem;
{
double cost;

   cost = 3*RR + MR;
   if (nteq > 0)
      {
        if (nsucc == 0)
          {
          /*
           * This case implies that the # of matching tokens was greater than 0.
           * Assuming that it maps into a hash bucket with exactly one token.
           */
            cost += RR + 2*MR + 2*CBR + 2*BRR + BRM + CBR;
            cost += C_DoTests(ntests,True);
          }
        else /* nsucc==1 and the opposite hash bucket would be empty */
            cost += CBR;
      }
   else
      {
        if (nsucc == 0)
          {
            cost += ntokOmem * (RR + 2*MR + 2*CBR + 2*BRR + BRM) + CBR;
            cost += ntokOmem*((C_DoTests(ntests,True)+C_DoTests(ntests,False))/2.0);
          }
        else
          {
            cost += ntokOmem * (RR + 2*MR + 2*CBR + 2*BRR + BRM);
            cost += C_DoTests(ntests,False) + CBR;
          }
      }
   return(cost);
}


double TaskProcCost(tptr)
Task *tptr;
```

```
{
bool primTask;
TaskPtr *tp;
double cost, tempc;
int nid, lces, rces, nsucc, nteq, ntests, ntok, ntokOmem, toksz;
Direction dir;

  cost = 0.0;
  primTask = tptr->tPrimaryTask;
  nid = tptr->tNodeID;
  tp = tptr->tDepList; nsucc = 0;
  while (tp) { nsucc++; tp = tp->tNext; }

  switch(tptr->tType)
  {
  case rootNode:
    if (nsucc)
      cost = (2*RR + 3*MR + CBR) + C_PushG;
    else
      cost = (2*RR + MR + CBR);
    break;

  case txxxNode: /* the cost for the &bus and txxx nodes is made equal */
    if (primTask)
      cost = (2*RR + 2*MR + CBR) + C_PopG;
    else
      cost = (2*RR + MR + CBR);

    /*
     * The following if-stmt is not a legal stmt in the language, and
     * has been added as a simple approximation to the actual form used
     * in the simulator.
     */
    if (nsucc > 0)
      {
        if successor_sched_thru_HTS   cost += 3*RR + C_PushG;
        else cost += RR + MR;
      }
    break;

  case andNode:
    lces = NodeTable[nid].nLces;
    rces = NodeTable[nid].nRces;
    dir  = tptr->tSide;
    nteq = NodeTable[nid].numTeqbTests;
    ntests = NodeTable[nid].numTests;
    if (dir == Left)
      { toksz = lces; ntok = tptr->tNumLeft; ntokOmem = tptr->tNumRight; }
    else
      { toksz = rces; ntokOmem = tptr->tNumLeft; ntok = tptr->tNumRight; }
    if (toksz <= 1)
      { /* alpha-activation */
        cost = C_PopG + C_HashToken(toksz,nteq) + CBR + (RR + MR + BRR);
        if (tptr->tFlag == Insert)
```

```
            cost += C_MakeToken(toksz) + C_InsertToken() + BRR;
        else
            cost += C_DeleteToken(toksz, nteq, ntok);

        if ((ntokOmem != 0) && ((nteq == 0) || (nsucc != 0)))
          {
            cost += C_LockTokenHT + MR;
            cost += C_NextMatchTok(nsucc,nteq,ntests,ntokOmem);
          }
        if (nsucc != 0) cost += RR + 2*MR + C_GetNewTokPtr + 2*MR + C_PushG;
      }
    else /* beta-activation */
      {
        cost = C_PopG + 2*MR + C_HashToken(toksz,nteq) + CBR + (RR + MR + BRR);
        if (tptr->tFlag == Insert)
            cost +=  RR + MR + C_MakeToken(toksz) + C_InsertToken() + BRR;
        else
            cost += C_DeleteToken(toksz, nteq, ntok) + CBR;

        if ((ntokOmem != 0) && ((nteq == 0) || (nsucc != 0)))
          {
            cost += C_LockTokenHT + MR;
            cost += C_NextMatchTok(nsucc,nteq,ntests,ntokOmem);
          }
        if (nsucc != 0) cost += RR + 2*MR + C_GetNewTokPtr + 2*MR + C_PushG;
      }
    break;

case notNode:
    lces = NodeTable[nid].nLces;
    rces = NodeTable[nid].nRces;
    dir  = tptr->tSide;
    if (dir == Left) toksz = lces; else toksz = rces;
    nteq = NodeTable[nid].numTeqbTests;
    ntests = NodeTable[nid].numTests;

    if (dir == Left)
      {
        ntok = tptr->tNumLeft; ntokOmem = tptr->tNumRight;
        cost = C_PopG + 2*MR + C_HashToken(toksz,nteq) + CBR;
        if (tptr->tFlag == Insert)
          {
            cost += 2*RR + 3*MR + C_MakeToken(toksz) + C_InsertToken() + BRR;
            if ((ntokOmem != 0) && ((nteq == 0) || (nsucc == 0)))
              {
                cost += C_LockTokenHT + C_ReleaseTokenHT + BRR;
                cost += C_DetermineRefCount(nsucc, nteq, ntests, ntokOmem);
              }
          }
        else
            cost += C_DeleteToken(toksz, nteq, ntok) + CBR;
        if (nsucc != 0)  cost += RR + 5*MR + BRR + C_GetNewTokPtr + C_PushG;

        if (toksz <= 1)  /* i.e., an alpha not-node activation */
```

```
        {
          if (tptr->tFlag == Insert)
            cost = cost - (RR + 3*MR);
          else
            cost = cost - (2*MR + BRR);
        }
    }
  else /* dir == right */
    {
      ntokOmem = tptr->tNumLeft; ntok = tptr->tNumRight;
      cost = C_PopG + 2*MR + C_HashToken(toksz,nteq) + CBR + RR + MR + BRR;
      if (tptr->tFlag == Insert)
        cost += RR + MR + C_MakeToken(toksz)+C_InsertToken() + BRR;
      else
        cost += C_DeleteToken(toksz, nteq, ntok) + CBR;

      if ((ntokOmem != 0) && ((nteq == 0) || (nsucc != 0)))
        {
          cost += RR + C_LockTokenHT + MR;
          cost += C_NextMatchTokNOT(nsucc,nteq,ntests,ntokOmem);
        }
      if (nsucc != 0) cost += RR + 2*MR + C_GetNewTokPtr + 2*MR + C_PushG;

      if (toksz <= 1)   /* i.e., an alpha not-node activation */
        {
          if (tptr->tFlag == Insert)
            cost = cost - (RR + 3*MR);
          else cost = cost - (2*MR + CBR);
        }
    }
  break;

case pNode:
  lces = NodeTable[nid].nLces;
  rces = NodeTable[nid].nRces;

  cost = C_PopG + 2*MR;
  cost += C_MakeCRCommand + C_InsertCRCommand + C_FreeTokPtr;
  cost += C_ReleaseNodeLock;
  break;

default:
  cost = 0.0;
  break;
}

if (MemConFlag) cost = cost/MemCon[NumActiveProc];
return(cost/1000.0);

}


double TaskLoopCost(tptr)
```

```
Task *tptr;
{
TaskPtr *tp;
double cost;
int nid, nsucc, nteq, ntests, ntok, ntokOmem, toksz;
Direction dir;

  cost = 0.0;

  nid = tptr->tNodeID;
  tp = tptr->tDepList; nsucc = 0;
  while (tp) { nsucc++; tp = tp->tNext; }

  switch(tptr->tType)
  {
  case rootNode:
    cost = RR + 3*MR + CBR + BRR + C_PushG;
    break;

  case txxxNode:
    /*
     * The following if-stmt is not a legal stmt in the language, and
     * has been added as a simple approximation to the actual form used
     * in the simulator.
     */
    if successor_sched_thru_HTS    cost = 3*RR + C_PushG;
    else cost = RR + MR;
    break;

  case andNode:
    nteq = NodeTable[nid].numTeqbTests;
    ntests = NodeTable[nid].numTests;
    dir = tptr->tSide;
    if (dir == Left)
      { ntok = tptr->tNumLeft; ntokOmem = tptr->tNumRight; }
    else { ntokOmem = tptr->tNumLeft; ntok = tptr->tNumRight; }

    cost =  RR + 2*MR + C_GetNewTokPtr + C_PushG + 2*MR;
    cost += MR + CBR + BRR + C_NextMatchTok(nsucc, nteq, ntests, ntokOmem);
    break;
  case notNode:
    nteq = NodeTable[nid].numTeqbTests;
    ntests = NodeTable[nid].numTests;
    dir = tptr->tSide;

    if (dir == Left)
      {
        ntok = tptr->tNumLeft; ntokOmem = tptr->tNumRight;
        cost += 5*MR + RR + CBR + BRR + C_GetNewTokPtr + C_PushG;
      }
    else
      {
        ntokOmem = tptr->tNumLeft; ntok = tptr->tNumRight;
        cost += RR + 5*MR + CBR + BRR + C_GetNewTokPtr + C_PushG;
```

```
        cost += C_NextMatchTokNOT(nsucc, nteq, ntests, ntokOmem);
      }
    break;

  case pNode:
    cost = 0.0;
    break;

  default:
    break;
  }

  return(cost/1000.0);

}



double TaskFinishCost(tptr)
Task *tptr;
{
TaskPtr *tp;
double cost;
int nid, lces, rces, nsucc, nteq, ntests, ntok, ntokOmem, toksz;
Direction dir;

  cost = 0.0;

  nid = tptr->tNodeID;
  tp = tptr->tDepList; nsucc = 0;
  while (tp) { nsucc++; tp = tp->tNext; }

  switch(tptr->tType)
  {
  case rootNode:
    if (nsucc != 0) cost += RR + MR + CBR + BRR;
    cost += C_ReleaseNodeLock;
    break;

  case txxxNode:
    if (tptr->tPrimaryTask)    cost = C_ReleaseNodeLock;
    else cost = BRM;
    /*
     * The following if-stmt has been added as a simple approximation
     * to the actual form used in the simulator.
     */
    if (nsucc > 0) cost += MR + RR + BRM;
    break;

  case andNode:
    lces = NodeTable[nid].nLces;
    rces = NodeTable[nid].nRces;
    dir  = tptr->tSide;
    nteq = NodeTable[nid].numTeqbTests;
```

```
    ntests = NodeTable[nid].numTests;
    if (dir == Left)
      { toksz = lces; ntok = tptr->tNumLeft; ntokOmem = tptr->tNumRight; }
    else { toksz = rces; ntokOmem = tptr->tNumLeft; ntok = tptr->tNumRight; }

    if (nsucc != 0)
      cost = MR + CBR + BRR + C_NextMatchTok(nsucc, nteq, ntests, ntokOmem);
    cost += C_ReleaseNodeLock + C_FreeTokPtr;
    if ((ntokOmem != 0) && ((nteq == 0) || (nsucc != 0)))
      cost += C_ReleaseTokenHT;
    if (toksz <= 1) /* alpha activation */
      cost = cost - C_FreeTokPtr;
    break;

case notNode:
  lces = NodeTable[nid].nLces;
  rces = NodeTable[nid].nRces;
  dir  = tptr->tSide;
  nteq = NodeTable[nid].numTeqbTests;
  ntests = NodeTable[nid].numTests;

  if (dir == Left)
    {
      toksz = lces; ntok = tptr->tNumLeft; ntokOmem = tptr->tNumRight;
      if (nsucc != 0) cost += MR + CBR;
      cost += C_FreeTokPtr + C_ReleaseNodeLock;
    }
  else /* dir == Right */
    {
      toksz = rces; ntokOmem = tptr->tNumLeft; ntok = tptr->tNumRight;
      if (nsucc != 0)
        {
          cost += MR + CBR + BRR;
          cost += C_NextMatchTokNOT(nsucc, nteq, ntests, ntokOmem);
        }
      cost += C_FreeTokPtr + C_ReleaseNodeLock;

      if ((ntokOmem != 0) && ((nteq == 0) || (nsucc != 0)))
        cost += C_ReleaseTokenHT;
    }
  if (toksz <= 1) cost = cost - C_FreeTokPtr;
  break;

case pNode:
  cost = 0.0;
  break;

default:
  cost = 0.0;
  break;
}

if (MemConFlag) cost = cost/MemCon[NumActiveProc];
return(cost/1000.0);
```

```
double TaskSchedCost(tptr)
Task *tptr;
{
/*
 * This is the time spent by the hardware scheduler, and corresponds
 * to the number of bus cycles required for servicing a request.  On a 64 bit
 * wide bus this would be one bus cycle, while on a 32 bit wide bus it would
 * be 2 bus cycles.  Assuming one bus cycle to xmit address, the total busy
 * cycles are 2-3.  Assuming 100ns per cycle, this corresponds to 200-300ns.
 * I assume a 64 bit wide bus (80 MBytes/s) and 200ns for the xfer time.
 */
double cost;

  cost = 0.2;

  if (MemConFlag) cost = cost/MemCon[NumActiveProc];
  return(cost/1000.0);
}
```

C.2. Cost Model for the Parallel Implementation Using STQs

```
/*
 * When software task queues are used, for large parts the cost model remains
 * the same as when a hardware task scheduler is used.  There are, however, a
 * small number of differences corresponding to when the tasks are enqueued
 * and dequeued from the task queues.  These differences are listed below.
 */


#define C_ReleaseNodeLock   (RR + 2*SYN + CBM)

/* cost for scheduling a task through the global schedulers */
#define C_PushG             (6*RR + 2*MR + CBM)         /* outside lock */
#define C_SchedTask         (3*MR + M2R + 2*SYN + BRR)  /* inside  lock */
#define C_SchedEnd          (RR + SYN)                  /* outside lock */

/* costs for popping a task from the scheduler */
#define C_SchedLoopStart    (MR)                        /* outside lock */
#define C_SchedLoop         (4*RR + MR + CBR + CBM + BRR) /* outside lock */
#define C_PopG              (MR + BRM)                  /* outside lock */
#define C_DeSchedTaskTxxx   (9*RR + 5*MR + M2R + 2*SYN + CBR + 3*BRR)


/* Costs when intra-node-level parallelism is used.        */
#define C_i_DeSchedTask     (9*RR + 9*MR + M2R + 4*SYN + 3*CBR + 5*BRR)
#define C_i_DeSchedFailLoop (10*RR + 2*MR + M2R + 2*SYN + 3*CBR + 5*BRR)

/* Costs when node-level or prod-level parallelism is used. */
```

```
#define C_np_DeSchedTask        (9*RR + 5*MR + M2R + 2*SYN + CBR + 4*BRR)
#define C_np_DeSchedFailLoop   (10*RR + M2R + SYN + CBR + 3*BRR)



double TaskSchedCost(tptr)
Task *tptr;
{
/*
 * This is the cost of enqueueing a node activation in a task queue.
 */
double cost;

  cost = C_SchedTask/1000.0;

  if (MemConFlag) cost = cost / MemCon[NumActiveProc];
  return(cost);
}




double TaskDeSchedCost(tptr, numFail)
Task *tptr;
int numFail; /* num of tasks looked before the right task was found */
{
double cost;

  cost = 0.0;
  if ((Grain == nodeLev) || (Grain == prodLev))
    cost += (C_np_DeSchedFailLoop/1000.0) * ((double) numFail);
  else cost += (C_i_DeSchedFailLoop/1000.0) * ((double) numFail);

  if ((tptr!= NULL) && (tptr->tType == txxxNode))
    cost += C_DeSchedTaskTxxx/1000.0;
  else if ((Grain == nodeLev) || (Grain == prodLev))
    cost += C_np_DeSchedTask/1000.0;
  else cost += C_i_DeSchedTask/1000.0;

  if (MemConFlag) cost = cost / MemCon[NumActiveProc];
  return(cost);
}
```